IT WON'T HURT A BIT

IT WON'T HURT A BIT

Nursing tales from the Swinging Sixties

JANE YEADON

BLACK & WHITE PUBLISHING

First published 2010
First published in this edition 2013
by Black & White Publishing Ltd
29 Ocean Drive, Edinburgh EH6 6JL

1 3 5 7 9 10 8 6 4 2   13 14 15 16

ISBN: 978 1 84502 533 5

Typeset by Ellipsis Books Ltd, Glasgow

Printed and bound by Nørhaven, Denmark

To David, Joanne and Mark

CONTENTS

ACKNOWLEDGEMENTS

Thanks to Diana Stainforth and Harry Bingham of The Writers' Workshop for their knowledge and help, the Black & White Publishing team for their grace, Mike Guild for his writing residence, Alister and Kenny my Brora wordsmiths, and medical experts and pals Roseann and James.

1

FUTURE PROSPECTS

I owe a lot to Alison-Mary Mackintosh – and even more to her nose bleeds.

In a classroom of such boredom that a sneeze would be an attention grabber, my friend was about to provide something a little more exciting.

'Alison-Mary! You're bleeding all over your desk and jotter.' Our teacher had grown as pale as my pal. 'Look, go and drip elsewhere. Take someone with you. And ok, take Jane if you must. At least she's showing a bit of interest in *something* for a change.' She shoved us out of the classroom at a speed suggesting First Aid definitely wasn't her subject.

Apart from her name, there wasn't much of Alison-Mary, and with the blood moving into a steady gush, soon there might be even less. I took her arm, piloting her to the nearest sink, unconvinced by her sanguine, 'Happens a lot. It'll stop in its own good time.'

I didn't want her to know I was wondering where I could get a stretcher rather than the chair I'd suddenly, with a surge of importance, grabbed from the classroom. Handing over my one clean hanky and turning on the tap, I went for, 'But not before the geography class finishes. Maybe if you feel faint we could stretch it till lunchtime. Here, sit down and lean over the sink. I don't want to clean the floor.'

In the end, Alison-Mary was right, but not before a conversation regarding our future.

'Think I'll be a brain surgeon – see where all the blood comes from –

and you'd be good at being a nurse, she'd said. 'You don't panic and must've registered I might faint.'

It would be nice to think that in my new, assertive chair-grabbing mode in the classroom I'd also shouted, 'And we need a basin!' That would have been even more dazzling, but in all honesty I can't remember. It was a long time ago.

The Swinging Sixties, actually. An allegedly wonderful time of sex, drugs and rock'n'roll. Whilst at home on a Scottish upland farm, only the calendar recorded those years, and the nearest I was getting to anything swinging was the udder of our cow on her way to the milking shed.

And certainly my 1962 school wasn't about to encourage reasoned debate with its young. I might have become Alison-Mary's regular accompanist during her nosebleed tours and been charmed to have been asked by the odd concerned teacher for an opinion on her state of health, but it went no further. Even the social interaction in a school bus full of pupils returning to their rural homes could bring trouble.

One particularly warm sunny day, with the beginning of a new school year stretching interminably ahead, I was summoned to the rector's office. I could have reached it blind-folded. With its dusty books and papers spilling over every surface, it had a sort of seedy charm, but this wasn't a social call and it wasn't a congratulations on Care of the Nosebleed Volume 5 either.

'Jane, you're over sixteen now but the bus driver's complaining about you . . . again. Going home in particular, you're acting like a kid, distracting everybody with your capering, teasing and shouting – shouting!' Behind his desk, the headmaster boomed out his fury.

Coming from somebody who used his own voice so frequently and to foghorn effect in the school corridors, I thought that a bit rich and went for a gentle correction, 'It's just high spirits.'

His face went so purple I thought he was going to reach for the belt, coiled like a waiting serpent beside him. I might be too old for that but, just as bad, he was stretching for the phone. His fat fingers trembled round the receiver.

'Rowdyism that's what it is, I'm going to have a word with your mother. It's a pity you're not like your conscientious sister and that she's left school – she used to keep you in order. Now, get out!' He was already dialling.

We lived two miles beyond the bus route, though the steep cycle run home never felt half as uphill as the schoolwork. Poor Mum, I thought, pedalling hard against the strong prevailing wind, another bad-news phone call and now that Beth's gone to university, there's nobody to help with an ever-increasing load of homework for subjects that are completely boring in a place that feels like a jail.

I'd grown to love the idea of being a nurse. Those occasional forays with Alison-Mary had made me feel important, useful, even valued, and I'd learnt that practical help could make an immediate difference. I'd even found a posh word for my friend's nosebleeds.

'Next time, tell the teachers you've got epistaxis,' I'd said.

She looked doubtful, but I thought it was a lovely word with an official stamp guaranteed to impress.

I pedalled on, consoling myself: schools didn't keep you forever and there must be some point when, exams over and aged seventeen, I could head to the Big City, hit the high spots, train to be a nurse and look after people too ill to be interested in Latin declensions or split infinitives.

There was little traffic or action on the quiet country road home, but for all its isolation, the words of Bill Hayley and the Comets should reach these northern parts. Aiming for the future I sang, 'One, two, three o' clock, four o'clock – rock,' the energy absent in school now powering the pedals so fast and throwing the words so high, they should have formed a vapour trail.

'Five, six, seven,' the last hill before home would need a gear change.

'Adios amigo,' I sang into the clear pure air of the back of beyond, reasoning that at the very least, Jim Reeves, the original singer, would've been impressed by a lung capacity which bounced off the hills.

Home at last, I threw the bike into the usual bed of nettles and was greeted by Bob the collie herding hens into a reception committee in our yard. They clucked outrage but Bob's bark was welcoming even if he smelt vile.

'Don't let that dog into the house,' my mother yelled through an open window, 'he's been rolling in something horrid.'

'Sorry, old thing,' I said, gently closing the door on him.

Mum was making porridge for the barn cats and seemed remarkably calm and intent on stirring a gluey mess over the stove. I breathed again. Maybe the phone call had been to someone else. Planning to take Bob for a walk to the river, where a dip in the water would sort out his personal hygiene and I could tell him how horrible the rector and school were, I tried to sidle past.

'Hold it, Jane! I had Old Man Shanks on the phone today.'

For someone who'd been at the end of what must have been an awkward call, she sounded amazingly calm, eyes as glued to the pan as the contents were to its bottom. Maybe so many calls had made her immune, but she looked pleased so I stopped looking for excuses and began to hope for a miracle.

There was a tantalising pause and then she blurted out, 'How'd you like to leave school?'

I sat down, stunned.

'There's a ward maid's job going in Grantown's Ian Charles Hospital. I spoke to the matron about it today and she said it might be a good idea for you to go there and get some work experience – see if you really want to go in for nursing.' The stirring had slowed down as if conveying doubt but she carried on, 'It's just a wee hospital and it'll be hard work but you're really going nowhere in school and I don't think I could stand another phone call. Old Man Shanks sounded as if he was going to have apoplexy and you wouldn't want that on your conscience, would you?'

'Um . . .'

'Very caring, I must say. Anyway, Matron says that Aberdeen's

Foresterhill will accept you for training on the strength of you passing its exam and having a decent interview. D'you think you'd manage that?'

I stood up, stretched and opened my arms wide, 'Of course! And leave?' I tried not to scream. 'Leave? Mum, you must know that's the best thing I could ever imagine. But when?'

'Now. Well, as soon as you've handed back your books.'

'And what did you say to the rector?'

The porridge was making a gentle boiling-point plopping sound.

'That's about ready,' Mum pulled the pan to the side. 'I probably sounded like that,' she mused. 'Anyway, it seemed to soothe him and to be frank, Jane, I think he's glad to see the back of you. You've really been disruptive and not only in the school bus apparently. Anyway, with your practical bent, you're more likely to get your education from the big bad outside world and he agreed.'

'Well then I do believe in miracles,' I grinned. 'That must've been some phone call, and what does Dad say?'

'We've been talking about it for a while now. He's all in favour. Says he can't stand the strain of homework either.'

'Damn tractor's broken down again and did I hear my name mentioned?' My father stood in the doorway carrying enough silage aroma to mask the smell of burning porridge. With his arms covered in grease and his dungarees caked in mud, he looked like a man not so much broken as disillusioned by the wheel. He mopped his brow and leant his back against the door lintel. 'My back's killing me too. Never mind the nursing, what about being a physiotherapist. That'd be real handy.'

'I'm not clever enough for that, Dad. I'd need lots of Highers. Anyway, it's easier getting into nursing *and* I'm really good at treating epistaxis.'

Mum raised an admonitory wooden spoon. 'I don't know why you don't just call it a plain nose bleed – and I imagine there'll be a bit more than that to deal with. As a career, nursing's no bed of roses. Blast! There's Bob!'

He bounded in, tail fanning the smell of old bones, to charge the air with a heady mixture of glue, silage and porridge. Mum was right. Stopping blood flows and dabbing eau de cologne to fevered brows in hospital would prove as unlikely as fragrance in its sluices. Still, leaving school meant freedom and a step nearer my dream.

2

THE FIRST LINE OF DEFENCE

Ten miles and in the other direction from Forres, Grantown was too far to cycle home from every day. I would have to live in at the hospital tucked away on the outskirts of a town whose douce exterior might, hopefully, hide an exciting nightlife.

Dad took me there. 'We'll be hearing from you when you've time and you be sure and hing in,' he said. Then, with an encouraging nod and valedictory toot of the car horn, he was gone in a cloud of black exhaust before I could say, 'I'll miss you.'

The hospital was set in grounds where there were fir trees, crouching shrubbery and a summerhouse. There was a thing like a smart henhouse jutting out at one side of a low-slung building whilst a modern square extension had been built on at the other end. With its small rather mean looking windows, air of watchful quiet and empty car park, the Ian Charles didn't exactly shout Emergency Ward Ten.

I was nervous. I'd never left home before but with no other option, I took a firm grip of my suitcase and rang the bell.

Outside it might have looked like a hermit's retreat but inside it was different. With its blue lino making a glittering river along a corridor the length of the hospital and paintwork a brilliant white, it felt warm, welcoming and definitely clean.

Having answered the door, Matron, by way of introduction, gestured to the mixture of polish and graft which had made every conceivable surface glitter.

'Hello, Jane, we're just hoping you can keep up these standards. Cleanliness in hospital is crucial and the first line of defence in medicine. So you see how important you're going to be.' She spoke in a rain washed voice, so soft and attractive it made you listen. I thought Mr Shanks could have learnt a thing or two from her about voice projection.

'Well now, our last ward maid had to leave to look after ill parents and we're anxious to replace her as soon as we can. So it's good you've been able to come at such short notice.' Behind the gold-rimmed spectacles, her eyes looked kind even if she seemed distracted. 'We're pretty busy just now so the quicker we get you going, the sooner you'll learn the ropes. Ah! Here's Sister Gordon.'

A figure bustled towards us. She was in a lighter blue than the navy so royally encasing Matron; and instead of the frilly confection cap, she had a nun-like veil, the similarity ending with lips red cupid painted, impossibly black hair and a waist-crunching waspie belt.

'Sister Gordon, this is Jane our new ward maid,' Matron gave a gentle shove. 'She's going to start tomorrow.'

'Is she now?' Sister Gordon had a sharp nose, which she twitched as if scenting trouble. She looked me up and down, then doubtful, 'Let's hope she's a good worker, because our standards are very high, aren't they, Matron?' She sounded as if she'd been force fed lemons. 'Well, I suppose she'd better come with me and I'll show her round the place. I know you're needing all your time to get yourself ready.'

Matron chuckled like a young girl, 'That's right. Very soon, I'm having a six-week sabbatical and going to Canada, leaving our Sister Gordon in charge and nobody could be more capable I know.'

Our Sister's chest visibly expanded. 'Well, I'll be looking to keep up her very high standards. We don't want her coming back to bedlam.' She narrowed her eyes, 'Like Matron I only expect the very best. Now come along and we'll let her get on with more important things. Quickly now!'

Recognising my place and frightened into silence, I padded a few paces behind her, worried that linoleum so highly polished could constitute a hazard – but now, even if as Matron said I was an important member of staff, might not be the time to say so.

Still, despite the perils of shiny floors, it must be a good thing to have all the patients on one level, even if they were at each end of a corridor which seemed to stretch forever. There were other rooms off it too but Sister Gordon seemed oblivious to the low whimpering sounds coming from one and surged past until at last she ran out of corridor and turned sharp left.

'This is the female ward.' She barged through a set of double doors as if they didn't exist.

Here it was less immaculate with the smell of baby powder competing with that of rubber and ammonia. Heavy-duty grey metal lockers on spindly legs flanked iron beds with blindingly white bedding tethering in the occupants. Whilst windows on one side gave out onto the hospital car park, the others offered a glimpse of the summerhouse full of stacked chairs. Beginning to get my bearings, I realised that through the door at the end must be the hen house.

Ignoring the patients and ten sets of eyes swivelling in her direction, Sister Gordon pointed, 'Through there's the sluice. You'll be responsible for keeping it spotless.'

I wanted to stop and speak to the subdued presences lying so quietly in their beds, but already we were retracing our footsteps.

'Male ward,' a pointy finger marked a ward opposite, 'same layout as the female – sluice likewise – but of course the boys,' she sounded almost fond, 'will smoke their pipes, so you'll have their sputum mugs, spit boxes to you, to empty as well.'

Between the male and female wards there was a two-bed unit with bigger windows and better views. The sound of friendly chat coming from it faded as we headed back along the corridor, whilst Sister Gordon said,

'They use commodes in there but if the patients are back in bed you'll have to get them bedpans from either of the sluices.'

Understanding we were on a toilet tour and that any interaction with the patients was going to be bottom-up, I postponed the idea of having a wee chat with the bed occupants and searched for something intelligent to ask, 'And the cleaning material?'

'In the sluices of course,' was the reply. 'Where else?'

The single rooms at the other end had adjacent toilets and bathrooms. 'They're for the fitter, difficult and sometimes private patients,' Sister Gordon explained. 'You'll not have much to do with them,' she gave a mirthless laugh, 'you'll be too busy cleaning around those who can't move, and of course, that's the outpatient department,' she nodded at the square extension part. 'The doctors come in the morning to treat them. Naturally, that's a medical and nursing responsibility and nothing to do with you.'

I was still carrying my suitcase. It gave the feel of a commercial traveller but unsure where to put it, I had to ask.

'Your bedroom's above the female ward. Silly girl, I didn't notice you still had it. Why didn't you say?' She clicked her teeth in exasperation, 'You could have left it at the stairs beside the female ward. There's a staircase leading up to staff quarters.' Taking in my figure, she screwed her face, 'I'll have to go and see what I can do about a uniform. I wonder if we've one that'll fit.' She sounded doubtful, then, pointing in the direction we had come from added, 'Off you go now. It's easy enough to find, and remember you start at six-thirty tomorrow and you'd better not sleep in either.'

My bedroom was a surprise. It was a sweet little *Anne of Green Gables* affair with low eaves, white painted furniture, and a wallpaper pattern of autumn leaves so richly coloured you might feel transported to a New England Fall. Through the small-paned window the fir trees moved restlessly whilst their cones bobbed in a dance as if trying to free themselves from their green and branch webbed captivity. In the distance the Cairngorms rose in blue unencumbered splendour.

Somewhat nearer were Wilma and Irene who shared the double room next door, and hearing noises, had come to interview the latest recruit.

'I'm the kitchen maid – I help Evelyn the cook,' said Irene by way of introduction. She was young with brown curly hair and had a cheerful managing way with her. 'But Wilma here's a ward maid like you. She's going out in a minute with her steady – been going with him for ages.'

Irene sounded envious but I was more impressed with Wilma's mop-holding capacity than her boyfriend-keeping power. With her slight figure and pale face she must be responsible for that acreage of cleanliness downstairs. I only had time to glimpse her hands, red and swollen before they swung behind her back on hearing Sister Gordon. 'I see you've met the girls.'

She hurried in with a large pink dress hanging over her arm. 'This'll have to do until the other frocks come back from the laundry – it's probably a bit big, but it's all we have at the moment.' She slung it over a chair. In her hand she had something white, plastic and round, 'You'll need it for a collar.' She placed it over the frock, gave it a pat of approval, 'Now that's you sorted.'

Sartorial matters achieved, she nodded at Wilma. 'Now Wilma is a good worker and will keep an eye on you – show you what to do. Isn't that so?'

'Uh-huh,' said Wilma in a non-committal way. She turned to a mirror as if seeking acknowledgement from the pallid reflection. 'Is she starting tomorrow? I won't have to waken her will I?'

'No,' I was keen to be part of the conversation, 'it won't be a problem.'

It was a foolish thing to say. I'd no difficulty waking early, but should have risen even earlier to deal with the problem of fastening the neck button of the frock to include the plastic collar, a four-hole conundrum. Listening hard for sounds of activity from next door I was eventually able to rouse Wilma to help.

Yawning and stretching, with love bites on her neck, she looked at my unmarked one with disfavour. 'It's a bit thick – no wonder you can't get the collar fixed.' She took such a firm grip of my collar I began to feel light-headed.

'Don't strangle her,' said Irene, looking alarmed, meanwhile climbing into a comfortable striped frock, and making a stirring gesture in her head's direction by way of hair care. 'Thank God I don't have to worry about dickeys. Evelyn wouldn't put up with them. Come on, you'll meet her in a minute and Wilma, count yourself lucky Gordie's off duty – she'd kill you if she saw that neck of yours.'

Wilma gave a mournful sniff. 'I know and I think you're going to have a hard day in that uniform, Jane, it's much too big – Gordie must've thought you were twice the size.'

There was a reveille-like sound of pans clattering coming from the wards as we passed.

'Night staff on bedpan round,' Wilma explained, 'then as soon as they get a cup of tea it'll be time for another round and it'll be our turn to dish them out.'

Her gloomy tones didn't exactly herald a bright new dawn but at least Evelyn, in a kitchen fiefdom full of steaming pans and running taps, was cheerful and welcoming. 'Well hello, Jane. And it's a fine morning for a first day too,' she said. She was buxom and bonny with a large teapot in hand. High heels castanet-clicking on the stone floor, she went to a row of mugs and started to fill them. 'You'll get breakfast later on but this should give you a jump start,' she said. 'Biscuit?'

I shook my head, retiring in the face of her oncoming bosom, 'Tea'll be lovely.'

In the wards, I'd an awful feeling I might see its return, for when Wilma and I got to them, I knew what our first task would be. Unsure if, this early, my stomach was up to the job, I followed her into the female ward sluice.

It was a small gloomy affair where bedpans were stacked on shelves as if on display whilst rubber mackintoshes were draped over rails to dry. The sinks were huge with one having a drainage hole apparently designed to cope with a flood, whilst nearby was a thing like a washing machine gaping its maw like a starving dragon.

'That's the bedpan steriliser,' said Wilma banging the door shut with her foot, pressing a button and tutting. 'There's a bedpan in it – night staff must've forgotten to do it.' The sound of rushing water playing on metal accompanied her as she took an armload of chrome from its shelf. 'Watch what I do,' instructed my minder, as she swished hot water over the pans, then with the expertise of a silver service waitress, placed a white cloth over them and returned to the ward. She'd a way of covering the ground at a tremendous speed in an effortless way. Whilst her top half looked immobile, her feet travelled with swift steps as precise as those of a windup toy. It was a struggle keeping up with her.

In the corner were wheeled screens covered in a nondescript and worrying colour of beige. With a deft flick of her ankle, Wilma manoeuvred them round each bed.

As she started to give out the bedpans, I thought she'd have as much trouble getting her patients up on their silver thrones as a lion tamer with his big cats at the circus. But within five minutes they were all enthroned and, now at the same level as Wilma, more aware of her neck than the job in hand.

'Good gracious, Wilma, have you been trying to hang yourself?' An old woman, her voice as creaky as her bones, struggled to point whilst squinting through spectacles greasy with finger marks.

'Mrs Grant, you're needing them cleaned,' Wilma declared pointing back, 'Jane here'll do them for you. Her first cleaning job, ha!'

The ward's attention changed direction subjecting me to the same scrutiny as Wilma's neck.

'New, eh?' It sounded like a croon, 'Don't worry, we'll keep you right. Just don't be like Wilma. We thought she'd a brass neck, but just look at it!'

3

STUBBORN BOOLS

Wilma was in charge of the electric floor polisher. It was kept in a special place unlike the other cleaning material far more readily accessible in each sluice and there for my complete attention. After reminding me of my importance in the cleansing department, Wilma headed off to maintain that lustrous gleam on the corridor.

'I won't hear any bells with the machine going so you'll have to answer them and as it's usually for bedpans you know how to do them now,' she'd said, apparently pleased with an unconventional training session where patients encouraged, Wilma disparaged and I'd got rather wet. 'And one good thing about the male ward,' she went on, 'is you haven't to do so many. Just be sure and clean their spit boxes, Gordie's really fussy about that.'

But not, I figured, about the atmosphere. Here, and despite the high ceiling, it felt overly warm with an all-pervading smell of tobacco smoke.

Fresh air might help, I thought, and feeling bold threw open a window. 'Good morning,' I said, all hearty.

'Shut that bloody window!' shouted an old man, his hand placed firmly over his bonnet as if it might blow off. 'It's freezing in here.'

Oblivious to this exchange, another cried, 'Nursie, nursie,' and beckoned with a finger the colour of a keen tobacconist, 'come ower here.'

I might have been a little crushed at so little appreciation for my toning up a ward's ambience, but delighted with such an early promotion to nurse status, I rushed to his bedside.

'How can I help?'

He furrowed his brow in real anxiety. 'It's ma bools. Ye see – they're nay working.' He patted his head as if to check it was still there.

'Bools?'

'Aye – hivna worked for a week. I'm thinking I should tell the doc.'

I gave an easy laugh. This was simple!

I soothed, 'Now you really shouldn't be worrying about them, though I suppose you must have a big farm with more than one bull. We've only got one on ours. Anyway, since you're in hospital I expect your family'll have got in touch with Mr Rafferty the vet.'

'Jane! That man's obsessed with his bowels,' said Irene, coming into the ward with plates of steaming porridge. 'Come on, it's time for your breakfast.' She twinkled, 'I can't wait till I tell Evelyn though. She's going to have a right laugh.'

I didn't think it was that funny and had a moment's sympathy for my mother who used to hear this so regularly when she asked me to recall a school day where jokes with my pals in the back row were all that seemed worth remembering. I just knew the bools story would figure at the breakfast table where staff, coming on duty at eight o'clock, assembled.

Separated from the kitchen by a hatch, the dining room had the feel of a best room with some oil paintings depicting Highland cows looking glum, probably because they were up to their knees in water. A cheerier sight was the table set as for a banquet with junket and rhubarb taking centre stage and floured rolls, butter and jugs of cream laid out in generous quantity. Large bowls of porridge were handed through from the kitchen by the disembodied hand of Irene.

'Have some porridge – good for the bools!'

'Poor Jane! They're only teasing,' said Matron who had appeared looking so serene and unruffled she must have gone to sleep standing up, 'but I bet you'll not make that mistake again.' As she took her place at the top of the table, a bell went off.

'That's for you,' mouthed Wilma. 'It'll be Mrs Davidson. She's in one of the side rooms. She always does that at meal times.'

It was from this room that the plaintive cries had come yesterday so I was curious to see the occupant. There was a red light outside her room, presumably to identify the caller, and it remained there until I was right beside her and had persuaded her to stop pressing the activating buzzer.

'You're new aren't you? Let's hope you get quicker.' Red hair streaked with grey was scraped back from a wrinkled face and secured by a ribbon, its red a lot cheerier than her expression. 'I hope you know why I'm ringing?'

I nodded.

'Well don't bring me a cold one or I won't use it,' she said, squirming down in bed, 'and you'll have to help me with it. I'm completely incapable of moving.'

A splendid ring glanced on her thin fingers. When I returned, it caught me as I tried to hoist her aboard.

'You're hurting me,' she scolded, 'and your hands are cold.'

'All that glitters is not cold,' I joked.

Mrs Davidson looked affronted. 'What did you say?'

I made to speak but she waved a dismissive hand. 'Oh, it's no use arguing. I know cheek when I hear it so don't bother making excuses. But when Matron comes round I'll tell her the new girl with the red hair and long frock is too impudent to be on any staff, especially here where you'd expect everyone to have a professional manner and then,' she gave a wriggle of pleasure, 'you'll have to go.'

Sick and worried, I returned to the dining room.

'Everything alright?' asked Matron.

'Yes, Matron,' I said, feeling like a prisoner at her last meal.

'Good,' she said, 'take a good breakfast now – you'll be needing to fortify yourself for your work. Sluice duties call for plenty energy.'

Meal over, I shot back to them. They hadn't felt so welcoming before nor did scrubbing and scouring seem such safe pursuits. Every time I heard a footfall I thought it must be Matron coming to tell me my number was up, but gradually as the morning went on and nobody came, and despite catching my heel on the frock and the collar persistently coming unstuck, I grew confident enough to come out of hiding and move into the wards.

In the absence of Wilma, intent on motoring her machine on the freeway, and keeping her neck out of scrutiny, everybody in the female ward recognised I needed help. The ward buzzed with their comments. All experts on cleaning, they were keen to advise and, making me feel less foolish, recalled their young experiences when they too felt strange and hopeless.

'But I've made too big a mistake and don't think I'll be here very long. I tried to make a joke with one of the other patients and she took umbrage,' I told Mrs Grant, who with the keen interest of a professional was watching me brush the ward floor, 'She says she's going to get me the sack.'

'Some folk are hard to please,' commiserated Mrs Grant. She crawled out her hand and patted mine. 'But Matron knows what everybody's like so I wouldn't worry if I was you. You don't look like a lassie who'd harm a fly and the way you're handling that brush tells me you're going to be fine but I think you've forgotten the dust pan.'

She was doing her best to console. It was humbling to think she could consider such an optimistic future when she herself, a thin body, riddled with arthritis, was stuck in bed and dependent on others for the most basic of needs. I'd never heard bones creak before but hers made a sound like a door needing oiled.

I said, 'One day when I've got the hang of this job, I'll take you on a tour of the sluice. The chromes will be so shiny, we'll throw away the mirror, and the U bend so spick and span, you'll want to take your porridge out of it.'

Mrs Grant laughed, 'Maybe I'll be pleased to be so stuck in bed.' She sighed and looked down on her misshapen fingers fumbling at her sheets.

'This is what you get from too much scrubbing though, so don't be a ward maid too long. Go for your training like you say you're going to, make it as soon as you can and get plenty letters after your name. Then you can come back here as Matron.' Her eyes crinkled in amusement.

'There's a lot of hilarity going on here and who's taking my name in vain?' Matron stood in the doorway. 'This ward's usually so quiet I thought I'd better see what's going on and here I find you all trying to get rid of me.'

A spot of pink rosying her cheeks, Mrs Grant retorted, 'You might go to Canada and never come back, so we're training wee Janey here – just in case.'

She'd difficulty nodding her head but with a slow movement, she managed it. 'And she could do with a better fitting dress and one with a collar. Look! One half of her's being strangled whilst the other's about to be drowned.'

Matron laughed. 'Well, it's obvious you're on form this morning but I'll see what I can do – even if I'm a bit pushed for time. I know Sister Gordon had a job finding one.'

'I bet that crabbed old spinster didn't try very hard,' muttered Mrs Grant's neighbour, but Matron continued as if she hadn't heard, 'I'm going away this evening so I thought I'd better come and say cheerio and I'll be back before you can say you've missed me.'

Whilst a universal sigh of resignation engulfed the ward, mine was of relief. At least I hadn't been given the sack. But after today, with Sister Gordon in charge, I thought we might all be in for a hard time.

4

STEPS IN THE RIGHT DIRECTION

A few weeks on, and following Wilma, I increased my stride. Approval ratings from both Sister Gordon and Mrs Davidson were still low but the other patients kept my spirits high, and even if Grantown's night scene was disappointingly confined to a café, the odd dance and a picture house made me truly happy.

Still it was frustrating that the best I could do was give out glittering, nicely warmed bedpans and wish all patients free from beds with rigid rubber mackintoshes and rubber smells no regular washing or talcum powder dredging could disguise. Since the soft ease of polythene sheeting in the nursing world was still a distant prospect, fresh air might make those sheets less ghastly.

Watching me pass the kitchen, laden, smelling like a tyre factory and heading for outside, Evelyn and Irene called out in cheerful banter, 'Is that you pretending to wash your dirty linen in public? We know it's just an excuse to meet Henry.'

Even if I was on my way to sluice down soiled stuff, I quite liked these forays to the grey stone building at the back of the hospital with its big sinks, Henry's garden implements and a washing line overlooking fields of well fed cattle. Henry had a craggy face, a kindly way and offered an affable diversion discussing his vegetable beds whilst I laboured over a sink sufficiently deep to drown in but blessedly removed from bell toll.

'How are you doing?'

'I was thinking I'd take my least favourite patient out here and see
she could swim.'

Henry laughed, 'No prizes for guessing who you're meaning. She
drives everybody daft. Just don't mind her.' He picked up a rake and went
off whistling with a blackbird striking up as if in competition.

Other than interspersing the moans with ringing her bell and
complaining, I couldn't see any reason why Mrs Davidson was in hospital,
but Wilma had said it wasn't a ward maid's business, whilst mastering
the vagaries of the floor polisher, scrubbing and high dusting was. Sister
Gordon would have said the same but less politely so I asked Evelyn. At
least she wouldn't bite my nose off.

In her tolerant way the cook explained, 'She's a lonely old woman –
plenty money but too difficult for the family to manage and you'll notice
she never gets any visitors. Shame really.'

It wasn't exactly a diagnosis. One day when I was a matron I'd keep
everybody informed so that at least ward maids would know as much
as the gardener and cook. In the interval there was a small matter of
training.

Sister Gordon didn't hold out much chance and used the back-up of
an audience to make her point. In Matron's absence she'd taken over her
flat, which was upstairs from the dining room. She didn't usually appear
until well on in the morning but one day she made a surprise early entrance
in a fit of fury and a pale blue negligee.

'This is disgusting!' A finger stabbed at the cup of coffee ordered to
start her day and which five seconds ago I had delivered. 'It's just as well
I tasted it first. If you'd given it to the patients they'd have thought you
were trying to poison them.'

Careless of the attentive gaze of the entire day staff, she took a deep
breath, then she was off again, 'Look here, Jane, if you can't manage something as simple as a decent cup of coffee what chance is there of you
making the grade as a nurse? Honestly, anybody accepting you for training
needs their head examined.'

'What's all this about?' Evelyn had come to investigate. 'Is there something wrong with the milk. I need to know in case it's off.'

'It's not off. It's weak and cold,' snapped Sister Gordon drawing her negligee about her with a dawning awareness that she might be a touch underdressed, 'so please will you make sure you make it so that at least I get a proper cup since I can't trust Jane to do such a simple thing.' She stamped off banging the door behind her.

'Even I've never had a row like that,' said Wilma in a voice just short of admiration, 'and I don't want to be a nurse.'

I bit my lip. Honestly that Sister Gordon was the limit. If I was accepted for training, I just hoped there wouldn't be too many like her. Every time I heard her, my heart would break into a canter – another couple of Sister Gordons might finish me off.

Still, a smug feeling lurked. She didn't know and I wasn't going to tell her that my interview was the next day, and since it was on a day off, nobody else in the hospital needed to know either. The secret powered me through work and off duty with a feeling of triumph. I'd show them!

But I'd forgotten the listening skills of the ladies in the double ward.

Mrs Spence was a blind diabetic and Mrs Fotheringham had advanced multiple sclerosis and was only able to get out of bed if helped. For two women so disabled you might think they'd enough trouble getting through the day, never mind collecting news of every colour. Maybe their phalanx of visitors kept them up-to-date whilst staff members under the spell of their sympathetic way and clever questions would unburden themselves of their own domestic affairs and never ask about theirs.

Whatever their methods, the duo seemed to know everything about everybody, but since I was always too busy trying to disengage Mrs Davidson's finger from her bell, and they were so undemanding, I didn't see them often. I wasn't even sure if they knew who I was.

'Is that you, Jane?' Mrs Spence, who might be blind, had nothing wrong with her ears. She must have heard my footsteps on the stairs.

'Good luck for tomorrow!' she called. 'We're keeping our fingers crossed for you.'

Slowly I went into their room.

'How d'you know about that?'

Mrs Spence smiled and tapped her nose, whilst Mrs Fotheringham chuckled, 'Didn't you know we read the cups?'

'I'm especially good at that,' said Mrs Spence.

'There's a simple answer to that one,' said my mother when I got home. 'Tommy, Coopers' van man must have told them. His wife visits a couple of ladies in hospital. He often talks about them and when he was here on Wednesday I told him. He's so much news himself, it was nice for me to give him some for a change.' She got defensive, 'I didn't know you wanted it kept a secret. Anyway, you've told Beth.'

'Well she's in Aberdeen and unlikely to bang into the odd Grantownian. Anyway, I'd be the last person she'd want to speak about.'

There was a long parental sigh. Then, 'Best get an early night, eh?'

The dew of an early morning had hung pearls on the cobwebbed bushes. It was early autumn and the countryside was beginning to show colour changes but I was too nervous to appreciate a sleepy sun's promise of a fine day. Had Sister Gordon been around, my heart couldn't have run faster.

My parents were taking me to Forres. 'Dad and I want to make sure you catch that Aberdeen train,' said Mum. 'Now that suit fits you fine even if it is short and tight. Still, green's your colour. Just remember not to run to catch a bus. We might even have to help you aboard at the station.' It was said with a twinkle but I was too nervous to respond.

The road was quiet but as we stopped at a crossroads I thought about my own. Maybe always wanting to be a nurse wasn't enough and what if Sister Gordon was right and I wasn't up to the mark? What would I do then? The very thought of her scolding tongue becoming a permanent feature was enough to decide that whatever happened, Grantown wasn't forever. I'd find a ward maid's job elsewhere.

'Drat! Look, Jane, you've got a ladder in your stockings.' Good old Mum. Perfect for boosting confidence, and how could she know that whilst sitting in the front and looking straight ahead? I'd counted and actually had several but at least she'd channelled my thoughts into a more immediate problem. I'd need to buy a pair in Aberdeen; was it not full of shops with wonderful bargains?

I boarded the train and waved as it steamed away from the station. They might have shouted something but it was lost in noise, clamour and the beating of my heart. Looking back, I suddenly saw my parents looking young and carefree, enveloped in the smoke as if in a cloud. How very strange. It wouldn't have happened with diesel.

5

A VISIT TO THE GRANITE CITY

'That's a nice suit, killer shoes though. You'll never last a day in Aberdeen with heels that high and look at your stockings already.' Beth was waiting at the other end and handed over a new packet as she spoke. All very well for her; being small and elf-like means there's less to maintain.

'How did you know?'

'I just knew. You're predictable in many ways and I suppose you've lost your comb too?' She scrabbled in a bag almost as big as herself. 'Here. Now come on, you've just enough time to change and make yourself tidy and then we'll get a taxi. You'll be late otherwise.'

The station waiting room was ill lit with a mirror reflecting so many freckles in an ashen face it was surely fly spotted as well. Aberdeen was cold and so were the toilets with a searching wind reaching through the gaps under the doors and blowing in a scrap of paper.

'For God's sake put these stockings on carefully,' Beth shouted. 'They cost me an arm and a leg.'

'Guy loves Meg,' declared a wall scribbler.

'Bully for Guy,' I said standing on one leg, handling the stockings with care and wondering if the visiting bit of paper also had a message. Already the shoes were beginning to pinch.

Out in the city the wind pounced on us, with the bustle of crowds and the roar of traffic overwhelming, but Beth seemed oblivious to it as she grabbed me and darted across a busy road.

'Are you trying to kill me?' I asked Beth and the shoes.

'Taxi!' Beth's imperious gesture stopped a cab in a squeal of brakes.

'Hurry up! We're stopping the traffic. Get in!' She shoved. The door slammed behind me.

'Are you not coming with me?' My cry was puny.

'No, you're a big girl now and I've classes to go to but I'll be up later and I'll be at the entrance, Foresterhill!' she cried, giving the door a bang like a starting gun. The taxi shot off. Aberdeen rattled past. In my agitated state it looked as if every building was hunched into one bleak granite blur until at last, the taxi pulled up at a complex of seriously grey buildings.

Set in their square jaws were barred windows suggesting captivity and surely if this was a hospital, the grounds would have more flowers and less tar?

'I'm sorry. There's a mistake. I didn't want to go to a jail.' Further along from the main building was another but smaller. Even if there was no barbed wire, it too looked like a fortress.

The taxi driver laughed and pointed to it. 'Well, some folk might call it that but it's actually the Nurses' Home.' He opened the door and pointed again. 'That nearest building's where you want to go. Look, it says Aberdeen Royal Infirmary. A.R.I. to us Aberdonians.' He sounded proud. 'Now the main entrance is below that funny looking thing like a cooker lid. I think it must be there to let in some light. Once you're in you'll see it's a fine place. Oh, thanks!'

At least the tip was right and once through the hospital's revolving doors I saw that so was he, for as much as it might be grey and cold outside, inside, warmth and colour made it the very opposite.

Green lino, stretching so far it looked like a long street, had a shine sufficiently impressive to have Wilma fainting with approval, whilst the commemorative plaques on the white walls were so bright whoever polished them deserved a mention there too.

Along the corridor came a gentle buzz of human traffic. Busy people all in different garb were going along on various life-saving missions; you could tell by their air of purpose. Nurses went along singly or in groups and were part of a world that I realised, with a sudden jolt, I was desperate to join.

Behind my mop, I'd watched and envied the comfort that the trained Ian Charles staff brought to their patients, and for all her sharp tongue and pointy nose it was obvious Sister Gordon knew something about care and a lot about nursing. My career prospects were being decided today but if I didn't get to be a nurse maybe I could relocate and ward-maid here. I'd love to be any part of a place that felt so alive and exciting.

Now where was Matron?

'Could you tell me where reception is please?'

The only person who looked as if he'd time to stop was a porter who directed me to something resembling a sentry box. 'Straight ahead, quinie. It's by that notice asking folk nay tae wear stilettos.'

'Thanks. I'll tiptoe there.'

I gave my name to a receptionist who spoke through the slatted window whilst ticking my name off a list.

'I hope there's not a mistake. A porter called me quinie.' I was anxious.

She laughed, 'You're lucky. If you'd been a young man, he'd have called you a loonie. It's just Aberdeen speak. Now, your interview's due any moment. Matron's room is up those stairs and to the left. You'll see her name on the door. Her secretary's office is just beside it and you'll need to see her first.' Her grin was impish. 'Just be sure and give a good knock, her secretary's hard of hearing and,' she leant over and whispered, 'them's funcy shoes! Good luck, quinie.' She was young, bright and so cheerful I couldn't help but feel encouraged.

It was easy finding the door next to the oak-panelled gold-lettered one and which I now gave the prescribed thump.

'OK, OK!' shouted a harassed looking secretary all tweedy and short and yanking the door open as if she were pulling a tooth. 'I'm not deaf you know. That wee brat of a receptionist downstairs must think I'm daft

– she does it all the time – the joke's wearing a bit thin.' The Cairngorm brooch on her jacket winked at her outrage. She checked a wall clock, then her watch, a stout affair with a man's strap, whilst I toyed with the idea of asking for a loan of her sensible brogues.

'Well, you're on time at least. Take a seat,' she nodded at an adjacent bench, 'you shouldn't have too long to wait. Matron's someone in just now but he's due out any minute. In the meantime, you'll need to excuse me. I must get on.' She sped back into her den.

I hoped she didn't have to sit on that hairy tweed skirt too long. It'd put anybody in a bad mood.

Time dragged by. The early breakfast was such a long way away, I thought I might faint with hunger, but then a man in a white coat with blue epaulettes came out of Matron's office and distracted me, leaving with so much bowing and scraping I wondered if we'd been relocated to Balmoral.

'Yes, Matron, I'll see to that right away. Yes, I realise this is important. Yes, immediately!' A snowstorm of dandruff landed on the epaulettes. He closed the door, righted himself, then barrelled in to the secretary.

Not fussed about privacy, he shouted, 'I'm afraid you're going to have to change tonight's rotas, there's a lot of staff shortages tonight. You'll need to phone the reserves list and' – jerking his head, he allowed another fresh fall – 'she wants it done *now*.'

The secretary's hand was poised between the phone that she had picked up and a box of chocolates that she put down. 'Yes, Matron, she's here and I'll tell her to come in.' As she nodded to me she carefully replaced the box lid then said in even tones, 'I think we should have this discussion with the door closed.'

Suddenly it seemed safer in Matron's office.

6

A SMALL MATTER OF
AN INTERVIEW

Matron sat at the far end of a room on a throne of padded red leather behind a desk big enough to rule the world from. She had the manner of a bored hostess filling in time until her proper guests arrived.

'Ah! Miss Macpherson, take a seat please.' She'd left her training days a long time ago and was plump, with a tinkling voice and a vague smile.

Her small fingers fluttered at the chair opposite as if they were practising fresh air arpeggios. How had such soft looking little sausages with their pale pink varnished nails ever survived sluice work?

I tried a soft shoe shuffle but on the parquet floor the stilettos moved in staccato. It felt as if she was a mile away and, oh God! There was something running up my leg, another ladder: and worse, I'd forgotten to curtsey.

'I hope you've had a good journey?'

Easy! Meanwhile, Matron sent her fingers on an improving mission checking her frilly collar, cuffs and a cap which on a lesser person might have resembled a meringue. Pinned on her Cresta run of a bosom was a medal. It shone like gold. I wondered had she herself polished it and if so, and I didn't get the next bit right, might she, before I left, be kind enough to share some handy cleaning tips.

'You realise that you're applying to become a member of a most noble profession. Yes indeed! And as you'll no doubt be aware, this is a very busy place. I've a lot of people to interview and time's at a premium,' she picked a sheet of paper from a neatly stacked pile on her desk, then anchoring those busy fingers together and arching perfectly shaped eyebrows observed, 'so I'll get straight to the point. You haven't any academic qualifications so you'll have to sit an exam after this interview. Your entrance depends on those two things.' She brandished her digits in the victory sign.

Swallowing hard, I tried for a reassuring tone, 'Well I hope that working in the Cottage Hospital has given me an insight into the profession and I've certainly learnt more about nursing there than, dare I say, I would have done in school.' I spread my hands as if to imply huge experience.

'Nursing's not just about practical skills, and if we accept you for training, you'll find this out in a very short time indeed. Many have come through this door thinking care and compassion are all that is required and had to leave because' – like an orchestra tuning up, her voice was interrupted by the odd squeak 'they couldn't accept the discipline of study.' She shook her head in disbelief whilst the fingers burst from release and fluttered back into action over the desk.

All round the room hung portraits of what I presumed were patrons, looking worthy if not quite dead: surely poor advertisements for a hospital. A small draught disturbed the chandelier right above her and chinked its dripping icicles as if conveying disapproval.

'Being a nurse is my dearest wish,' I tried.

Matron suddenly leant across the desk with the smile of a tiger baring teeth. 'Why?'

The question was predictable. I'd been preparing for it for all the years I could remember. Yet when the reply came, it was as unrehearsed as it was terrifying.

'Brown boots. Old shiny brown boots.'

Matron's eyebrows raced upwards at the same time as her jaw dropped. Even the oil paintings looked shocked and the chandelier was silent.

I plunged on, 'They belonged to a Mr Matheson. He was an old shep-
herd who was admitted to the Ian Charles. You know, where I work. He
was pretty confused but if you could imagine you were out on the hills
with him, he made sense. Sometimes he'd put the boots on and sit in his
hospital pyjamas trying to get the other patients to herd his long-ago
sheep, but of course, they weren't interested.' My laugh was fond if trembling. Matron was now looking bemused but at least she was listening.
Were we moving out of the land of permafrost?

I struggled on. 'After all, as you would understand, they'd their own
flocks to mind. The boots were hidden because the staff thought they
just added to his confusion but I thought they were so much part of his
personality that it was a shame. Then he had a stroke and we never heard
him speak or whistle again.'

'And the boots?' Matron picked up a pen and held it like a gun over a
clean sheet of paper.

'When Mr Matheson died, I'd to pack his belongings. He didn't have
much, but the boots were his and they just lay there as if waiting for him
to put them on. I hadn't realised how fond I was of him. The boots seemed
to echo a sadness I didn't know I had and I wished I'd had nursing skills
to look after him. I'd have felt better about him dying.'

For a moment even Matron seemed to accept that death was a force
mightier than her as she gazed heavenward in silent contemplation. Then
her knuckles went white as with renewed vigour she squeezed the pen.
It spluttered into life to allow her to dash out a scrawl.

'Right! Well thank you, Miss Macpherson, I'll let you go now but,' she
consulted her watch, 'have you any questions?'

'Will it be long before I know if I've been accepted?' I couldn't think
of anything cleverer to say.

'No,' she said and arrow-aimed a smile at the door.

The secretary was hovering outside. She greeted me with a grin reminiscent of a whist player with a winning hand. She must have won that
rota row.

'Now for your written.' She took me past a girl, her church-going hat and lacing shoes making her an ideal candidate with matching academic qualifications because, tussling with syntax and number questions, I sat the exam alone and in a small airless room.

'You'll be glad that's over; it can be daunting.' The secretary's unexpected kindness made me blink. 'Why don't you go and have a cup of tea? There's a café downstairs and I do hope you have a safe journey home.'

Returning along the main corridor and unsure of my future, I considered throwing myself under an oncoming trolley. At least I could stay in this bustling and exciting place, even if it was at the receiving end being put back into shape. There were nurses passing by, so casually and at ease, they didn't seem to realise how lucky they were to be in uniform, here, in this fabulous place.

Meanwhile, a cross Beth was waiting at the entrance, her bag loaded with learned-looking tomes.

'Come on!' she said. 'I've been waiting ages. These books weigh a ton. See!' She took one out and thrust it at me.

'Thanks for asking how I got on,' I said, catching it, reading its title and promptly holding it in such a way that people could see it and think I was a medical student. 'I didn't know you were studying adenoids.'

'It's actually Virgil's *Aeneid* – if you'd bother to read properly,' Beth chuckled. What a little rib tickler my sister could be.

'You don't fancy a cup of tea here? There's a café near the entrance.'

Beth looked horrified. 'No thank you! It's the last place on earth I'd want to visit. Hospitals give me the heebie jeebies. Honestly, Jane, I think you must be nuts wanting to spend any time at all in there. Look at it, it's just like a prison.' She swallowed nervously and hugged her bag close as if to ward off evil.

'Yeah, that's what I thought until I went inside, but it's a different place altogether.'

Already I felt territorial about the place but Beth wasn't convinced so we made for a nearby bus stop. Despite the best efforts of some dedicated smokers, my initial impression of Aberdeen, became clearer from the front of the double-decker taking us into town.

A cheerful conductor whistled 'Annie Laurie' as he winked at us, then punched out half fares. The coins clinked in his bag as he took the stairs two at a time and in time. As yet, The Beatles weren't around to expand his repertoire. Maybe I could become a clippie, I mused. I could count, practise the whistling, I'd be good at stair jumping and the conductor sounded as if he was happy at his work.

'Now tell me how you got on.' There was a book on psychology on Beth's lap. What about becoming a case history?

'The written bit was ok. I don't think they're looking for an Einstein, but put it like this Beth: if I needed the kiss of life and yon Matron had the chance to do it, I think she might turn down the offer.'

'Ah!' said Beth in an understanding way, then the bus jolted, throwing us together enjoying a collective mirth. It was great when she appreciated my jokes and didn't pursue unpleasant subjects. For a moment, the interview and exam were forgotten and I could just enjoy the bus ride.

Below, and behind their glass frontages, shop haute couture mannequins adopted improbable poses. That malicious wind had more luck plucking at the clothes of the pavement people as they hurried past. Whilst a boy dressed in fifties Teddyboy style seemed better attired for the weather in his thick brothel creepers and long jacket, the girls in their short skirts should have had medals for endurance.

'This is a great way to window shop,' I said but Beth was already on her feet, gathering her possessions and plunging down the aisle.

'Come on, if we're quick, we'll catch the traffic lights. It'll save a big trek to Marks & Spencer and you owe me a pair of stockings, though I'd prefer tights – they're the latest thing.'

7

A DRESSING GOWN GETS
A DRESSING DOWN

'So how did you get on?'

It was amazing. Mrs Davidson's bell had fallen silent whilst Sister Gordon was fully occupied at the far end of the hospital with a new patient. I'd a nag-free moment to spend with happy people.

'I don't know why you're asking.' Mrs Spence's sightless eyes gazed into the distance like those of a mystic. 'Jane'll have come up with all the right answers. She's a natural comedian too,' she leant forward and a note of excitement crept into that gentle voice, 'but tell me, does Marks & Spencer really sell black underwear?'

Mrs Fotheringham chuckled, 'I don't know about that but if you're wanting any, Miss Kerr'll give you some of hers.'

There was a huge chainlike affair above her bed. It looked like a gallows, was called a monkey pole and gave her a handy grasp for pulling herself up. It clanked as she hoisted into full chat mode.

Breathless with the effort, she wheezed, 'Elsie Kerr's got to come into hospital every now and then. She lives at the back of beyond in a house with no running water. Sometimes she lets herself go, doesn't eat, then gets admitted so we can build her up. She doesn't like it but it's for her own good.'

Mrs Fotheringham had been in hospital so long she regarded herself as a member of staff. Maybe it made her incarceration bearable and certainly she bore it with greater grace than Mrs Davidson. Perhaps I should go and investigate. The silence was beginning to shout for attention.

Anxiety was well founded. The room was as full of snores as the bed was empty, its usual occupant located by a pair of bunions sticking out from under it.

'Mrs Davidson! What on earth are you doing there?' It was difficult trying to reach her and worrying that a snore was the only response.

She felt cold and must be unconscious because she wouldn't want anyone to see her with her fallen teeth grinning beside her and a nightdress hugging her neck. There wasn't much point in ringing for action. I'd be ringing myself.

It must be my fault she'd fallen out of bed. Even if she did complain, maybe I should have tucked her in better. Sister Gordon would be furious but I'd just have to find and tell her. I threw a blanket over Mrs Davidson and hurried to get help.

Funnily enough Sister Gordon, with a patient looking a long way from cooperation, was having problems of her own. She seemed almost pleased to have a bigger better emergency on her hands.

'There wis nae need for that bath. Look! Ah'm shivering. I'll get ma death o' cold.'

This must be Miss Kerr. She was minute with a hook nose and the ferocious look of a trapped hawk. Black nails which must have escaped Sister Gordon's attention curled over her fingers.

'Leave me alane, ye brute!' She pulled on her dressing gown cord with a force suggesting a strong free mind.

Having seen the poor thermal quality of a flimsy nightie on a patient currently under a bed nearby, I thought that even if the dressing gown Miss Kerr was wearing was held together by grease, she should keep it on. But Sister Gordon, backing out the door, had other ideas: 'After you've given her a cup of tea and tidied the bathroom, we'll lend her a hospital dressing gown. That one needs a wash. Now I'll see you later, Jane, but right now I'd better go and sort out this *other* problem.' Her tone was grim.

'An' dinna come back,' called Miss Kerr, looking pleased.

I picked up some towels. Sister Gordon must have given Miss Kerr a wipe down before getting her near the bath for they were as black as flue rags.

'Now what about something with your tea?'

'Hiv ye bananas?' Miss Kerr sounded hopeful.

Compared to her alleged staple diet of week old porridge, maybe they held a touch of the exotic.

'Pop into bed and I'll see what I can do, but you'll have to give me that dressing gown first.'

Like a trophy, I carried it and the towels under my arm and hurried to the washhouse before Miss Kerr could change her mind. There was a pile of soiled draw sheets waiting to be sluiced down but they were left to the side as I filled the deep stone sink and added enema soap.

Along with its usual use it was supposedly ideal for fragile fabrics, a fact disproved by the dressing gown, which, even if it was a sad cerise, leaked colour like a haemorrhage.

'Mighty me! I came to put away my rake and what do I find but a bloodbath.' Henry had arrived and sounded so shocked you wouldn't think he'd been a war veteran.

He stroked a lantern jaw. 'Are you doing operations here as well?'

'Blast!' I lifted out the sopping heap. 'Here, hold this please. I'll need to change the water.' I foraged for the plug but in haste tipped the sheets into the water.

Their change to pink was immediate and could have been a magical transformation had their future not been so clinical.

'Damn!'

'A bonny colour,' said Henry fatuously, laying down the dressing gown

[35]

and beginning to edge away. Whilst it looked diminished, the other stuff soaked up the dye like blotting paper.

'You can't leave me now, Henry,' I wailed. 'This is an emergency. Who ever heard of pink hospital linen?' But he'd evaporated and I was alone with only two singularly unattractive pink bundles for company.

We could have had a shared joke about cabbage patches but with Henry gone after suffering an unusual attack of diligence, I'd to deal as best I could in a sort of single parent way and, feeling disappointed in them, hung my children out on the washing line.

'Well I see we're in the pink.' Evelyn had arrived and was rubbing her eyes. 'I'll say one thing about you, Jane, at least you bring a bit of colour to our lives but this is carrying things a bit far surely. Actually I came out to tell you we've managed to get bananas, and that Miss Kerr's shouting for her tea but maybe I'll get Irene to do the needful, give you time to hide that lot. If Gordie sees it, she'll have a fit – and so will Miss Kerr.'

With a sepulchral cough and sigh so big it should have dried everything, she went back inside whilst I shoved my problem children into a bag, stashed it under the sink, then went to get a good relaxing row from Sister Gordon because I hadn't had one for a while.

'Your trouble is you've no common sense,' my mother sighed when I went home with a tale of laundry smuggling and a missing patient. 'I suppose it's all in there apart from the lady under the bed.' She nodded at the poacher's bag. 'It's a wonder you weren't caught taking it out of the hospital.'

I followed her into the scullery and watched her fill the Baby Burco recalled from its usual W.R.I. tea urn duty. 'We're not going to boil the dressing gown as well, are we? It might leave a horrible flavour.'

'Watch and learn.' Mum was testy. 'The dressing gown should go on the pulley. It'll be dry by tomorrow. I think it'll be fine.' She considered it thoughtfully. 'Shabby chic actually. Now, hand me that other stuff.' She threw it in, bringing the mixture to a nice rolling boil and stirring with an unusual cooking enthusiasm until at last the sheets gave up and went back to white.

'That should do.' She dried her hands on her apron. 'You do the finishing off and then you can make the tea, but Jane, I hope to God you get accepted for your training soon, I'm not cut out to be a laundry maid and neither, obviously, are you.'

8

RESULTS!

Miss Kerr had been reunited with her dressing gown and Mrs Davidson with her bell, but whilst Miss Kerr had begun to bloom, Mrs Davidson's grip along with her speech, had gone, taken by a left-sided paralysis.

Sister Gordon was brisk. 'For goodness sake, Jane, don't be so melodramatic. Her landing under the bed had nothing to do with you. She's had a stroke and couldn't help herself falling. One side of her body gave way. That's all. Now that she actually needs nursing I must go and attend to her.'

Personally, I'd rather be looked after by a piranha. No wonder I fretted, and even though my activities were confined to cleaning her room and she lay in bed so quietly, I was unhappy to see complaining Mrs Davidson reduced to a dumb impotence.

Then, one morning, I went to clean the room and found it empty.

'Gone,' said Wilma on a floor-polishing constitutional. She switched off her machine, sighing at the interruption and my distress. 'Went last night.'

'The way you talk about her you'd think she was catching a train and surely somebody might at least have mentioned it at breakfast. The poor woman's dead. I thought she'd have put up a better fight.'

'I never get that involved with the patients,' declared Wilma, pulling on the flex and looking righteous, 'saves a lot of grief. Anyway, I expect the nurses discussed it at their report and that doesn't include you, Jane.'

'I suppose not but maybe one day.'

Wilma was frosty. 'There's worse things than being a ward maid. Why don't you look on the bright side? Without that damn bell ringing all the time, think how much more time we've got to get on with the real work. Here, pass me the floor polish and tell me what d'you think I should wear tonight. Billy says he likes me in pink.'

'You could ask Miss Kerr to leave you her dressing gown. She doesn't like its colour – prefers grey I suppose.'

'Well at least she's likely to be getting home and not leaving in a box.' Wilma dismissed the subject with a flick of her duster.

'I hope I never get that hard hearted,' I said, returning home one day and reeling off a litany of complaints, 'but at least Matron's back and bringing more than sunshine with her. Honestly, Mum, the place is different when she's around. I'd love to be like her.'

My mother looked distracted and pointed to the mantelpiece.

'Let's see if you get the chance.'

There, behind the canary yellow clock painted to match its surroundings, was an official-looking envelope with an Aberdeen postmark.

Dry mouthed, I lifted the letter as if it were a bomb and with shaking fingers opened it.

Bob, snoozing by the fire, yawned largely, showing the teeth of a dedicated carnivore, then returned to the rabbits of his dreams whilst in the yard hens clucked as if in disapproval. I looked at my hands so Lysol worn they could do serious damage and stretched my neck. Somewhere in the distance came the cough of an unhealthy sounding tractor keeping Dad well distant.

I scanned the paper, kicked a log to a safer place in the fire and dropped my shoulders. It had been such a long time since I'd passed any exam I wasn't used to success, then looking down on fire flames leaping, dying and rising again, remembered Mr Matheson, grateful for his memory which too must have played a part in my acceptance.

'Yes! I'm off to Aberdeen and I *am* going to be a nurse.' I waved the paper in triumph and hugged Mum.

'Och I knew you'd be fine,' she said and uncrossed her fingers.

Sister Gordon would have disapproved of the air punching, and even if all the other staff were delighted, she wasn't about to change tack.

'What do you think you're doing?'

I was back in harness and she'd appeared at my shoulder. 'Since when were you allowed to test urine?' Tucking her fingers under her belt she beat out a drum roll, a sure sign of displeasure. 'You're supposed to be cleaning the clinic floor. You've nothing to do with anything above it.'

'Ssh! I'm counting.' I measured five urine drops into a test tube. 'Now, ten of water. Yes, Matron said I could.' I dropped a tablet into the test tube and watched as it fizzed and changed colour. 'She said it'd be good practice for when I'm training.' It was hard not to sound smug. 'And look! Good news. It's blue.' I consulted a colour chart on the wall. 'Negative. Mrs Spence'll be pleased. There's no sugar.'

I eyed her thoughtfully and held up the tube. 'Now there's a funny thing. Look! Same colour as your eyes, Sister.'

'It's a pity you're leaving so soon, doubtless in another month, you'd be doing brain surgery,' her voice was as sharp as a knife, 'but in the meantime, the toilet in the men's ward needs cleaning.'

She stopped to look out the window onto the grounds where Matron was speaking to Henry. Tap tap, went the fingers whilst she made a line of her mouth. Gardeners and cleaners must be part of her fiefdom. Maybe he'd lent her his secateurs to cut Miss Kerr's nails before she went home and Henry needed them back.

She turned on her heel. 'I'm going to have a word with Henry. Mind and you do that toilet properly,' she said as she pointed a finger. 'Your work is so slapdash, I don't think you'll find your training such an easy billet.'

I hoped she wasn't right. It might be hard going back to study, especially as the recommended books were heavy going with illustrations explicit enough to make Dad blench and Mum ban them to my bedroom. Along with some paper nylon petticoats, I'd put them in a suitcase and closed the lid.

Time wore on with the patients clocking a countdown in case I forgot to leave.

'How time flies!' they said, as if their days were full of action.

'Not long now,' said my parents, consulting the calf feed calendar and marking off the days. 'One more week.'

What's in a week? I had known longer minutes.

'Don't tell me they're making you do the washing on your last day!' Henry, hedge clippers in hand, watched as I pegged it out in his prescribed way. 'You've certainly learnt a thing or two. That's a perfect line,' a light breeze got up and made the washing move and dip as if in acknowledgement, 'and now you're going and I'm going to have to train someone new. Me and Sister Gordon.' He scissored the air by way of exercise.

'I'd prefer you any day, Henry,' I said and went to say goodbye to the patients.

9

NEW ARRIVALS

It was different coming to Aberdeen this time. Had I not been a Grantown sophisticate with a doctorate in cleaning I'd have jumped for joy. Instead, I was cool and soignée, assuring Beth that I'd easily find my own way to the Nurses' Home.

'We can catch up at the weekend then,' she said. 'We're thinking of having a party.'

This time I didn't need to be told I'd arrived. Up a small incline offering an easy view over the hospital, the Home had lost nothing of its barrack-like exterior but as I'd already learnt, outward appearances can be deceptive.

Some yards away was a tennis court disused except by seagulls for target practice. A keen wind whistled through the rusting mesh with a monotonous whine and so chilling to the backbone, I rang the bell fast.

To my surprise, the door immediately burst open and a girl carrying suitcases tumbled out.

'My mind's made up and I'm never coming back!' she called to someone over her shoulder. She was tall but with the defeated slump of a hockey captain whose team had just lost.

'Why won't you give it one more go?'

'No. And it's no good you trying.' The girl's tone softened, and she paused for a moment, the wind tugging at her skirt as if trying to hold her back. 'Sister Cameron, you've been a wonderful support and done your best, but if I did stay,' she thought for a moment then grimaced, 'I'd murder Sister Gorightly, and she's ruined enough of my time already.'

She had startled the gulls into flight, their cries echoing her distress. They wheeled high above as she ran down the stone steps oblivious to the bulk of her luggage.

'Wait!'

But she'd fled, going so fast I thought she might overtake my taxi. Her heels clattered down the road until the noise faded into the distance.

'Yes – well, well – by Jove! Not quite the welcome you expected. I hope you don't think this happens every day. A clash of personalities – that's all.' There was concern in the voice of the small trig woman presumably Sister Cameron though her badge only said Home Sister. She held up the oiling can in her hand. 'Maybe I should have used this on the lassie instead of the door,' she sounded rueful, 'but och, don't you be looking so worried. Yon nurse was always homesick and I'm thinking Sister Gorightly was a grand excuse.' She twinkled a welcome and held open the door. 'Come away, come away.'

I stepped in and the door slammed behind as if on a spring.

'At least the oil's worked there then. Now what would be your name?'

The big entrance hall was imposing, impersonal and empty with a bust of Florence Nightingale dead-eyeing proceedings. Sister Cameron's shoes clicked on the marble floor as she went to her glass-fronted office, like a jailer's headquarters with all its keys.

She picked one out and ticked a list.

'Nurse Macpherson!' She handed over a key marked 321. 'That should be easy to remember,' she chuckled as if numbers were hilarious. She picked up a suitcase. 'Here give me one. I'll take you up to your room and because you've luggage we'll take the lift.'

There was a classroom and a cloakroom area aggressively bristling with coat pegs nearby. 'You'll be there for the first three months. It's the P.T.S., short for Preliminary Training School. You see they wouldn't be wanting you near the patients just yet – and you with heather still between your ears.' She had the bright-eyed look of a Skye terrier.

A feeling of dutiful learning followed us to the lift, an ugly ironwork tucked in a dark corner. Sister Cameron marched towards it holding the suitcase as if it were feather light then, putting it down, gave the door a good shake. 'It's not for everyday use. You young girls are fine and fit and the stairs are grand exercise. Anyway, it's just a touch temperamental.'

A well-aimed kick at the whole contraption seemed to do the trick, though it needed a small ankle nip to get me aboard.

'Okey dokey!' sang my minder, following with a carefree spring and clanging the door shut whilst posting herself a pandrop.

Slowly and with a lot of murderous creaks, we inched heavenward, eyeball to eyeball, whilst the suitcases jostled for position: reluctant travellers in a peppermint world.

Meantime and between pandrop crunches, Sister Cameron explained, 'I've put you on the third floor beside another new girl. She's here already and I'm thinking she's a wee bit homesick. No medical cure for that you'll know. I expect the others will be here shortly too but they'll be on another floor. We like to mix older students with the new but don't tell them I said that.' She clapped her hands. 'There's actually not so many in your class so you'll make chums all the sooner for that of it. Ah! Here we are.'

Grateful for survival, I followed as she went along a corridor, which, compared to downstairs, was livelier and brighter with towel-draped bathrooms, cluttered pantries and singing kettles. Behind some of the bedroom doors drifted sounds of transistors, chat and laughter.

'321!' With the air of a conjuror, Sister Cameron threw open a door. 'And it's all yours.'

Even if it didn't have the same charm as my Ian Charles room, the yellow curtains, light furniture and red rug made a cheerful statement. Unlike patients, nurses weren't expected to throw themselves out of windows, which were wide and looked over the city, its granite glitter so clinically clean it could, itself, have been a huge hospital. Beyond was the colourful edge of the North Sea: hard blue in the March light.

'First and foremost, you'll need to be reading these.' An oily finger stabbed at a notice so big it practically obliterated the mirror. 'We don't want you burning to death so there'll be no smoking either, and then you'll need to unpack and mind you do it tidily, the maids don't like cleaning up after other folk's boorachs – it's a fine Highland word for mess as you may well know. And then you could mebbe call on the lassie next door I was telling you about and don't forget,' she consulted her fob watch, 'tea's at five in the staff dining room in the hospital.'

With a kindly nod and in a menthol vapour, Sister Cameron headed back to the lift, ears pricked and presumably preparing for the next incarceration.

The suitcases had been dumped at the door and made the room feel temporary. I wasn't in the mood for unpacking so I threw the rest of my stuff on the chair and sat on the bed savouring my title. Nurse Macpherson! I tried a bounce but the mattress was unyielding. I tried a few times more and was working up to a nice steady rhythm when there was a knock at the door.

'Hello?'

A girl with hair even redder than mine stuck her head round the door. 'Hi! Are you ok? You sound out of breath.' She had mauve-rimmed spectacles which she adjusted by a combination of finger pushing and nose twitch. 'I'm Maisie.'

'I'm Jane and I was just celebrating being called Nurse. I'm trying to knock this bed into shape but it's resisting. Come on in and have a seat.' Cheered by the newcomer's corkscrew curls and pink furry mules, I leapt to clear the chair.

'Well that won't fall any further.' She stepped over the heap. 'I'd done a fair bit of unpacking and was just starting to wonder if I was going to be the only one here when I heard you and Sister Cameron.' She thought for a moment then added, 'Actually the wall's are so thin, I heard your conversation and then the crashing so I thought I'd better see you were alright. Anyway, I thought it might be your first time away from home too and you'd be bound to find it strange.'

Sister Cameron had hinted that Maisie might be homesick but there was something about her jaw which suggested certainty whilst she looked a little old for this to be her first time away.

'I'm delighted you're here. It is all new and a bit scary.' I didn't mention the runaway girl in case my new friend escaped as well. 'It's such a barn of a place I can't imagine ever getting used to it.'

Maisie got up, smoothed her skirt and realigned her spectacles. 'My folks always say not to be frightened of the unknown, maybe offer a wee prayer then go and see what's what. So why don't we do that? I'm dying to have a nose. Come on, Jane, there'll be plenty time for you to unpack later.' Beckoning, she made for the door. 'A wee adventure, eh?'

Her giggle was disconcerting but, grateful that I wasn't expected to fall on my knees, I meekly followed and as we headed for the great unknown, asked Maisie what she used to do.

'Worked in a corsetry department at home. I eventually got curious about what went on under the whalebones and left before the *All In One* got me.' Like someone looking for change, Maisie felt about herself then twanged something elastic. 'Peterhead's alternative to the strait jacket.'

Her heels clopped gently as we tried the next landing, then stopped at big notices threatening dire reprisals should night staff be disturbed. The corridors were long, dark and so suffocatingly quiet, a snore could have started a riot. I found I was holding my breath.

'I've got a terrible urge to scream,' whispered Maisie clutching my shoulder. 'Maybe we should try somewhere else. Let's go downstairs and see if there's more action there.'

Everything in the Home was on a big scale except for a small library which wore a learned air with rich blue carpet, red velvet curtains and by the look of their dull covers, improving tomes, stacked wall to wall. The sole occupant was a bluebottle frantically trying for freedom. Frustrated swears filled the room until Maisie threw a window open to free it and let silence back in.

We moved on to a huge sitting room complete with grand piano. The view over the hospital grounds was astonishingly boring unless you liked flat grass with uncomfortable-looking garden seats regimented round it. The indoor chairs were the same, planted and unloved upon a swirly patterned carpet.

'It's not very homely is it?' Maisie tried out a chord on the yellow keys, but the sound was as bad as her accompanying warble whilst the long chintz curtains shivered as if in horror.

'Next time we're back, we'll put on our tiaras. Come on, it's time for tea.' I closed the door with its Strictly Private sign. 'I wouldn't want to miss it. I'm hungry.'

'I miss the slippers.' Maisie's impressively polished flat black shoes twinkled alongside as we reached the hospital. She looked earnest. 'I've bought two pairs. I hope that's enough. They say nursing's really hard on your feet.'

But I was too busy to respond savouring the joy of walking along that green-floored corridor remembered from my interview. Sister Cameron had said we were to go to the *staff* dining room and now we were actually part of it.

We followed the smell of boiled cabbage, went upstairs and found the dining room, a drab hall with dark wood panelling meeting walls the colour of jaundice. A portrait of the Queen took pride of place above the food-serving area. She was dressed for a grander occasion and looking over rows of apparently colour-coded nurses sitting at tables.

'They're the staff nurses,' Maisie whispered as we crept past a line of serious pink with white caps bent over their plates in single-minded concentration. 'You know the students by the grey uniform and yon stupid hats that look like foolscap. Ha! Dead right! I wonder how they stay on.'

A maid in green noticed us and directed us to a table right at the back where there were others, conspicuous by their ordinary clothes.

'Come and sit with us. We're new too,' a small plump girl beckoned.

With blonde corkscrew curls exploding round a red-cheeked face, she was a cherub taking time off from a Christmas card.

'Come and sit by us.' With her dimples and little hands a blur of instruction and organisation, she was clearly one of God's really useful little helpers. 'Hello. I'm Rosie and,' the hands whirled into action, 'this is Isobel, Sheila, Jo and Hazel. See, I've remembered!' She looked round the table in triumph.

'You forgot me – everybody does,' sighed a girl patting mousy hair as if to remind herself she was actually present.

'I have not!' Rosie was triumphant. 'It's Morag and it rhymes with toe rag. See!'

In a sensible grey suit with her self-effacing way it was hard to imagine anybody less like a tearaway, but Rosie's attention had turned to the mince and cabbage lying in a terminal state at the side of Isobel's plate. 'You not hungry?'

Isobel pushed it aside. 'No, not really. I'd my tea before I came.'

'Are you from Aberdeen then?' I asked, thinking with that elegance, height and cloud of black hair she should be on the front cover of a fashion magazine.

Isobel opened her mouth but Rosie was quicker: 'She is. Hazel, Jo and me too. It's a bit daft but living in's the rules.'

'Maybe the idea is for us to get to know each other. I'm really chuffed I've a room to myself. I'm looking forward to settling into it and the food's fine if you're hungry.' Hazel spread a large dollop of butter onto a slice of white bread and bit into it with perfect teeth.

Whilst it was impossible to think of Isobel on frontline duties dealing with unmentionables in a sluice, Hazel, even if she was as elegant, was a bit more substantial and with a jolly manner – and her hair was straight.

'Yer right, Hazel, an a droppie salt maks the difference.' Sheila had a placid voice that wrapped around us like a comforting shawl. 'An if, like me, ye hivna eaten since the 2:30 fae Inverurie, ye fairly tuck in.' Food bunched her cheeks into downy peaches whilst she patted hair lacquered into a crash helmet. 'So, eat up quines. It's a lang time til breakfast.' Her easy way was enviable.

Jo ate tidily and daintily. Her eyes were dark and watchful. 'You must have arrived before me but how come you're last here?'

We explained about our tour of the Home.

'That solves that mystery,' she said in her demure way. 'I heard you when I was in the lift with Sister Cameron. She was going to stop it to investigate. I nearly died at the prospect of that old crate doing anything so efficient, though I did wonder who was making that bloody awful racket.'

'That would have been the piano – it needs tuning.' Maisie was quick.

Another table close-by had more recruits at it, their laughter and chat making a friendly noise and echoing ours, though Isobel was more impressed by my empty plate. 'You must have been hungry.'

Aware she was twice my height and probably half my weight, I tried not to sound defensive. 'I'd an early start.'

'Me too,' said Morag, sounding forlorn. 'It's a long, long way from Tain and by comparison, Aberdeen's enormous. I feel a proper little country mouse.' She nibbled her finger as if it was a corn ear.

Sighing but unable to compete, Rosie stacked the plates and marched us out of the emptying hall.

'The maids need their time off.' Her short legs pumped to keep up with Isobel's easy lope. 'Now let's see if we can cheer you up, Morag. When we go back to the Home we'll make a cup of tea and have it in your room – it'll be a bit of company for you.'

Morag looked like my favourite auntie faced with a busload of relatives arriving unannounced and looking for refreshment. 'No! Please don't bother. It's in a right old mess – there wouldn't be room for you.' In an agitated way, she squared her box jacket. 'I've loads to do. Look, I'll be fine.' Still protesting, she hurried after Rosie.

'We'll go to mine then,' Maisie called after her. 'Come on, Hazel, Rosie's about to give us a row. We're falling behind.'

'There's plenty time. Three years in fact,' said Hazel as we left the hospital. She nodded in the direction of the courts, 'Anyone for tennis?' Her laugh was like a drain being cleared.

We dawdled behind, taking in our surroundings. I hadn't noticed the flowers bordering the side of the hospital. Their heads were turned to catch the last rays of a late sun. The wind still blew but came from a kinder direction. It stirred my hopes. I hadn't expected the hospital or new faces to feel so familiar so soon. I was sure we were going to be nurses – good nurses, all of us.

'Come along,' sang our leader and we lengthened our steps to please her and arrive at the Home together.

'Well, well now, girls, have you had a nice tea?' Sister Cameron bobbed out of her office. Her eyes missed nothing. A pandrop crunched.

'Thank you, it was lovely,' Isobel lied, not missing a beat.

'Isn't that grand, and I'm glad to see you're making friends too. Now you be making sure you all have an early night now, so you'll be fresh as fresh tomorrow. By Jove, yes.' Highland valedictions followed us up the stairs.

Taking the steps two at a time, Maisie passed Rosie. 'Wee leggies!' she chuckled. 'And it's my room, Rosie, Morag's not ready for a site visit.'

'Well I'll be your first visitor,' said Rosie, sounding annoyed and running to catch up with her.

'Isn't this a lovely evening?' Maisie sang as she threw open her door. For someone who didn't appear that organised, her room had a military tidiness.

'I've had plenty time to get sorted.' She made an apologetic wave at the book shelves stacked with precision, the cosmetic bottles lined up on the dressing table like a firing squad. A bible lay on the bedside table. 'I'll have you know I keep immaculate drawers too.'

There was a bonding snigger then Jo suggested, 'Maybe singing lessons could be more fun.'

As Morag sat primly on a hard chair, Hazel hunkered down to look at the mules peeping out from under the bed.

'I bet Sister Cameron doesn't know about the animals. What do you feed them on?'

'Jane likes them too. Hey, folks, I'm sorry there's not more room, but I'm sure the floor's clean enough to sit on.'

'Hmph!' sniffed Rosie, plumping down and ruffling her celestial feathers. 'We should have more chairs but the rooms are that pokey there wouldn't be space.'

'I don't know. A crowd around me makes the place feel more alive. Until Jane arrived, I thought I was stuck on this floor on my own, but now I'm beginning to feel it's quite cosy here.'

'Well it's maybe ok for you – you're much older, but it's not like my own wee bedroom at home.' Two fat tears rolled down Rosie's cheeks. 'Och I'm sorry but I've never been away from home like this and I just can't help thinking how much my dog, Mam and Dad will be missing me and I know I don't live so far away as Morag or even Jane, but – o-o-oh.' Rosie was lost to grief.

We exchanged glances. We hadn't expected this and for a moment there was an uncomfortable silence. I wondered if it might set off Morag but she was already on her feet and taking charge.

Earning her place as the first caring angel, if not in heaven, at least in the locality, she said, 'You were quite right, Rosie. What we need is a nice cup of tea so why don't you come with me and help me make it. Come on and, look, here's a tissue.'

10

A LEARNING CURVE

We might have one cherub and one kindly angel in our group but that didn't count for much in the eyes of Miss Jones.

God may well have started as a medical student and with diligence become a doctor, shedding that title on his surgical way to becoming a Mr and eventually jettisoning that for the top job, but Sister Tutors had also taken a difficult route to power. From humble student nurse origins, they qualified to become staff nurses, onwards to ward sisters, then finally back to their original titles but now in charge of nursing destinies.

So, and on God's behalf, Miss Jones and Mrs Low, a double act running the Preliminary Training School, were about to rule our universe: Mrs Low by saintliness, Miss Jones by quite another method.

Blessed in ignorance, we hung about the classroom, our first day chat enlivening the dull chalk-laden surroundings and making connections with the rest of the students. Isobel, idly manicuring her nails, was already seated whilst Rosie set about organising the rest of us.

Maisie, ignoring the traffic control signals, chose her own spot. 'This is like school. I've always to be near the front so that I can see the blackboard.' She drummed her fingers on her desk and looked about her. 'I wonder where the tutors have got to.'

As if on cue, a tall angular figure in bottle green strode into the classroom. 'Quiet!'

In a missile sort of way, she was impressive.

I hid behind Sheila whilst the rest scuttled to the nearest desk and Isobel put away her nail file.

'Since you're new, you might not appreciate how noise carries, but do you realise night staff might be trying to sleep? I could hear you miles away. This class is smaller than usual so I wasn't expecting it to be twice as noisy.' Her eyes flashed. 'I just hope its mind doesn't match its size. I don't want a racket like this again. Is that clear?'

'Yes, Miss – er –'

'Jones!' It came like a battle cry.

'I'm your tutor for anatomy and physiology and by the end of three months, I'll have hopefully instilled in you all there is to know about the human body so that by the time you go into the wards you should at least know how it works properly. Of course and so that I know I'm doing the job properly and you've been listening, there'll be the weekly tests to check your progress. The exam at the end of P.T.S. will prove both your and my worth.' Her smile was mirthless as she raised her eyebrows. 'Now! Has anybody any questions?'

Jo raised her hand. 'What happens if we fail?'

'That's it.' The tone was final. 'The first three months are crucial and allow us to see if you really are committed, and don't forget, we'll be looking at your practical work as well. There's no point in time being wasted either for you or for us. Nursing is a profession that isn't worth doing unless it's taken seriously.'

Apart from the minute niggling sound of Morag worrying her fingers, you could have heard a pin drop.

'Of course, there is the option of a repeat P.T.S.,' the tutor said, moving towards a tall thin cupboard. She smoothed her hands on its handle. 'But we'd have to think about that very carefully because there's a lot of new recruits eager to take your place. Right! Let's get started right away.' She opened the door. 'This morning, I want you to meet a colleague of mine.' In a smooth movement, she pulled out a skeleton hanging from an extending rail so that it dangled before us like a puppet.

'Meet Skellie,' she said and stroked, twiddled and twirled its long dead bits.

Maisie screamed and Sheila cried, 'Ma Gode!'

I had never envisaged a real corpse for educational purposes but Sheila with her ashen face closely resembled one. She slumped over her desk whilst we craned forward to get a better view. This was some lecture.

Miss Jones was unperturbed. 'Dear, dear, I shudder for the profession if this is what's likely to happen. So what do you think we should do, girl behind the body please?'

I got up slowly, adjusted Sheila's scarf, fiddled tentatively with her neck buttons and hopped on one leg by way of diversion.

With a sigh of exasperation, the tutor strode over and laid the patient on the floor with a gentle ease.

'You put an unconscious patient like so, and her legs like so. We call it the Sims' position. If she's put like this, she won't choke. Just take a note of that will you? I hadn't expected to use the term so soon but you'll meet it often enough when you're in the wards. And remember that the patient's dignity must be maintained as much as possible. I don't suppose this patient really wants to be like this.' The hand movements were quick, sure and practised. Sheila's suspenders were hardly affected and the 'A Present From Inverurie' emblazoned on her knickers surely a figment of the imagination. She looked so comfortable we quite envied her, especially as it was hard not to join in Rosie's fit of nervous giggles. Laughing might be a health hazard.

Maisie had been despatched for a drink of water or a breath of fresh air, whichever got rid of her quickest, and when she returned still ashen-faced but spectacles glinting with renewed health, she was in time for Sheila's recovery.

'Ah gott an affa fright. Naebody expects skeletons tae cam poppin oot like that. Weel, nay in Inverurie ony road.' She got up slowly, shaking her head as if to check the contents, hair remaining in concrete. 'Fit next?'

'Ok? Right!'

Treating Sheila's faint as mere detail, Miss Jones surged on. She held up a plastic model of something you might order from the butcher. 'Everybody listening? Let's move on shall we? We'll be finding out about the liver and the heart of course. I know you'll find them quite fascinating.' Her teeth, reminiscent of the Home's yellowing piano keys, flashed as she delved into a drawer, its contents rattling like dice. Then she lifted out a heart, which opened like a joke apple. 'Marvellous realism here, Nurses, I thoroughly recommend you use it when studying.' She smoothed over the plastic as if it needed a polish.

'I might eat it,' said brave Jo.

To our surprise, Miss Jones laughed, lightening the classroom atmosphere a little. Still, the coffee break came as a relief.

We gathered in an adjoining room to discuss survival prospects.

'I wouldn't put it past that wifie to do open heart surgery just for a laugh,' said Rosie, looking around nervously.

'Yes, Sheila, you were lucky to come round when you did. You might have woken up with a plastic one,' Hazel laughed.

Isobel shrugged elegantly. 'Well, we can't say it's been a dull morning. I haven't felt so alert since putting the kitchen on fire in the nursing home where I used to work.'

'How did you manage that?' Fire raising had not occurred to us as a way of entertainment.

'I found a quickie way to do a poultice by grilling it, but I wouldn't recommend it. It can set off the fire alarm and ruins the taste of toast.'

One of the girls chuckled and patted her pocket. 'Talking of fire, I'm dying for a fag. Anyone coming out for a breath of fresh air?'

'For goodness sake! We haven't time!' Rosie tapped on her watch. 'We don't want to get on the wrong side of Miss Jones.'

'Yeah – I'll come,' Maisie said. 'I think my head'll burst if I don't and don't worry, Rosie, we'll be back for the next execution.'

'On your own head be it.'

Morag pursed her lips looking like a conscientious secretary. 'Well I'm going back. I've already missed half of the stuff she was saying. She's going so fast I'm worried I can't keep up with my notes. If I go back now I'll get a chance to catch up.'

I said, 'Notes? Crikey! I was so taken aback by her introductory spiel I never thought to put anything down. Let's have a shufti at what you've written.'

We sped back and were surprised to find that the sun had broken out with Miss Jones replaced by a tutor who sounded genuinely welcoming. 'Ah! There you are, Nurses, come and take your seats please. Have you had a nice break?' She had grey curly hair, a motherly way and a smile like the stir mark left on thick custard.

'I'm Mrs Low and delighted to be your practical work instructor. I know we are going to enjoy these three months together and that you will leave here able to take your places as caring representatives of this P.T.S. That is of paramount importance.' She clasped her comfortable bosom and looked upward with such sincerity she should have been accompanied by a burst from a heavenly choir.

'Now our first practical lesson is,' her inhalation could have hoovered up the dust particles dancing round her halo, 'how to properly fill a hot water bottle. Yes! A hot water bottle! It is of paramount importance,' a waggish finger waved, 'that we learn to do the simple things well. We can then proceed. We shall do this in the practical procedure room. If you would follow me please.'

'This is heavy stuff,' grumbled Jo, as we cheeped light discontent in the tutor's comfortable wake. 'My brain's going to burst with the challenge. Still, she's a friendly old soul. I wouldn't like to upset her.'

The other classroom was large, light and full of draughts, with a life-size doll in a state of advanced decline in the hospital bed placed centre stage. There were cupboards, sinks and enough trolleys to mobilise the entire caring concept. For the patient's view, long poorly-fitted windows gave out onto seagulls tap dancing for worms on an unbroken length of stunted anaemic-looking grass. Somewhere in the distance, the city grumbled, its moans carried by a chilly wind through the windows and demanding a presence in the room. It wasn't the best prospect for a patient exposed to the care of a novice army.

Mrs Low gathered us round the bed.

'I want you to pay close attention to my technique. It is of paramount importance,' Maisie dug me in the ribs, 'that you tell the patient what you are about to do, otherwise they can get an awful fright. I know this personally.' She put her hand on her heart and rolled her eyes with the drama of a prima donna. 'You see, Nurses, I was once a patient and had to have my appendix out. As soon as I was admitted, a nurse came to my bedside with a razor. In my anxious state I thought she was going to do the operation right there and then.' She winced at the recall, then, 'You see, Nurses, she didn't *explain*.'

'So what did she want to do?' asked Isobel.

Mrs Low's look was as sharp as the alleged razor, but Isobel's look of dedicated interest sent the tutor on a mission to explain about cleanliness and how being shaved from stem to stern guaranteed hygiene for an operation.

'And six months stubbly discomfort,' murmured Isobel, lips fixed and looking dreamy.

Still, Mrs Low's lecture was long enough to stop anyone wanting to hear more. There were no further questions.

Our tutor now advanced upon the dummy, face aglow and arms outstretched.

'Good Morning, Mrs Brown. I hear your hot water bottle's cold. Now I know it's not easy for you to move, so if you'll excuse me, I'll just get it out for you. I think it's under the bedclothes somewhere.'

We watched, becoming interested, as she prepared to climb aboard whilst Rosie went red and searched for her hanky.

Mrs Brown, plainly overcome by the exertions of her carer foraging, clucking and explaining, flopped drunkenly to the side.

Jo frowned at Rosie who was having some difficulty in breathing. Meanwhile, the rest of us were mesmerised by the sight of Mrs Low's sturdy calves and the sound of her voice muffled under the blankets.

'Goodness me, Mrs Brown, I think you must be hiding it!'

When all but the tutor's heels had disappeared Isobel gave a gentle cough. 'Excuse me, but is this what you're looking for?' She pointed to a bottle lying on a table beside the sink.

'And doesn't this just prove how important it is to have a real dialogue with your patients? Listen, listen and listen!' Not missing a beat, Mrs Low emerged, fixing her cap in a composed way and beaming at her patient. 'Isn't that so, Mrs Brown?'

We looked again at the dummy and thought Mrs Low should spend more time with real people, especially as we now had to emulate her demonstration. Under her dedicated eye, we explained, we listened, oh how we listened and filled the hot water bottle as a water-play bonus. Time tripped by, and we got wet and bored enough to stop pretending our patient was capable of dialogue.

'You will have a written examination on this on Friday just so that I'm quite sure you understand this procedure.' Mrs Low momentarily sounded as fierce as Miss Jones. 'So you see it is important to concentrate.' Then she smiled and normal service was restored. 'But I can see you've all been working very hard and with a little diligence you will manage very nicely. I think you've earned your break.'

As she left the classroom, Isobel stretched and, waving her fingers to the ceiling, sighed, 'This could be a long week.'

She was right, for, whilst Miss Jones filled the days juggling, levering and raining anatomical wonders up to a bilious point, Mrs Low continued to smile and radiate benevolence and paramount importance. Subjected to so much care, Mrs Brown seemed to have uncooperatively aged decades and begun to leak stuffing. Morag agonised over every move and filled reams of paper in her neat handwriting, but as I had filled a few hot water bottles in my time, I figured a question on Mrs Brown's one would be a doddle.

I wondered what I should wear to Beth's party.

'Are you nervous about tomorrow's exam?' Bored in the evening with bedroom and study, I went next door where Maisie was lying on her bed surrounded by a pile of books with her eyes shut and the occasional twirls of her mules to indicate life.

'I'm sick to death of Mrs Brown, our tutors and the great and good works of the kidney.' Maisie, reaching out for her spectacles, knocked over her bible. 'Damn!' She swung her legs over the side. 'Tell you what, Jane, I really fancy going to the pictures. Fancy coming?'

'Great idea. What about the others?'

'Let's just go,' Maisie was already up and throwing on outdoor clothes, 'otherwise Rosie will turn it into a military manoeuvre and I don't want to be marched into town.' She thought for a moment then bobbed her curls. Cheerful as they might look, they were also signs of determination. 'Why don't we take the lift? Then we'll avoid seeing anybody and having to explain where we're going.'

'Do you think we should?' I was doubtful. I hated that lift but didn't want to appear soft in front of a worldly twenty-one-year-old fae Peterheid.

'Honestly, they treat us like kids around here.' Maisie applying lipstick like a guided missile caught my worried look in the mirror. 'What's the big deal about this lift? Anyway, I wouldn't put it past Rosie to be out patrolling her floor and I for one think we all need a break from each other.'

'What about Morag then? She's in a permanent state of anxiety. When she hasn't got her nose in a textbook, she's down at the kiosks with her ear to a phone. I think she's really homesick and we should ask her. We're supposed to be learning to be members of a caring profession. We could practise on her.'

'Ok. Just go and see if you can find a whole pair of stockings and get your coat.' She blew herself a kiss in the mirror. 'We'll just nip into the lift and go down to her floor.'

Like burglars, we stole along the corridor and pressed the lift button as if it were red hot. Slowly, like a wakening monster, it creaked into view.

'Sshh!' I covered my ears whilst Maisie opened the gate then, as soon as we stepped in, crashed it shut. 'Quick! Turn off the lights – we don't want to be seen.' I screwed my eyes shut in case throwing the switch light off hadn't worked.

The descent was painfully slow.

'We'd have been quicker taking the stairs,' I grumbled, 'and why are we stopping here anyway?'

'Because I've pressed the stop button,' said Sister Cameron glaring through the latticed ironworks at us. 'The pair of you. Get out, now!'

11

EXAMS AND PLANS

'We've just had an awful row.'

Apart from a framed photograph of a tweedy-looking guy on her bedside table, every other surface in Morag's room was covered with handwritten notes and books whilst bean-shaped illustrations enlivened the walls. Instead of the dreaded suit hanging like a repressed clerkess on the back of a chair, Morag had changed into an Ovalteeny in her flannelette pyjamas.

It wasn't easy finding room to sit and, plainly getting ready for bed, she looked flustered at our visit.

'Crumbs! You've been busy.' Maisie perched one cheek on the side of the bed. 'We were actually coming to take you away from all this to the pictures when Sister Cameron found us in the lift and sent us packing.'

Maisie didn't add that, instead of going to a quiet prayer meeting she'd invented as the reason we were leaving so discreetly, we'd been roundly told to do something a little more Christian.

'I'm worried about that nurse from Tain,' Sister Cameron had said. 'She's homesick enough to leave. Just you go and give her a bit of your company instead and don't let me ever see you in this lift again.' She'd put her back against the door as if barricading it.

No problem, I'd thought.

So here we were, back where we intended to be, but with the extra baggage of a lie between us.

Doubling it, I offered, 'We thought we'd take the lift for a laugh.'

Morag looked shocked at the very prospect of fun and the lift in the same breath. 'I'd have persuaded you not to take it. Honestly, you're a right pair of rascals. I'd have thought you'd have been studying anyway.' She nodded at the beans, 'I just hope I remember where to put the ureters tomorrow.'

'Well, maybe we'll get back to our studies too.' Maisie squinted at the drawings and looked startled. 'Is that where they go? In that case I might have a problem with mine. Maybe we should get back to our studies after all.'

Next morning, Miss Jones handed out paper with the smug expression of somebody with all the answers. 'Now I'll find out who's been paying attention and grasped the concept of study. There will be no speaking throughout the examination and remember, it's facts we're after.' She pointed to the wall clock. 'You will have half an hour for each question.'

The kidney question didn't come as a surprise and already Sheila was using coloured pencils with artistic skill: cute cartoon-like figures having personalised her notes all week.

'They're sperms,' she'd explained. 'Affa easy tae draw.'

I hoped she didn't feel Miss Jones needed the same light touch on her exam paper, but since I didn't want her bored, I wrote about the great and good works of the kidney, recommending one with plenty ureters as the best plumber in town.

The hot water bottle question was so much easier, we considered it an insult to our intelligence. Still, we didn't want to disappoint Mrs Low and wrote with a diligence surely enough to please her.

Gathering the finished papers, Mrs Low beamed upon us. 'Now, Miss Jones and I want you all to have a lovely weekend and to come back fresh, rested and ready for next week. We'll be doing lots of practical procedures and we must get them absolutely perfect, or Mrs Brown will be asking for the Complaints Book, won't she?'

'Tae pot wi Mrs Broon.' Sheila's artwork had obviously consumed her, leaving her wilting and homesick. 'Ah canna wait tae get the bus hame an' I'm nay sure if ah'll be back.'

'Oh surely you will,' Hazel said, chucking her under the chin. 'Don't you let that old Jonesie put you off.'

'Ah'll see.' Sheila, looking unhappily into the middle distance, picked at a cardigan button and sighed. 'Ah'm nay makin' any promises an' whativver happens, Ah'm only buyin' a single ticket.'

'I know what you mean but Tain's too far and I can't afford the fare.' Morag's little face was creased in misery. 'Anyway, I've made such a mess of that exam I'll be asked to leave without sitting any more.'

'Ah doot it but fittaboot coming tae Inverurie wi' me, we've great dances on a Saturday an' at least it'd tak yer mind off yer studies?' Sheila was already brightening but Morag looked aghast. 'I couldn't possibly. My boyfriend wouldn't like me enjoying myself, especially when he's saving to come and visit me in Aberdeen next weekend. No thanks, Sheila, I'll just stay put.'

Maisie however had no such reserve. 'Well I'd fancy some fun. Could anybody come?'

Sheila was pleased. 'Aye an' fittaboot you other quines? We could mak a right do of it. Ye could a' come oot in the bus tomorrow night.'

But Maisie was the only taker and having consulted the runes about timetables and fixing up a time, said she was already getting excited and what about us all going to the cinema to celebrate it was the weekend.

'There's a good film on. *Billy Liar*.'

'No. I'm going home to see my dog. Anyway, I don't think it's my style.' Rosie fluffed her curls. 'It's supposed to have a sad ending.'

Linking arms with Morag, I said, 'Well in that case it sounds perfect. Come on, a nice bit of gloom will do us the world of good.'

12

PARTY PREPARATIONS

Next morning, smoke was issuing from the pantry on our floor where Maisie, hedgehogged in rollers, was throwing charred remains into the sink.

'Quick! Shut the door.' She turned on the taps and let the toast sigh into sappy oblivion. 'There! That sorted that, I don't want Sister Cameron thinking there's a fire.'

'Coo, Maisie, you live dangerously.' I watched as she slung more Sliced Pan into the still glowing toaster.

'Don't worry.' She was supremely confident. 'It'll be fine. Just relax. It's Saturday, we've got this super wee place so we don't have to go trailing into the hospital for breakfast, and with a bit of luck, Sister Cameron's off duty.'

She cleaned her hands on her dressing gown, then rubbed them together in glee. 'Isn't it great it's Saturday? I can't think why you're even dressed. Cuppa?' She switched on the kettle, looked out two thick white cups and banged them down on the formica-topped table.

I wished I'd such a leisurely approach to time. All week I'd been looking forward to a lie-in, yet I was already up and ready for action in a young day, unsure if I'd time for that cup of tea.

Maisie said, 'Go on! You can do it. Take a chair and while you're at it, tell me about Beth's digs.'

Reluctantly, I sat down trying not to check my watch.

'She's got a great setup. Rooms in a big house which must have been grand once, but it's old now and a tad decrepit. I bet the road was built after it. It's cobbled with such a narrow pavement, step out the door and passing buses could trim your toes.'

Maisie twirled her mules as if to reassure them. 'It sounds oldie worldie.'

'Well, the University must think it's worth saving. It's near King's College in the old town quarters. They've bought it from Mrs Ronce, Beth's landlady, giving her life rent. It was a good deal, especially as she was able to tell them about the leaking roof a month after signing the contract.'

'How many?' Maisie held a large spoon over a sugar bowl.

'Just two please. I'm thinking of dieting.'

'And what about inside?'

'Well, they don't make front doors like that anymore.' I recalled a huge heavy affair which opened into a dusty entrance hall that might have looked classy had the marble floor not been cracked and the grandfather clock missing the minute hand. 'And once inside, you have to watch out. The rug's so threadbare I tripped over it the first time I visited Beth. I'd a weekend with her, thought I'd suss the City before I started training.' I rubbed my neck. 'I could have broken this instead of becoming the city slicker I am today.'

Maisie squinted down her nose. 'You've a while to go yet. And Mrs Ronce?'

'She's quite a character. Posh but chirpy as a sparrow. According to Beth, she must live on fresh air: it's certainly not on the rental pittance she asks her and her pal. I suppose it's all a bit basic and cold but Mrs Ronce doesn't seem to feel it and on the rare occasion she does, she buys a woolly from the charity shop where she sometimes works, and as for transport – well – she's got a pensioner's pass.' I stirred my tea, feeling the syrup underneath. 'D'you know, there's enough sugar here to last her a week.'

'And does she cook for the girls?'

'Sometimes she knocks up what she calls savoury messes. Beth says they're great, but she cooks mostly for her cats. They're the most valued residents and very partial to fish, so the place can stink a bit. According to my sister, you don't notice it after a while.'

'Gyad,' Maisie wrinkled her nose, oblivious to the lingering odours in the pantry. 'And is there a Mr Ronce?'

'Apparently there was one, but long ago. I gather there was a favourable divorce settlement, enough to fund fancy cat food anyway.'

'So why take lodgers?'

'She's very young at heart, loves the company and likes to know what's going on in their lives.'

'Nosey then?'

'A bit, I suppose, but Scrabble's her passion so she's never short of players. She'd engineer anybody into playing it but it's not a big price for allowing parties and unlimited numbers of young folk around.' I mused, 'I certainly couldn't imagine my parents putting up with a houseful of young folk, let alone enjoying their parties, but Mrs Ronce even plays the piano for them.'

I drained the cup and got up, shoving on my anorak. 'Unfortunately, hospitality rates fairly low in farming routines when everybody's to be up at the crack of dawn. Anyway – I'll need to go. I've promised to go down early and help get the place ready. If you hadn't opted for Inverurie's bright lights you could have come tonight.'

Maisie poured another cup of tea and yawned deeply. 'What it is to have a crowded social diary. I'm exhausted already. I think I'll have to go back to bed.'

I caught the bus to Old Aberdeen.

A planet away from the sixties city high rises, the area wore a look of ancient dignity with its narrow, winding cobbled streets, walled gardens and King's College, standing some way from the road, regal in its learned past. Apart from the sound of buses rattling over the uneven stones, it was very quiet.

I got off at Mrs Ronce's house where it was noisier, the old lion's head over the doorknocker seeming to try for a roar, albeit in a lacklustre way.

Still, what was the want of Brasso compared to the sparkling welcome of Mrs Ronce?

'Janey!' she cried, lugging open the door. She looked pleased though odd, with something like a snail curling halfway across her forehead. 'Come in! I'm in the kitchen – in the middle of something actually. Now, mind the cats.' She scampered on ratty legs, back into a room leading off the hall.

It was a shame the university hadn't stretched funds for some redecoration. The high corniced ceilings and mouldings deserved better than the present flaking distemper, yet the house retained a charm reminiscent of a kindly dowager relaxed amongst fading treasures.

Two ginger cats were parked under the stove, keeping vigil over a big pan of fish boiling on the gas, with enough room left for a faintly glowing gadget. It could have been a branding iron but Mrs Ronce was now using it on her fringe to produce a matching snail. The smell of fish mixing with singed hair was a unique combination and enough to alert Beth, who stuck her head round the door.

Her eyes watered as she said, 'My, but you're up early, we haven't had our breakfast yet.'

'I could fry you some kippers,' Mrs Ronce offered. Both cats and Beth looked horrified.

'Thanks, but we'll fix ourselves up with something when we go into town. Sally and I are going now to beat the crowds and get stuff for tonight.'

Sally, petite, blonde and beautiful, joined us. 'Hi big little sis, good to see you. So you've come to help. Great! It should be fun; nurses like a good time.' Her friendliness was genuine, so I wondered why such a chance remark should make me cross. Ok, I might dwarf Beth, but what was wrong with a size fourteen? I sucked in my stomach and supposed malnutrition mustn't figure in any of their lectures.

'You'll see we're off on a big errand?' Sally waved two large shopping bags. Then, listening intently, she cried, 'Quick! There's a bus coming. Come on, Beth, if we hurry we'll catch it.'

'Ok.' Beth grabbed her duffel. 'You'll probably still be here Jane, when we come back, and we'll catch up then. I'm dying to know how the caring world is progressing.' The door slammed and they were gone.

I sighed. 'Honestly, Beth and her pals make me mad. They're always going on about nurses liking a good time as if that's all they think about and did you hear that sarky crack about caring?'

Mrs Ronce had looked out a package with faded lettering and was pouring the contents into a pan of boiling water. 'Personally, I think nurses are wonderful, and much as I respect the would-be academics of this world, they won't have seen half or any of the stuff nurses have to cope with,' she stirred vigorously, 'so I suppose some nurses might think parties are a good way to let their hair down and as they're not patients, that's all that students see of them. Of course, you won't be like that, Jane.' She held up an admonishing wooden spoon. 'You're far too stable and sensible. Now I'm going to have some porridge as a special treat. You can either have some or go and check the cellar.'

Unsure if I liked the recent accolade I asked, 'The cellar?'

Mrs Ronce nodded at the grandfather clock. 'There. Open the door and see if there's anything in it.'

An array of quality sherry bottles as good as any bar's stock stood around the pendulum.

'I have them to make my Scrabble parties go with a swing, you'd be amazed how it loosens people's vocabularies, and of course, I have the occasional morning constitutional.' She smacked her lips. 'So let's put them somewhere else so there's room for tonight's surplus. And before you ask, sometimes people carry a surplus and don't know it. Storage like this is all in the name of charity and preventative medicine. As a nurse, I'm sure you'll approve.'

The sitting room was opposite the kitchen. I took the bottles out and stored them in a coffin disguised as an ancient cupboard and looked at the fire. There was a rug in front of it, so old and tatty there should have been a preservation order on it.

'Will I get in some coal?' Some pathetic-looking embers were on the edge of expiry.

'Good God, no!' Mrs Ronce threw down her spoon before coming through to seize a poker and give the cinders a hearty extinguishing whack. 'It's absolutely boiling in here.'

I was glad that I'd asked, surprised we couldn't see our breath in front of us and suddenly aware that I might have to shop for something warm to survive. Setting about clearing the sitting room, I thought something cute but not sensible in flannel should do the trick.

The cats, abandoning all hope of food, had departed to the untamed garden and had taken to glaring in from the sitting room window sill.

'I'm afraid they're no party animals. They always know when there's one on.' Mrs Ronce flicked a grimy dishcloth in their direction, shouting after them, 'Just you go and find a home in the summerhouse.'

She meant the converted wardrobe at the bottom of the garden. It looked like a step up from the trysting byre of home, but Mrs Ronce declared it out of bounds and only for pussy cats made homeless by selfish people wanting to sit on sofas and have parties.

Beth and Sally had come back and were in time to help replace the caster wheel dislodged from the piano during its trundle to a whole floorboard area.

'Good! I can't play on a slope.' Mrs Ronce, with a toothy grin, rattled off 'Three Little Maids', her foot hard on the accelerator.

'It feels like a bomb alert in here.' Beth threw aside a list, found a chair and tidied herself into a small corner.

Sally said in her elegant exhausted way, 'Saturday shopping's hell but that's the main part of the work done. Now what we need is a nice cup of tea.' She raised eyebrows so finely sculpted they must have been done under general anaesthetic. 'What say you, Oh Jeannie of the Magic Lamp?'

'Hey, that's a good one,' said Beth, perking up. 'Perfect name for you, sis. Go and do some magic in the kitchen.'

'No thanks.' I was sour. 'The lamp's left in the Nurses' Home. Anyway, I'll need to get back. Maybe give it a polish too.'

I should have added, 'Now that the heavy work's been done,' but only thought of it stepping off the Union Street bus.

Out in Aberdeen's main shopping area, the shops were full of clothes for rich mannequins unlikely to move, catch buses or be anywhere cold. Maybe it was the prices or even the lack of breakfast, but suddenly I felt dizzy.

I leant my forehead against the cool window of a chemist shop and practised the deep breathing acquired when I finally accepted that Beth could hit harder then me. It worked in as much as the street stopped reeling, but I saw from the reflection in the glass that I was a perfect contrast to the advertising picture inside of a tanned, fit and lovely looking model declaring, 'You too can be a golden girl; what's more, it's Fantanstically simple!'

Apart from those who had trowelled on the Panstick foundation or were a red raw colour scoured by the April wind, the faces on the Aberdeen crowds were as colourless as mine. I had never ever had a tan – freckles ruled – so on an impulse, I went into the shop and bought a bottle the model assured held such promise.

13

A FANTANSTICALLY GOOD TIME

It was night time and Maisie was still in her morning gear, hairnet firmly in place.

'You look ready for bed you lazy thing,' I said.

Along the corridor outside her room came the sound of nurses getting ready for that good time Sally and Beth spoke about. Even if Morag had been robust in her stay-at-home policy, the air of Saturday night excitement must have made her feel isolated with only a photo for company.

There was something black stretched over the back of Maisie's bedside chair. 'And what on earth's that? It looks like an antimacassar.'

'It's to accentuate my lovely figure. It's a new roll-on I bought today.' Maisie stepped over to ping it, looking disappointed when it snapped right back. 'Drat! I think it's still going to be a bit tight.' She sucked her lip. 'But at least it proves I've been downtown and not slobbing about all day as you're so unkindly implying.'

There was a light tap on the door and Isobel came in.

'Hey, great timing! Jane's deaving me with her questions. We thought you were away with the others having the weekend at home.'

Isobel drifted in, sat on the bed, and despite an air of disgruntlement, transformed it into a chaise lounge.

'I've just finished with my boyfriend,' she said. 'We've had such a big row and now I don't want to go home as my folks would be asking all sorts of silly questions.' Her sigh was worthy of a fine actress. 'They did say he was a weasel and it's a bit soon for me to admit they were right, so I thought I'd come and recover in good company' – she stopped short as Maisie slapped on face cream –'Good God! What's that? It makes you look like a corpse.'

Maisie peered into the mirror as she realigned her spectacles for a better look. 'The bright lights of Inverurie demand the best and you wouldn't know anything about having to use this clarty stuff, but I'm just searching for a perfect complexion with a bit of natural colour.' She slapped her cheeks hopefully.

'Stop that, Maisie. I think I've got the answer – the very dab in fact.'

I ran to get the Fantanstic. 'Look.' I showed the bottle and, like Sally's genie, explained its magical properties. 'There's plenty here – for you too, Isobel, if you fancy, in the absence of a better offer, being sun kissed.'

Isobel's smile was tolerant and it was good to see her perk up, but Maisie was more interested and grabbed the bottle.

'"Put on evenly and in a few hours you'll have your friends asking you where you acquired that deep Mediterranean tan."' She read carefully, her finger following the small print, then she scrutinised me. 'You haven't tried it yet?'

'No.'

I didn't want to admit the preliminary trial, minutes before visiting. Anyway, the stuff had seemed pretty innocuous and I had only put on a little, which in the muted light of Maisie's bedroom, didn't seem to have had much effect.

'It says it takes a few hours to develop so I need to do it now.' Maisie squirted out a quarter-bottle load, which she divided between her face and arms. 'It's not got the best smell,' she said. 'Still, one has to suffer for the sake of –'

'Art?' Isobel murmured in a gentle tone of disbelief. 'Well, folks, thanks for the company but I'll need to let you two get on.' She got up and drifted towards the door.

She looked so forlorn I blurted out, 'If you're not doing anything else, why don't you come to Beth's party with me?'

Isobel whirled round. 'I couldn't possibly.' She didn't sound convincing.

'Och, you'd be welcome. From what I can gather, it's pretty much open house.'

I hoped I was right and now, completely incapable of wiping out her happy look, I got hearty. 'The more the merrier and you'd be company for me too.'

'Well, if you're sure.' Isobel was already halfway down the corridor and calling back. 'I'll just go and throw on something and be ready in a jiff.'

'You'll need more of this stuff, Jane.' Maisie returned the bottle. 'Now for the big fight.' She squared her shoulders and I left her advancing on the chair with the concentration of a sumo wrestler.

It was disappointing that Fantanstic had not, as yet, fulfilled its promise, so I put on more, hurrying now, for it was getting late. Beth might be wondering where we were.

As I knocked on Maisie's door, two nurses passed; their conversation floated back.

'Off on the ran-dan then?'

'Aye. I've Sister Gorightly next week. I'm dreading the old bag. With a bit of luck tonight, I'll be able to forget about her.'

'Well, I hope you've a good time.'

The sound of their laughter faded whilst Maisie appeared, walking with care, her curves miraculously contained.

'I can just breathe,' she complained, 'but I'll never be able to sit down.'

Already she was heading for the stairs, 'D'you think Isobel's ready? If she is, I'll get down in the bus to Union Street with you, come on.'

I was so impressed by her sashaying walk I didn't look at her properly, and since my own mirror only showed the fire notice and Maisie wasn't wearing her specs, Isobel would have to give us a sun tan progress report.

'Maisie, have you heard of a Sister Gorightly?' I'd to hurry to catch up with her.

She shook her head. Then, as if I'd been holding up the works, she said, 'Come on, slow coach, Isobel'll be giving up on you. You can ask her.'

She was waiting in the main hall. It may have been my red screaming with her pink and Maisie's bright green, but as soon as she saw us she took a step back.

'My height makes me feel like a maypole beside you,' she explained, adding cautiously, 'Do you think your tans will even up?'

Curiosity about Sister Gorightly was now replaced with a heightened anxiety, especially when, moments later, we caught the bus and the conductor, familiar from the interview day, took one look and started whistling *Runnin' Bear*.

'That bloke really fancies himself.' Maisie's tone was disparaging. She seemed unaware there was any connection between us and a song about a Red Indian. 'It might be different if he could hold a tune.' She squinted at me in the half light. 'Hey, I think you've actually got a tan. What's mine like?'

But she was getting off and I was too busy watching the cheerful cheeky conductor help her off with a care that suggested undue interest to answer.

'Wish I was coming to the fancy dress with you.' He laughed and tinged the bell three times.

We got to Mrs Ronces'. Isobel, as inconspicuous as a model on a catwalk, followed as I rattled the door knocker, its noise just audible above the noise of a party in full swing.

Beth let us in where the grandfather clock was holding his own but the rest of the house was rocking. Mrs Ronce was issuing dance floor instructions from the piano with a big crowd milling around her.

A tall chap helped me hang up my coat whilst a thin one with a predatory look took charge of Isobel and led her off to a dark corner of the sitting room where dancing appeared to be the last thing on his mind. Before I could thank my helper, Beth pulled me into the kitchen.

'Who's the dolly bird and what on earth's that on your face?' Beth sounded cross. 'See if you can wash it off,' she added, her attention beginning to wander in the direction of the sitting room, 'you look as if you've got jaundice.'

Avoiding the amused look of passers-by, I hurried upstairs to the bathroom and stared in the mirror.

There was a huge gas geyser beside it: an ancient model with smoke marks surrounding the yellow-flickering pilot light. Every now and then, it would go out. There would be an ominous silence then there would be an explosion of flames so volcanic, strangers to its eccentric timing would flee in a state of deshabille.

In the mirror, a large patchy freckle with eyes looked back and rather like the geyser, and despite my best scrubbing efforts, the blob had all the frightening signs of further eruption.

Bleach might be an option but it wasn't likely that Mrs Ronce had any. I didn't want to go back into the kitchen where I could hear Sally's bloke chatting to a girl, so I sat at the top of the stairs planning my exit strategy, hearing people having fun and remembering that Morag had a photo at least for company.

'So who's the ginger nut?' The girl's voice, sharp with curiosity, floated upstairs.

'Came with that gorgeous piece of stuff everybody's falling over. A wee scrubber – though plainly not scrubbed enough,' came the laconic reply.

I thought that cheeky coming from someone with a tatty moustache and a greasy manner, but I didn't care to eavesdrop on an exchange where the squeak of a chair and a giggle was followed by silence, so I crept downstairs and sneaked out into the garden.

A ragged moon enchanted the ancient apple trees into another life and turned the overgrown shrubbery into something more exotic than laurel, even the summerhouse looked exciting. I walked towards it, reckoning that with a face the colour of marmalade, I qualified to be the third outcast.

The cats were perfect hosts with one giving up his bed for my knee, whilst the other stretched out his head so that I could give his ears proper attention.

Time passed. We sat in the dark in a companionable way with the occasional bursts of music and laughter spilling out into the garden and telling me I was missing a good party.

'Jane?' The voice was unknown but someone was coming down the garden. I opened the door feeling a bit daft. It was the bloke who'd helped me hang up my coat.

His accent was as soft as Morag's but at least he sounded happy to be here. 'Hello, I'm Douglas. I'm in Beth's English class and she's asked me to find you. What are you doing out here? Hello, cats.'

He crouched in front of them, stroking their heads in the way that cats love, then straightened, looking round the garden in an appreciative way. 'It's nice out here but you'd barely arrived before you disappeared. Are you alright? As soon as I saw you come in I recognised you as Beth's sister and wanted to say hello – but then you were off.'

'I thought the cats might be lonely and wanted to check up on them, and then' – I waved an arm at my surroundings – 'it was so lovely out here, I thought I'd stay here a wee while.' In the dark it was easy to lie.

'Good! I'd hate to think it was because of the Fantanstic. Your pal Isobel was giving me a right laugh about it but I hardly noticed it. At least it'll fade.' He rubbed his legs carefully. 'Know anything about psoriasis? Beth tells me you're student nurses.'

'We only started this week so we're sticking to something simple like toenail extraction, basic of course.' I stood up, careful not to fuss the cats. 'And maybe I should have my head examined for missing all the fun.'

'We both should. Alness is alright to grow up in but I wouldn't be at this party if I'd stayed there, so come on back!'

In the hallway, Isobel's skinny guy was helping her into her coat and tying up the buttons with the flying fingers of a pickpocket.

'I thought you were lost, but obviously Douglas found you.' She nodded towards the sitting room. 'I think Mrs Ronce's losing speed so if you want to dance, you should get in there now.'

Then she took me aside and whispered, 'I'm getting a lift home.'

With a Presbyterianism worthy of Rosie or Morag, I said, 'He looks a bit dodgy to me. Fast.'

'That's what I'm hoping. He's got a sports car,' said Isobel, giving a conspiratorial giggle. 'Anyway, I can look after myself. He's really good fun and makes me forget about bloomin' kidneys. Don't you worry about me. I'll be ok,' and she left in a flurry, door slamming. Outside, the sound of the engine revving must have done wonders for neighbourhood harmony.

Then I forgot about Fantanstic progress since Douglas's dancing and mine needed more attention. Maybe his legs had been affected by psoriasis. I'd need to read up on it when I'd a minute, but after some toe crunching and inadvertent knee knocking, rest on the sofa monitoring the legs seemed safer. And when someone switched off the main light, recovery at some time in the – preferably distant – future seemed reasonable.

Mrs Ronce gave up to concentrate on some stock-piling whilst someone with an appetite for folk music took over with a guitar.

'I love this kind of music,' said Douglas, his arm carelessly slung over the back of the sofa. 'I go to a folk club in Aberdeen. You might like to come with me.'

'Sure.' I was thrilled but tried to sound as casual as if my diary were crammed with social engagements. Then, since Douglas had a long lean form that looked as if it could do with filling, aimed for consideration, 'Let's go and see if there's any food left.'

As we chewed some long-dead sausages in the kitchen, Sally joined us looking pale but brave.

'What about a dance, Douglas? I could do with a good dancing partner. Mine,' she bit her lip, 'seems to have disappeared.'

Have a good time, I nearly said, but settled for clattering dishes into the sink instead.

The party was winding up and I was sorry. With a belated feeling of responsibility I started emptying ashtrays into a sulking fire. With a bit of luck they might even bulk up the heat.

Beth, ushering some people out, shut the door one decibel short of a slam. 'Phew! What a work a party is – and now there's the clearing up.' Her sigh was about the same size as herself. 'Has anyone seen Sally?'

'She's gone to bed. I think she's upset that her bloke went off with someone else.' Mrs Ronce poured something from her bar into a large glass, 'Just a little reviver.' She looked at the glass reflectively. 'Never trust a man with a mouser, particularly one who cheats at Scrabble. Cheers!'

'Well, Jane, you can't go home on your own, there's lions and tigers out there,' Douglas was already putting on his anorak, 'and they need protecting, so I'll come with you, but by the look of things, we'll have to hurry. You might get locked out.'

I didn't ask how he knew about the Cinderella hours of the Nurses' Home, but said, 'Actually I'm staying here tonight. Mrs Ronce's letting me stay.'

'D'you sleep on the sofa?' he asked hopefully and put down his scarf.

'No, she's upstairs in an attic bedroom in a single bed,' said Mrs Ronce, handing him his scarf, 'and it must be time for you to go to yours.'

'So how did last night go?' It was Sunday afternoon before I left Mrs Ronce's, but as soon as she'd heard me, Maisie appeared. For once, curler free and with normal colour restored, her inspection was in the manner of a kindly G.P. 'You'll be sorry to hear you're losing your sun tan. In fact you're a bit pale. Lack of sleep I suspect.'

'Come on in, Doctor, do. Yup, I'd a great time. What about you?'

Maisie gave a skittish laugh, threw herself into a chair, crossed her legs twice and rubbed her nose. 'Inverurie was terrific. They're not used to suntans so mine was something of a novelty. I suppose they didn't know what to expect. I was popular alright, but not quite as much as Sheila. She'd disappeared for a while and I thought she'd gone, but she came back looking pleased, if dishevelled. I asked where she'd been and d'you know what she said?'

'No.'

'"Ootside backit" up against a lorry!"' Maisie giggled. 'She suggested I stay overnight in Inverurie but I thought I'd better come back by bus, in the absence of any more lorries.'

'So you got back alright?'

'Yup – last bus. In fact, I could have been locked out if I hadn't met Isobel.'

I was relieved that Isobel had made it back to the Home. 'And was she alright?'

'Och, fine! Said she'd met a bit of a lecher but he'd been good fun. Actually, we were both late but she'd arranged for someone to open a window so we could both get in. Her bloke had wanted to come back with her but I gather he got the elbow before his leg got over the windowsill.'

'Goes to show what a live-in boarding school education teaches you, but what a good thing she did, you'd be in so much trouble if you'd been locked out.'

'Yeah, well, that's what friends are for. What are you looking for?'

I was thumbing through the Nurses' Dictionary.

'How do you think you spell psoriasis?'

'With a *c* or *s* I should think. Why?'

I attempted a careless shrug. 'Chap I met last night says he's got it. It's a skin condition. Says he's waiting to go into hospital to get treatment for it. He says he gets flare-ups when he's been under stress.'

'In that case, Jane, if he's been near you he should be in intensive care.' Maisie looked over my shoulder and continued with her jokey theme. 'Try looking under mange. There might be a connection.'

I thought about someone cheerfully coping with an affliction and turned the pages.

'You'll never find it under *p*,' said Maisie.

'That's because I'm looking up pest.'

'Ooh! Puss Puss!' She grabbed the book and slammed it shut, then put it with my other books, marshalling them into a neat row. 'That's better. You never know what you might discover. Actually, Isobel told me he's a great looking bloke, nice – even if he's keen on politics and likes Mr Wilson. I heard you were outside with him too, so don't think you'll get away with skinny little details.'

Annoyed at being a subject of gossip, I changed tack. 'Have you seen Morag?'

Maisie looked remorseful, 'Actually, no. I'd forgotten all about her. Maybe I should go and look for her,' and with the strains of 'I Could Have Danced All Night' echoing flatly in her wake she left whilst, hugging the memory of last night, I hung up my red frock.

I was just about to retrieve the dictionary when Maisie came back sounding worried.

'She's not in her room. Sister Cameron says she decided at the last minute to go home. Blast! I wish we'd persuaded her to come with us.' She looked at her watch. 'There's no trains on a Sunday so we'll just have to wait till tomorrow morning. I just hope she does come back.'

'So do I. She's our shining hope in the class. Knows all the answers and keeps Jonesie from going into meltdown. Och, Maisie, I'm sure she'll turn up. She's a hardy Highlander after all.' I wished I sounded more convincing.

14

SETTLING IN IF NOT DOWN

We were curious about Jo.

Last week we had nosily watched as, shoehorned into trousers, she piled her long hair under a crash helmet every night and headed off into an exciting world with her biker bloke. She never talked about him but he made her happy, evidenced by her silence and smug face – even on a Monday.

'Good morning, Jo. Nice weekend?'

'Very nice. And you?'

'Come on, folks, Miss Jones's waiting for us,' Rosie cried.

We'd only been here for a week but already Rosie was well on the way to splendour; but not perhaps, this morning.

Miss Jones presided at the blackboard, arms folded and grim faced. There was a pile of papers on a desk in front of her. They looked like our exam results, as much a matter of concern as the two empty desks.

'Sheila as well?' I muttered, feeling a need for that friendly presence.

'Quiet!' yelled our tutor. She picked up the papers and shook them at us. Covered in red marks, they looked as if they'd measles and the way she held them suggested something even more unpleasant. 'I have spent the better part of my weekend correcting these,' she crashed them back on the desk, 'and what a waste of my time that was. So, will you now please come and collect them.'

There were two papers left, one of which was blemish free. I bet it belonged to Morag, presumably absconded to Tain, which suddenly held a great appeal.

'Very disappointing.' Miss Jones, having no problem with voice projection, sought to better it as she pulled her shoulders back, drew breath and jutted her chin. 'Considering the amount of information given last week, I am amazed how little has come back. The kidney description deserves far more than what you've given me. Frankly, Nurses – and enjoy the title for it may be short-lived – you will all have to do much better than the rubbish I've had to wade through.' She finger-jabbed the air. 'Remember, your time here is short and we expect you to make the most of it.'

I was gutted. I thought I'd done a fair job and had been sure my little plumber analogy would charm. However, the 'facts not fiction' scrawled over my paper said otherwise.

'When your kidney knowledge wasn't minimal it was inaccurate, and as for your diagrams . . . Well! Words fail me.'

At last! Something in common, but not for long. 'Remember what I told you about your weekly tests?' Miss Jones picked up speed again. 'Well, this is a poor beginning isn't it?'

Mrs Low appeared, sparing us the indignity of a reply. We bucked up. Surely she brought good news, but she spoke with such sorrow it moved Miss Jones's tirade into happiness zone.

It had started to rain and water tracked down the windows like the tears Mrs Low was apparently fighting.

'Last week,' she began, her chin wobbling, 'I was sure I'd managed to convey the necessity of precision, a step-by-step description of a professionally-achieved procedure,' her sigh was immense, 'but I fear I have failed.'

She handed us our papers with the solemnity of an undertaker. 'I am so very, very sorry that something of such paramount importance was ignored. Some of you seemed to think that such a simple procedure could be dealt with in a very careless manner, whilst others treated it so lightheartedly, I found more than one joke in it!' She was scandalised. 'Were I to follow some of these details, poor Mrs Brown would be either scalded, drowned or suing the hospital for lack of proper care.' She crunched a hanky, then, dabbing her brow with it, gazed upon the weeping window as if it were a happier prospect. 'Read my remarks, then I suggest you go, have your coffee break and think about whether or not you're really serious about this great profession I, for one, am honoured to represent.'

We dragged ourselves out to gather in a shocked little group. The coffee tasted bitter.

'I think that pair go a bit over the top,' Isobel at length remarked, 'and I think Miss Jones must have a bit of kidney trouble herself; she drinks an awful lot of water and have you seen her ankles?' She stretched out her own perfectly shaped ones, which cheered no one but herself. 'I hope it's not going to be like this all the way. I'm sure old Florence wasn't half as fussy.' She caught Rosie's worried look and added, 'I don't think we'll ever get out of this classroom. Think of the disgrace – the only P.T.S. stuck here for years on end.'

Chewing mechanically and thinking deeply, we swallowed the plain biscuits and coffee, as free and attractive to nursing staff as the hospital's Government Property toilet paper.

'And on top of all that,' cried Rosie, 'we've lost Sheila and Morag as well. What do you think's happened to them? Where could they be?'

'Probably having a fine old time at home.' Hazel was gloomy. 'Honestly, you do wonder how anybody manages to get through all this and qualify. Maybe those two had the right idea and jumped before being pushed. That is except for Morag, and she's not even here.'

'Hey, quines,' the voice from the door was as welcome as it was unexpected. 'The Inverurie bus wis late. Hiv ah missed much?'

I said, 'No, Sheila, but we're down to the last biscuit. Looking on the bright side, I suppose that one good thing about Morag not being here is you'd have had to share it with her.'

'Somebody mention my name?' asked Morag, stepping out from behind.

'I was on the same bus that Sheila got on at Inverurie. Haven't you girls heard that troubles don't come singly?'

'That sounded like a joke,' said Hazel. 'Quick! Let's get you back into the classroom before you change your mind about training.' She threw her arm forward. 'Lead on, Morag Macduff!'

With Rosie chirping brightly in the rear, we trudged after Morag, hoping that the sight of her would give us all a break.

'Cheer up! It'll get better,' a passing nurse called as she swung out the door, an enviable skip in her step.

And she was right. As the weeks passed, and even if Morag persevered with pessimism, we began to make progress, gradually recognising that our tutors were there to help even if their teaching methods seemed peculiarly based on the inanimate qualities of a big doll, a skeleton and a drawerful of butcher's offal.

One day Miss Jones said, 'Nurse Macpherson, come out here and describe the humerus.' She stepped back smartly as I leapt to the floor, grabbing a ruler and advancing upon Skellie.

'There's nothing funny about the humerus,' I said, giving the old bone a good whack.

'Facts, Nurse. Facts.'

But I hadn't spent all night mugging this up to be so interrupted. I held up the ruler as if it were a baton and continued, 'It is the longest bone of the upper limb. It presents as –' I was just getting into my stride when Miss Jones checked her watch.

'Well now, it's time for Mrs Low. Thank you, Nurse Macpherson. We'll hear the rest of the lecture from someone else tomorrow.'

A snigger swept the class but I didn't care. The humerus and I were good pals and I knew how it worked.

Today was remarkable. Even Mrs Low seemed pleased.

'Do you know I really do think this group has made great strides. I like the thoughtful way you've been dealing with Mrs Brown and what's more, some kind nurse has actually stitched her arm back on again. She's really looking ever so much better. Whoever did that, thank you.'

She put her hands together in a prayerful way and looked around the class but nobody was admitting to this outbreak of compassion, though I suspected Hazel. With her eye for labour saving, she resented time spent sweeping up stuffing after our caring forays in the practical classroom. And her father was a surgeon, so she's plenty access to needles and thread.

Wearing my own particular brand of care, I went to visit Douglas, now in hospital.

He was in bed but despite the carbolic surroundings his cheerfulness was undimmed whilst he laid down a betting slip to give me a warmer welcome. Sunshine spilled over the long ward.

'The nurses are great. I'm thinking of asking if I can stay on for another week. My skin's clearing, I haven't got half the discomfort or itch, there's telly, I've made some good mates and all I have to worry about is what's for tea – and that's always great too.' Apparently pleased with his lot, and beaming at a passing, teeth-grindingly pretty nurse, he lay back on the pillows. As he moved his legs, they rustled.

Apart from sounds, rather than signs, of treatment, none of this tied in with my idea of a hospital patient racked with pain or discomfort and I wondered what would have been Mrs Low's take.

'Observation is a key skill,' she'd said.'Nursing skill's incomplete without it.'

But we'd had no set of rules for patient visitor behaviour and I didn't want to look or ask too much in case Douglas got coy. Anyway, his legs were under the bedclothes and apparently in good enough order, if noisy.

Was it time for a cool hand on a fevered brow then? If I'd thought, I'd not have worn the wool mittens. Compared to that annoying nurse I felt like a woolly mammoth.

'How did you manage to get in?' Douglas asked, looking round at a ward of patients who, having no visitors themselves, were interested in his.

'It's one of the perks of the trade.'

I should have shouted, it would have saved everybody lugging in, so it wasn't the best time then, even if I had the courage, to ask discreet questions.

'Do you see that bonny nurse? She puts cream all over his legs, takes ages to do it, then wraps him up in a polythene bag. It's a wonder he doesn't slip off the bed,' Douglas's neighbour was keen to inform. He poked around in his locker and tossed over an intellectual magazine; you could tell by the cover. 'Just returning your mag, Doug.' He settled back, pleased to have contributed so richly.

'Don't mind him.' Douglas laughed. 'He's only jealous I've got a bonny visitor.'

Between hearing about Douglas's treatment and reading up about it, I wondered if this might be the time to add to it, but mid neighbour and the rustles, I still wasn't quite ready to get that personal.

'What are these two so engrossed in?' shouted a patient across from us.

'Can you believe? Politics! It's riveting stuff apparently. Cor! They must be stuck for something to say.'

Douglas told me he'd been on a C.N.D. march and how important it was we banned the bomb.

I could have told him how certain members of nursing staff went nuclear quite frequently but he'd become serious. Actually, our class had had a lecture on what we should do in the event of a nuclear war and we were so scared we'd all wanted to run home. Since this didn't put any of us in a good light, I kept quiet whilst the rest of the ward lost interest and normal shouting was resumed.

'They might get sore throats as well,' I suggested at length.

'They'd certainly prefer it.' Douglas's tone was sombre as he nodded at a patient with a face that looked as if it had been scorched. 'That chap's been in for skin grafts but they're not taking. He's been here for ages, poor guy.' Then he brightened. 'You'll come back soon won't you? It's great having a visitor and I think we can talk about anything, and' – there was a busy rustle as he stretched his legs and put his hand out – 'I've been telling everybody what fun you are. Cuddly too.'

'Give us a twirl, Doll,' shouted the neighbour, proving that whatever problem he had, his ears were fine.

On my way out the pretty nurse said, 'We've heard a lot about you from Dougie and what a laugh you are. I expect he's told you about the new stuff we're trying. It seems to be helping; you'll have seen how well he's looking.'

'Yes, he smells like a newly tarred road,' I said, keen to put her off, and supposing a carbolic derivative was the main ingredient of Douglas's embalming ointment and rather wishing she wasn't so nice and I wasn't such a laugh.

I'd a pang leaving Douglas but when I got back to the Home I was caught up by our group dashing in and out of Maisie's room in a state of excitement and undress.

'Why is our mature and thoughtful group playing ghosties?' I asked Hazel, who was shroud-winding a sheet round Rosie.

'We've had such an overdose of Miss Jones today, we've prescribed ourselves some fun therapy. Hold still, Rosie.' She dredged her with talc. 'Look! Now you've grey hair, a sure sign of wisdom – and where's the raspberry jam? You'll need that for blood.'

'Just the thing for caring specialists.' Jo was painting fangs on Isobel. She stepped back to admire her handiwork. 'We need somebody to do blood-curdling yells.' She looked speculatively at Maisie. 'You could do that, I think you've got the voice.'

'Great to be so valued, and I suppose the same applies to my room. Look at that talc. It's everywhere, and where's Morag?'

'Phoning home or head under the blankets. It's why we're in your room.

[87]

If she'd got wind of this lark she might have tried to dissuade us,' said Jo. 'Honestly, she takes life far too seriously. She'll have a nervous breakdown if she doesn't start to relax. Anyway, you lot. Come on! What's it to be. Victim finders or outriders? Choose your title. Now, girls, are we ready?'

Support team at the ready, Rosie and Isobel set off, so realistic even I got a chill as they moved silent and phantom-like along the corridor.

Some very satisfactory screams and the occasional dead faint with Sims' position trialled encouraged us to go global and stalk any old corridor, spurred on by the time and signs that the Night Staff was not moribund, and thus fair game.

'I think it's time for a break,' said Hazel at length. 'It's the stress build up.'

'And I fancy a cup of tea. My voice is hurting,' said Maisie.

'Too right.' Rosie couldn't resist it.

She turned to Isobel and beckoned, 'Come on, Iso, one more and then we'll join you.'

We should have gone with them. It might have spared Sister Cameron from an ill-judged pounce, and Rosie and Isobel from a consequent and very big fright indeed.

'You'll never guess what happened.' Rosie appeared in the pantry, looking even more the part. 'We were both caught and Sister Cameron's mad and says she knows who else was with us. She says she's going to tell Miss Jones and we must be the worst P.T.S. the hospital's ever had.'

'Just wait till Miss Jones hears this,' Isobel – always pale, now ethereal – murmured.

'Just wait till Miss Jones hears this,' we parodied to show bravado before stepping into the privacy of our bedrooms and offering up deliverance prayers.

15

A LITTLE PERFORMANCE

'I believe some in this class have a flair for drama.' Miss Jones was in brisk Monday morning mode.

Her ankles were a normal size though, always an encouraging sign, the nostrils, no smoke – so far so good. Still, we kept quiet. Even the floorboards held their breath because Miss Jones had that sort of presence.

'There's a lecture cancellation today so Mrs Low and I thought you could put a more constructive use of your talents to some role play. So, this afternoon, we want you to demonstrate the care of an asthmatic patient taken in an acute stage to a – what kind of ward?'

'A medical ward,' we Good-Girl chorused, apart from a random Sheila who promoted Inverurie Casualty in case lightning had wiped out Aberdeen.

'You can spend the morning preparing and then we'll see you later. We're trusting you to do this on your own, so use the time profitably.' With a flash of her teeth she was gone.

The promised lecture by a roving parasite officer cancelled, and the chance to have some fun. What an opportunity! Control at last.

Whilst the rest of the class moved into intense, earnest little groups, ours was casual.

'If they like our performance, we could move on to "The life cycle of a louse",' said Isobel in her dreamy way. 'Hazel, you could be the school nurse and I'd be the visiting medical officer. I could ask all sorts of personal questions.'

'Private education gave us a great insight into pest control,' Hazel agreed. She patted Rosie's head, 'but I don't know that it's working here.'

'So, how are we going to do this?' asked Jo, chalk in hand, followed seconds after by Rosie who grabbed it from her.

'I'll tell you.' she tapped the blackboard with authority. 'I'll be the ward sister, Sheila, you're the patient, Hazel, you be the staff nurse, Isobel, you the resident doctor, Maisie, you've got to be a student nurse, Jo, you take over from me, it's a split shift and I'll be off half-time. We need to share the responsibility.'

'I see you've been studying power structures in your spare time,' Maisie observed.

But Rosie raced on, 'And, Jane, you'll be a difficult relative – that should be easy,' she gurgled, 'and you could doll up Sheila a bit so that she looks blue.'

'Easy.' I rose above Rosie's jokey moment, diverted by the sight of a bottle full of the most gloriously coloured liquid nearby, a drop of which would be ideal for make-up.

'Ah'm nay sure.' Sheila looked dubious.

'I've thought of something good,' I promised, 'really authentic.'

'And maybe I could be a secretary,' said Morag in her diffident way. 'They're really important you know.'

All eyes swivelled in her direction. 'Eh?'

She blushed, and checked her finger waves. 'Well I think so anyway. How else can doctors' notes be deciphered?'

'Is that what you used to do?' I asked, rather ashamed that I'd never bothered asking Morag what she did in her previous life, but then again, she wasn't about to give away much.

'I was learning,' she said obliquely.

'Sounds good,' said Rosie, sounding unconvinced. 'So maybe you could move around the stage taking notes.'

'I couldn't do that!' Morag was appalled. 'I'm definitely backstage and even then I'd have a problem if I didn't know what I was doing.'

'Join the club. But life, in case you hadn't noticed,' said Hazel, chewing gum, 'is dealing with challenge.' She put an arm round Morag and blew a bubble. 'And yours will be prompting us when we get stuck, but since we're likely to be making it up as we go along you shouldn't find it too difficult.'

That settled and names on the board, we relaxed, checked with the others we could go first, and discussed our tutors and where they might have gone. Then we tried to winkle information out of Jo about her boyfriend, and, failing, recalled our own real life dramas and left rehearsal for the lesser. At lunch break, some trolley setting and trial dialogue made us think it would be alright if we worked as a team.

'You've certainly been putting a lot into this,' enthused Mrs Low, over-hearing our conversation on the way back to the classroom, 'and my good-ness, you've set up the place so it looks like a first-night performance. I like the way you've made the screens like curtains. What do you say Miss Jones?'

'We'll see.'

'Just come this way.' Between hand-scooping gestures and herding the audience to their seats, Rosie had hit an all-time bustle record. Her cheerful welcome and introduction set a good, if ambitious, tone. I didn't remember bed-baths or constipation being discussed but maybe, bored with so much of her instructions, I'd tuned out. Full of confidence, Rosie bounced backstage.

'You should have charged them. You sounded like a compere-cum-ticket-officer.' Maisie had had time to consider her role and was smarting about her lowly position.

Rosie's sniff was so profound, it might even have impressed Beth.

Hazel now drew back the screens, their little wheels screaming like those in a car rally. Isobel followed, more Sarah Bernhardt than Dr Finlay, and beckoned to Rosie who, complete with clipboard and eager expres-sion, re-entered.

'Um, Sister,' Isobel raised a hand to her forehead – a fine portrayal of an artist in thought. 'There's an asthmatic coming in – emergency – can you get things ready? You'll know what to do. I'll have to dash now – there's another emergency coming in.'

She drifted off.

'Staff Nurse!' shouted Rosie. Hazel ambled on.

'There's an asthmatic coming in. You'll need to get a bed ready and trolleys, you know – just the usual.' Her hands waved like small propellers.

Hazel tapped her teeth thoughtfully, checked their stability and giving a very good impression of quiet authority, beckoned Maisie who had started to hum 'The Red Flag'. Still, she appeared on cue and gave a proper imitation of servility, battening down her curls with such an armoury of hairpins she looked as if she might have a problem understanding life, never mind instructions.

'Now, Nurse, prepare a bed and set a trolley please. There's an emergency asthmatic coming in and – look! She's arrived. My goodness that was quick.'

Sheila's entrance was made in a high-speed trolley driven by Jo, aiming rather than steering since nobody had thought the role of a porter with transporting expertise relevant.

'Merciful Heavens! What has she on her face?' gasped Mrs Low. 'If that's gentian violet, she'll never get it off.'

'We never thought about makeup,' said someone in the audience.

'Maybe just as well,' said another.

'I'll kill that bloomin' Jane,' gritted Sheila putting an appalled hand to her face and beginning to breathe in short bursts.

'Let's lift the patient altogether now,' called Rosie, and those who were team players assembled round the patient, astonished by how featherlight she was. As she flew from caring clutches to the far edge of the bed, she was stopped from a crash landing by her own keen instinct for survival and a 'Mind oot!' scream.

Apart from reassuring Morag, who was plainly bringing stage fright to a new art form and being banned from action except make-up artist until now, I was ready for a role to be relished. With a busybody walk I got on stage.

'You'll mebbe find ma auntie a bittie confused. She's been affa difficult lately, winna tak her pills, winna stick tae her diet. Ah canna sleep at night fur her coughin' an' I've a right sair back lookin after her – an' as for her bowels, weel that's anither story. Noo whaur's Sister an' whaur's the Complaints Book. I've plenty tae pit in it.'

'Sorry, but you'll need to wait in the waiting room. We're far too busy dealing with your aunt just now. You can see how breathless she is.' Jo appeared at my elbow and gave a discreet shove.

Stopped from getting into full stride, I was offstage quicker than I intended, which was a pity, for being such a caring relative was fun.

Jo now assumed Rosie's mantle of authority and addressed the air very clearly.

'Let's have the oxygen shall we?'

'Oxygen! What oxygen? Oh! Just a minute.' Maisie stifled a scream.

Mutterings and curses followed, then an unaccompanied trolley appeared so fast the attached *Oxygen* marked flag flew from it in a straight line.

'Where's a' the nurses an' fit kinda corners are these?' The relative had sneaked back and was pointing to the feeble mitres. 'In ma young day, beds were made properly. That's a disgrace, an' she'll need mair pillows an' mind she's allergic tae feathers.'

'Check the patient's pulse.' Morag must be on the mend for that was her voice even if it was interrupting my observation.

'An' dae ye nay think she's an affa funny colour?'

'My goodness, that is a difficult relative,' murmured Mrs Low, sneaking a look at her watch and inflating her chest. Miss Jones seemed to be checking her ankles.

Once more Jo helped a rapid exit.

'Do not come back on again,' she murmured, then for the audience's benefit, 'And what about a cup of tea, dearie, before you speak to some nice person who could help you,' adding through gritted teeth, 'I think an almoner's available right now.'

'I think you're overdoing things,' whispered Morag, 'and look at Sheila, Jane, she's really beginning to look distressed. I'm getting worried about her.' She pointed, but already Maisie was bearing down on our hapless patient with a trolley heaped high with enough equipment to kit the world. It was crowned with a large but unmistakable enema funnel.

She advanced upon Sheila who had been playing dead with a faraway expression and a blue look not entirely gentian.

'Can I just explain what I'm going to do to you?' she asked, squaring her jaw and smiling into Sheila's face while pushing up her spectacles for a better look.

Suddenly, Miss Jones looked very alert and made to stand up. Sheila, however, proved that one look at the trolley was enough to re-energise her.

'Ah'm nay comin back here ivver again,' she gasped. 'Ah'll stick tae ma inhaler an' Inverurie.' She got out of bed and fled with her bedclothes billowing behind like a storm cloud.

Isobel sauntered on to have the last word. 'I see our patient has fully recovered. You wouldn't think a woman that old could move so fast.' She leant on the trolley, her regal air transforming it into a carriage. 'Come along, Staff, let's see if we can get rid of that obnoxious relative. Look, we've got a spare bed now. Ready for that emergency I was telling you about.'

Her exit was elegant and ended the performance. Backstage, Morag discouraged us from banging Sheila on the back and suggested that if we left her alone she would breath easier, whilst Rosie drew the final curtain screens and waited for the call.

Outside, the sun suggested spring was well underway and like an old dog warming its bones, the Home seemed to be basking in it. The colour of those dour grey walls softened in the light. A few nurses strolled past without their capes, allowing them individuality and easy strides. There might have been happy chat, but we couldn't hear them. Anyway, our attention was elsewhere, as with some shoving and pushing we shuffled out to face our audience.

A small outbreak of clapping was stopped by a glare from Miss Jones who, ensuring everybody's attention, turned to look out the window. Mrs Low followed and for a while they both just stood, watching, whilst small tittering bursts came from the rest of the class.

At last Miss Jones said, 'Do you see these nurses?' She pointed to some serious striders. 'They were also in P.T.S. you know, and I remember some of them had a very light-hearted casual approach indeed. Once they were in the wards, however, that had to change and they had to learn very quickly that hospitals are not places for burlesque.' She paused whilst Mrs Low nodded her head and looked agonised, then continued, 'There must be professionals and professionalism at every level and so, nobody, but nobody, gets out of this classroom unless we personally are sure it's safe for them to do so. At some time you will all be dealing with life-and-death situations and you will all have to learn to recognise the signs. Do you realise your patient was in grave danger of having a real asthmatic attack, brought on by your antics? You could have killed her and as far as we could see, not one of you recognised that – not even Nurse Munro,' she gave Morag a baleful stare before training it on the class,' nor anybody in the audience either. I thought at the very least we could rely on you to be sensible, so frankly that's very worrying and I think you all should be considering your future prospects here, very, very carefully.'

This was some curtain call. If there was any power in prayer, the floor should have swallowed us, but the only miracle was that Sheila was breathing normally and we hadn't killed her.

I groaned inwardly. Why was it that a bit of daft jollity always seemed to go wrong?

Miss Jones continued, 'Of course, there is a place for fun and I must say this group's got a particular flair for it, but here's not the place. We really do need some serious application from now on. Have I made myself clear?'

'Yes, Miss Jones.'

The flat chorus must have touched Mrs Low for she stepped forward and said more cheerfully, 'I'm sure everybody's learnt a few things from today's exercise and using the experience, we'll see how the other groups fare tomorrow, but in the meantime, I think we've had enough of drama.'

Then she got out her 'Kiss Me Quick' hat and said, 'Don't forget that tomorrow as well, we'll be having that visit from environmental health, so you can learn all about parasites and ask intelligent questions of the gentleman who is giving up a little of his rodent-roving role to speak to you. It'll make a nice change, I'm sure.'

'Yes, Mrs Low.'

16

MOVING ON

'Well, at least after this exam you'll be out in the wards and looking after real people.' Douglas hunched his shoulders against an east wind accompanying us on our walk along Aberdeen beach. 'Honestly, Jane, I can't think what possessed us to come here today. It's freezing.' He looked out at the waves, grey as granite, hitting the sand in a monotonous thump, and shivered. 'Just listen to that. They even sound mean. You wouldn't think it was summer. Let's go back to the café.'

'I need to clear my head – it's so full of anatomy, I doubt I'd make sensible conversation.'

I didn't want to swap the wide space and absence of people for a greasy shelter. Of course, the warmth of thermal underwear helped, but the blue look of Douglas hinted that without the polythene, he hadn't the same protection.

'Maybe you're feeling the cold because you're just out of hospital.'

'And maybe I don't want to be back in again with hypothermia.' The wind whipped his hair across his face as if teasing him, but he was unamused. Then, face brightening, he caught my hand. 'I know! There's a pipe band playing in Union Street Gardens today. Why don't we go and listen. At least we'd be warmer.' He searched my face eagerly but I liked it here. It suited my mood. It was where I thought I could put my world and the prospect of the end of P.T.S. exam in perspective.

'You go, Douglas. Look, I'm sorry, but I'm probably better on my own. I really need to shift the "facts, facts" tutor drone to somewhere else in my brain and then I can deal with the worry of failing and having to go back home without so much as seeing one patient, apart from yourself.'

'And maybe I don't count,' Douglas managed, despite the teeth chatter.

The sound of the waves was dismal. A herring gull strutted past, his yellow beak a cruel hook and the brightest colour on the beach.

'And I didn't realise you were such a senseless worrier.' Douglas held up his hand to stop denial. 'Of course you'll pass, but if walking on a beach in Arctic conditions on your own helps, then I'll leave you to it.' With that he turned, and muttered, 'And that's a fact,' before hurrying away.

My returned hand was the only bit of me that felt cold. I was sorry he'd find a skirling pipe band a better option and that I couldn't explain how this place with its raw power might disentangle my mind, but the long walk to the other end beckoned. I put my hand in my pocket and headed there, enjoying the way the wind robbed me of all thought except breathing.

Eventually the sky began to clear so that a small patch of blue showed. The wind dropped and, as if on cue, the waves grew quieter and made a hushing companion as I walked beside them. I'd begun to perk up and hoped that Douglas was at least feeling warmer. The three-month haul in P.T.S. was coming to an end. Our amateur dramatics had made us realise we would never progress if we didn't take study seriously, a fact we had at last accepted.

There was a telephone kiosk at the end of the beach. I should call home. My father answered and sounded so pleased, warmth reached down the phone. 'You seem grand. How's things?'

'Fine, Dad. Just fine,' and funnily enough I wasn't lying. 'I'm down at the beach at the moment – it's really wild but bonny. I thought I needed a break from the studies.'

'Quite right. Want to speak to your Ma?'

'No, but tell her the big exam's tomorrow and I'll call after it.'

'Good luck then. I'd better go. We've got Maudie calving.'

I put the phone down and thought as the sun broke out that I was in a good enough place, better than Maudie anyway.

But where was Douglas?

Back in the Home, Maisie asked the same thing but I couldn't tell her. Searching for him, I had gone to the Union Street Gardens but got an overdose of piping laments instead.

'He'll have gone back to his digs. Maybe you've inspired him to study.' Maisie, pulling her dressing gown closer and hugging her head to her shoulders in an impression of cosy talk, continued, 'And after tomorrow, we'll all be fine, just as long as we remember it's of paramount importance to stick to the facts, facts, facts.'

Sitting our exam in that dull classroom with its posters portraying everything helpful but what was asked, we bent our heads, aware of the mechanics that drove that movement.

Thanks to Miss Jones, we now knew there was a life of such complexity under our skin, we could only trust that our brains conformed and transmitted the right facts to paper.

On and on we wrote, drew precise anatomical diagrams and described in clinical terms the importance of caring in a professional way. When at last the bell rang, Mrs Low gathered in our papers with such big capable hands, I suddenly thought that behind a wet facecloth, they could make a bed bath swift if not unpleasant. Maybe her brand of care was best confined to the classroom.

'We'll have these corrected for tomorrow, and in the meantime, and after Matron's visit, you'll be measured for your uniforms so that they'll be ready by the end of the week when, hopefully,' she pointed to the papers, 'you will all be ready to go into the wards. And now we've asked Matron to come along and give her customary end of P.T.S. lecture.'

Impresario-like, she opened the door to Matron, who sailed in as if on wheels. Plainly in a hurry, she took the floor in a running movement then, braking, checking her cap had survived the speed, stopped. Breathless, she faced the class.

'After today, Nurses, your tutors,' she ducked her head and sent a vague smile in their direction, 'will be finding out how much knowledge you've retained – that's their job, and it's mine as Matron to remind you that each and every one of you is going to be a representative of a profession which cannot afford anything but the highest standards of behaviour.' She stopped for a moment as if to contemplate a fine view or catch breath, then continued, 'And not only at work. I have had,' the medals jangled, her voice moved into a squeak, 'tears in my office, because some nurses have not taken anything seriously. Nor have they put a value on themselves.' She mine-swept her gaze round the room before letting it fall upon Mrs Low who was nodding so much her head should have fallen off. 'As a matter of fact, and it grieves me to tell you this, I've had to let such girls go because very soon they would be facing the consequences of irresponsibility.'

A bee droned by, the bravest bee in Aberdeen but now sensibly escaping through an open window. Mrs Low looked at her feet, Miss Jones at her fingernails. We moved uneasily. She couldn't possibly be speaking about pregnancy could she? Blimey! If this was a centre for caring, what was happening in the back streets?

In silence, we watched those fingers butterfly play as she went on, 'Nursing work is so physical, pregnancy is not an option, and anyone in that condition could do irreparable harm, not only to herself but the child as well. And then of course she will have the responsibility to look after it – a full and lifetime commitment.' Her tone was final. 'I can't imagine anyone here has a problem with this? No? Very good then and whilst we're on the subject of suitable behaviour I'm aware of the present fashion of wearing frills rather than skirts and whilst I have no jurisdiction over what you wear off duty, your uniforms must conceal the popliteal space at all times.'

Mission completed, Matron left with a hasty if regal nod, voice squeak and finger twiddle, whilst we were sent to be measured for our uniforms, where we tried to redefine popliteal to a thin-lipped seamstress.

17

MORAG MAKES A STAND

We were in the dining room and filling up on stodge prompted by tape measure readings just recorded and surely too generous.

'Has anybody seen Morag?' I asked.

'She said she was going to her room and not to wait for her,' said Jo. 'I thought she looked a bit upset after that talk by Matron but presumed she'd turn up later on. I didn't see her getting measured – did anybody else?'

'No.' Maisie, carefully arranging a token green on the last of her macaroni and cheese rissole, shovelled it down, then jumped up saying, 'I hope she's alright. You know how serious she gets about everything. I thought for a moment she was going to take on Matron about that pregnancy stuff. Honestly, the way that woman spoke, I'm surprised we weren't fitted for chastity belts as well. You'd think we weren't capable of looking after ourselves never mind others. This is the sixties for God's sake! Come on, Jane, let's see if she's alright.'

At the Home entrance, Sister Cameron pounced. She seemed unusually pleased to see us. 'Ah! You two, I've just had a word with Nurse Munro and she says she's leaving. Something about Matron's talk being the last straw.' Behind the round specs, her eyes were anxious. 'Now get up these stairs quickly and stop her doing anything silly. I'm counting on you, mind. Tell her I'm expecting her to show Highland grit,' her voice floated after us.

'Oh for goodness sake, Morag. Open up!' Maisie's knock and voice were demanding.

Reluctantly, Morag opened the door. Apart from the photo of her boyfriend rustically smouldering by her bedside, Morag's room had always looked half dead and now, with only a waste paper bin stuffed with screwed-up papers and a small suitcase facing the door, it was as empty as if she'd already gone.

'Don't try and make me stay. Lord knows Sister Cameron's done her best. And for that of it, so've the tutors.' Morag had been crying, but despite the blotches she sounded determined. 'When you went to get measured I told them so. They tried to dissuade me but I'm going and that's that.' Never had she sounded so positive.

Despite being impressed that anybody would face up to Miss Jones and survive, I said, 'Morag you're the best nurse in the class. It'll be a real waste if you go and surely you've not come all this way just to chuck it in because a silly old wifie's got a bee in her bonnet about pregnancy.' A thought suddenly occurred, 'You're not –?'

'No, I'm not,' snapped Morag. 'I've been thinking about leaving for a while now but if I was actually pregnant, I'd have been bundled out the back door at the first missed period and we wouldn't be having this conversation.'

For Morag, this was quite radical stuff. Maybe she was more interesting than the strait-laced exterior suggested. Who knows, she might have been about to admit to the joys of a previous life as a stripper in Tain, but the sound of running footsteps followed by a hail of door knocks interrupted. It was the rest of the group, headed by Rosie.

Racing in and seeing the suitcase, she started to dance up and down as if about to take flight. 'You're all packed! You can't really be serious, Morag.' Turning to the others, she cried, 'You're not allowing this surely? I can't believe you're letting this happen.'

'Nor me,' Maisie said agreeing for once. 'It's such a waste. Matron's heartless and this place stinks.' She shook her head as if to get rid of flies. 'We should all be walking out.'

'Dinna be daft,' said Sheila. She ambled over to the window, breathed on it then drew a face on the glass with a frilly halo on top, a sad mouth under. 'Matron jist minds me on yon gossipy wifies wi' their hats, hivvin' tea in Watt an' Grants in Union Street, but nay a'body's like her. I dinna see Miss Jones there somehow an' she's jist as important. Ye shid jist bide an' gie it a chance. Ye hivna even met ony patients yet!'

Morag sounded fierce: 'But have you not noticed, nobody really discusses patients' feelings inside.' Dramatically she beat her chest. 'Not even Mrs Low. Oh we explain alright and observe – my God! How I've observed – and do you know what? What I've actually observed is that nobody seems aware that patients have lives outwith hospital and how they might feel about things going on at home which might be relevant to their recovery. Now that can't be right.' As if giving up, she dropped her shoulders, managing a watery smile. 'Anyway, you girls need to stay and train and learn to be Matrons yourselves.' She picked up a small piece of fluff off the floor, threw it in the bin and looked round the room in a final way. 'And maybe by the time you do, times will have changed and if not, then you could do something about it.'

'And what about you?' Isobel looked depressed. 'What'll you say to your parents?'

Morag smoothed her skirt, dabbed her eyes with a folded hanky and looked down at her sensible shoes. 'They never thought I'd make it. Thought I was too soft – and how right they were, but just maybe in the head. So I'll probably finish that typing course I was doing in Inverness. It's nearer home and the boyfriend.' There was a hint of mischief in her smile. 'Who knows, he might even make an honest woman of me. I'll certainly try and avoid the perils of becoming an unmarried mother.'

'Well then, we'll come and see you to the train. At least we've got the afternoon off so our blessed tutors can mark our papers.' Hazel went to pick up the suitcase. 'Though in your case they'll probably keep yours and frame it. Come on! Let's get you past Sister Cameron. After all the bother you've caused we wouldn't really want you murdered. Not really.'

18

ON OUR WAY

After today and with our exam results announced, we would know whether or not we were to join Morag and head for the hills. It was our last P.T.S. day and already our tutors were lined up with the air of generals about to despatch final orders. We tramped into the classroom and sat down in silence.

If they'd any apprehension about meeting a group upset by the loss of one of its members, our tutors hid it well; then Miss Jones swung into action. In another time I bet she'd have relished gladiatorial sport. She looked about, seeming to enjoy our fear, then taking her time, drilled out, 'We have your papers here – and . . .' she tapped them in a final way and looked about as if enjoying an audience's complete attention.

Time stood still. Just in case I might shortly need the skill again, my hand gripped my pen with the same grasp needed for a mop. The class held its breath. Seldom had Miss Jones so transfixed us. Then, allowing a pleased if surprised smile to escape, she said, 'We are pleased to tell you that you have all passed.'

Mrs Low's beam engulfed the classroom in sunshine whilst the sigh flooding the classroom should have made the building collapse.

'Well done, Nurses. You're on your way.' Miss Jones cleared her throat and dropped her voice, 'We're sorry Morag chose to leave. She'd have made a fine nurse.'

Mrs Low looked stricken whilst Miss Jones's tone was as genuine as it was unexpected, but it was sad that the use of her first name separated Morag from the group and formalised her departure.

I was torn between exasperation that she hadn't stayed the course and relief at the exam results, whilst the memory of Sister Cameron's words still lingered.

'She can't be a real Highlander,' she'd said. 'Now you'll have to prove normal ones are worth the effort.'

What's normal, I wondered. Certainly not what's going to happen here in a minute and courtesy of our group.

'Right! Let's move onto these papers.' The tutors started to hand them out. 'The results were good, but there are some misconceptions, particularly about the femur – Mrs Low, would you mind?' She nodded to Skellie's house.

Isobel and I exchanged glances whilst Rosie searched for her hanky.

Mrs Low swung open the door. There was a pause. Then, instead of Skellie, a long-dead nurse swung before us. The silence was profound and even though I knew it was the skeleton dressed in uniform, he still looked scary. Mrs Low gave an impressive leap and Miss Jones took a step back, whilst those in the class who weren't in the know screamed.

We'd become slick at treating faints and were eager to demonstrate, but disappointingly nobody collapsed. We must all be growing battle hardened. Instead, Miss Jones picked up a ruler and tapped the apron with its 'Nursing can damage your health' notice written in Sheila's perfect copperplate. 'So can tutoring,' she murmured. 'Now, about the femur –'

'Fancy Old Jonesie having a human side, and with a sense of humour too,' said Maisie as we walked out of the classroom at the end of the day, 'but that Morag business has put me off and I don't even feel like celebrating. What about you, Jane?'

'Stunned.'

'Me too.' Rosie turned briskly on our group. 'I know! Why don't we phone her, see if she got home alright. Then we can tell her about Skellie.'

She held up an index finger straight out of Miss Jones's personal development book. 'That'll cheer her up. Now! Come along, everyone.'

Reaching the telephone booths, she fledgling-flapped her arms over her pockets. 'Has anyone any money?'

'Yup.' Hazel slapped a handful of change on the shelf. 'And look, Jane, there's a note here for you.'

The booths were festooned with notes for people who hadn't been there to take their call by people who had.

I read the note: 'Would Jane Macpherson please phone Douglas.' It had a number and a yesterday time. Blast! I got so few calls I hadn't bothered to check.

'Ooh,' cooed Maisie. 'Now there's a cause for celebration.'

'Ssh!' Rosie waved her finger, fresh from dialling. 'Morag?'

We grouped round and heard that soft voice reassuring her that all was well.

'We'd a right laugh with Skellie. You'd have died laughing. It might even have cheered you up,' Rosie, that mistress of tact, ignored Maisie screwing up her face and held the phone tighter, 'and Jonesie even said she was sorry you'd left.' Rosie could apparently think of no higher praise. Then whatever Morag said pleased her and brought the dimples out. 'She's going to finish that course in Inverness and her boyfriend's delighted she's going to be near,' she relayed, twirling the telephone flex round her fingers so much she was now having to stand on her tip toes to reach the cradle, 'and she sounds happy. Different girl.'

'Well, Dr Rosie, that's fine,' Maisie reached for the phone, 'but maybe we could have a word too.'

But our captain said we all had to dash, said goodbye on our behalf and hung up.

'Rosie!'

'I didn't want to use all Hazel's money. You can phone her yourselves with your own money,' Rosie retorted, scooping up the change and slapping it into Hazel's hand. 'Now what about that celebration?'

A cleaner came pail-clanking down the stairs, muttering about a dismal job mopping up talcum powder dredged bathrooms, and though I was still mixed up about Morag and a hospital's apparent indifference to its staff, I was relieved I wasn't going back to cleaning – yet. Success needed to be marked in some way, but not in the present company. Maisie and I crept away.

'Rosie is that bossy, I could scream,' Maisie grimaced as she vented her frustration on her bedroom door handle making the door fly open.

'Yeah – but she has moved us out of the doldrums,' I clutched my bit of paper, trying to memorise the number, 'and she's put me in the mood for catching up with Douglas. What were you thinking of doing yourself?'

'I think I'll go and catch a bus tae Inverurie,' said Maisie with a sly grin. 'Sheila and I have plans for the weekend and after that, Jane, we'll be out in the world of reality.'

'I wouldn't count on it.'

I went to make my phone call.

'You've just missed Douglas,' his landlady said, 'but I'll tell him you called.'

There was a better result with my mother accepting a reverse charge call home.

'Jane! How lovely to hear from you. We've been thinking such a lot about you and wondering how you got on.'

Bob was barking in the background and my mother sounded so cheerful, a wave of homesickness washed over me, making my good news sound wobbly.

'That's marvellous, but are you alright? What about coming home for the weekend? We're dying to see you. We'll stand you the fare.' I could tell she was smiling.

'Right, Mum.' I was suddenly decisive. 'I'll just do that. I'm longing to see you too.'

As soon as I hung up, the phone started ringing again. Despite an uncharitable wish to leave it, I lifted it.

'Douglas!'

'Jane! That's a stroke of luck,' he sounded frustrated. 'I've been trying to get a hold of you for ages. I'd to nip back to the digs for a second so I knew if I was quick, I'd catch you. How's things?'

'I passed.'

'I knew you would.' Douglas was dismissive, as if it were pre-ordained, then he rushed on, 'Look – I'm in a bit of a hurry but there's a folk concert on tonight. D'you fancy coming?'

A group of nurses passed in a chattering group. I waited to let them pass. The phone suddenly felt heavy. 'Douglas, I'm sorry, I'm set up to go home.'

'But there'll be other times.'

'I know. It's just that they so seldom put on any pressure – and they're paying the fare.'

'Oh well, I can tell you've made up your mind. Another time, maybe. I need to dash now but will you phone me when you come back? At least someone answers the phone here.' Douglas's voice grew fainter, as if he was already gone.

'Yes, Douglas.' I put the phone down slowly, wishing he'd sounded more pleased I'd passed and less casual that I couldn't make that date.

19

IN THE WARDS

'I wonder if the girls are as busy on their hems as us,' said Maisie, squinting in her efforts to thread a needle. 'They'll be settling into their Nurses' Home. Apparently it's really modern, even if Woodend Hospital's supposed to be ancient.'

During our training we would be sent to various hospitals, most of which had their own nurses' homes. Woodend, regarded apparently and somewhat scathingly as the last outpost of the hospital empire, was on the outskirts of Aberdeen. It was a smaller, if more rural version of Foresterhill, and Jo, Sheila and Rosie had gone there.

We were in Maisie's room and taking up hems on the uniforms waiting for us in well-organised bundles on our return from the weekend.

'Everybody does it,' said Hazel. 'Honestly, the sewing department must have served time making tents. I could have broken my neck wearing something that trailed the ground. Look! I've had to take my hem up by a mile.' She held a dress against her. An optimist would have said it just covered her knees.

'Yes, but I saw one nurse the other day wearing a thing like a pelmet,' Maisie said with admiration. 'Good for her but it might get draughty round corners. I was surprised she was allowed to operate if you get my drift. Ouch!' She sucked a newly-pricked finger. 'Blast! I've marked an apron.'

'That wouldn't look good first thing arriving on the ward,' Isobel chuckled, 'but never mind, we've been given plenty.' She nodded at Maisie's pile of all-enveloping aprons that had a white boiled-in-bleach brilliance and conveyed a promise of cleanliness and starchy purpose. 'We only wear them in the wards and they look easy enough to put on, though I can't say the same about the caps.' She sighed. 'I've tried putting mine on but my hair hates it and tries to shove it off. Nightmare! I've had to buy two cards of kirby grips to anchor it.'

Coloured belts marked the different training years, the first being the same sober grey as the dress, the second was purple and even if the final year blue seemed an eternity away, at least we were heading in that direction. We sewed on, then, final alterations completed, we tried on the new clothes and saw strangers.

In the morning, torn between the excitement and fear of finally arriving in the wards, I suddenly wished we were back in the classroom. At least there we knew where the challenges lay. Oddly, we might even miss them, but having readied us for this moment, Miss Jones and Mrs Low were already turning to a new P.T.S. intake and Hazel and I were heading for the surgical unit.

'Trust you to get the cushy number. I'll be dishing out the bedpans whilst you'll only have bottles to think about. Men's plumbing arrangements are definitely better designed for hospitals.' Hazel sounded genuinely envious as we parted at the common corridor. 'I'm really nervous about this, aren't you?' She re-secured her cap, straightened her dress, sighed, then sprang away, showing confidence and the backs of her knees with every bounding step.

I put on my apron in a small cloakroom, then went and hovered at the entrance of a ward so full of bed-ridden patients, there didn't seem room for any more. There were even beds down the middle into which countless trolley-borne casualties moaning and spluttering under masks, tubes and bed clothes were being transferred.

I'd have been first in the bunker if I'd known war had been declared and thought Douglas, with his C.N.D. contacts, might have warned me. In the classroom, the lecture on nuclear war had suggested little hope for survivors, but in the absence of complete wipe-out and with people still breathing, I realised this was just an ordinary war and Ward Eight, its field hospital.

'Take care,' cried a student nurse directing a travelling bed near the entrance.

'Mind out!' called porters, heads down and arms full out as they sped out of the ward, their trolleys laden with rigid cargo.

'Can't stop!' shouted a harassed-looking staff nurse. 'Just try and make yourself useful or see if you can find Sister.' She bent over a form huddled in his bed. 'Come on, Mr Sim, you've had your operation. Can you hear me?' she tapped his cheek in a brisk way and seemed happy when he moaned.

In a stationary bed, a knight in a suit of shining purple threshed. It was difficult to make out his face, what with the stubble, crust and swollen eyes, but neither his tongue nor his vocal chords were affected and he was chanting in the same medieval tongue my father used before he got the hang of making silage.

Watching over and on high from a pile of air cushions was his neighbour, an old-looking little man so ethereal in appearance, he could have been a ghost.

'Excuse me, Nursie. I think Alex's needing medicine,' he piped in a clear boy's voice. 'His burns are awful sore and that blue stuff's not helping.'

He was looking at me with such urgent appeal, I forgot anxiety and promised to find someone – anyone – if he'd hang on a minute.

'That's what they all say,' he said, turning an anxious gaze back at Alex.

'Thanks for trying, Gordie,' the knight said clearly to the boy.

Determined not to disappoint, I looked around the ward realising this was not war. It was Operating Day and contributing to the bustle and drama were doctors and nurses, some of whom were preparing patients for theatre whilst others were tending recovering returned ones. Everybody was very intent and busy but I spotted the frilly cap of a Sister and flagged it down, noting her nametag.

'Ah, Nurse Macpherson. I wondered where you were.' With her blonde tousled hair and distracted air, Sister Miller looked a bit scatty, but she sounded brisk and had a bright smile. She took Gordie's message then pulled out a crumpled note from her pocket.

'Here! I've made out a list for you. As you can see, this is our busiest day, so you'll just need to get on with this as best you can. I'll get back to you later. Yes, Gordon, I'm coming,' she called, then, as she hurried away, added, 'After the coffee break, you'll come and help me with Alex. He'll need more gentian on his burns. I understand you've some experience in this field.' I hadn't expected to hear this or her amusement.

I looked at the note. It said simply, 'sluice duties'.

Easy! I followed the sound of plumbing noises coming from a huge cavern of a room, its shelves crammed with sanitary ware, where the Ian Charles experience came into its own. Diligently, I set about my tasks. Sister Gordon would have been impressed as I bent over a sink big enough to give ample scope and admiral status, and figured out some damned clever navigational manoeuvres for cleaning the urinals stacked beside it. I was lost in a blockade of soap when an auxiliary dashed in.

'When finished, you go. Coffee break,' she said commandeering the sink and filling a large metal bowl with hot water.

'I wash purly pegs,' she explained, adding a dash of antiseptic.

I must have looked bemused for she added, 'It's ok – I'm married. Must dash. Ta ta.'

Her cap, perched on a black French knot armoured in hairpins, blazed as much importance as the bunion-shaped shoes flying out of the sluice.

I left my fleet and caught up with Hazel, also heading for the dining room.

'How's it going?'

'Ok, I suppose. I'm dying for a break. You?'

'It's not what I expected, but in a changing world, sluices remain the same.' I was thoughtful. 'Um, Hazel, what do you think purly pegs are?'

'They're not in the female side that's for sure.'

'That's what I suspected. See, there's an auxiliary running amok in our ward with a huge basin and surprising a lot of men behind the screens. She speaks in staccato and I think she should have a licence.'

'Did you happen to notice her name?'

'Yeah. Cockburn.'

'Well that figures.'

No one from our group was in the dining room.

'Probably running the wards by now,' said Hazel, throwing down her coffee and jumping up from the table. 'Wonder how Rosie's doing.'

'Giving Woodend a fright I bet.'

There were some nurses heading purposefully for a small room just off the dining room. Hazel looked at them. 'They're going for a smoke. Fancy going to see what it's like.'

'No thanks. I've got a ward to run.'

'Ah! You're back and in time to watch.' Sister Miller pulled a screen round the blue knight who was considering her covered trolley with apprehension, heightening as she donned a mask and gloves. Turning a swab purple with gentian from a gallipot, she advanced.

'Now, Alex, we need to put this on to keep out more infection. The fire's left you with some very nasty chest burns and look at your poor face. We'll get something else for that.' She gestured at the trolley groaning with lotions.

It was going to be a long session, but Mrs Low would have approved of the way the sister dressed Alex's weeping sores. Her light touch and soothing manner could have had the angels singing if Alex had been more appreciative but, unfazed, she carried on, her hands flying over and applying the various lotions with such adroitness, even the bottles clinked in disbelief.

At the end of it all, our patient said in plain English that he thought he felt rather better and was glad that the shiny armour plate caused by the gentian violet would slough off, allowing his manly chest to reappear to the joy of one and all.

'The hair might take a while to grow in again,' said Sister Miller, shoving a lock of her own behind her ear.

Alex gave a toothless smile.

'That'll be ok. The wife'll give me some of hers.'

'You can usually tell when a patient's getting better when they start to make jokes,' she returned, 'and some are better than others.'

The clatter of the departing trolley drowned out his reply.

By now, a ceasefire had been declared and some kind of order restored to the ward. Patients coming back from theatre were reviving and their demands immediate but clear.

'Daftie!' chortled Mrs Cockburn, replacing my tumbler with a urinal and giving it to a patient. 'Get it back soon eh?' She winked then, black eyebrows shooting upwards. 'Somebody's up! Shouldn't be. Catch him.' She nodded at a naked sprinter carrying the intra-venous bottle connected to his arm like an Olympic torchbearer. He was heading for the toilet and going so fast I had to run to catch up with him.

Staff Nurse had been so diligently observing patients on the horizontal she hadn't noticed anybody on the vertical. 'Emergency?' she called and for a moment took her eye off the blood pressure monitor.

'Could be,' I mouthed, aware that running was only for special occasions.

'You were all too busy, I didn't want to bother you,' said the patient limping back to bed.

'What a relief eh?' shouted Alex, proving Sister Miller's restorative touch; but she had adjourned to her office, from which there now issued the proper caring sounds of relaxed chat, fag reek and real coffee.

'You're supposed to be the watchman, you should have let us know we had a streaker,' I chided Gordon, who looked crestfallen and admitted that he had been unable to resist a new comic supplied by Alex.

'Don't give him a hard time, Nurse,' said Alex. 'How would you like to be stuck in here 'cause there's no spare beds in Sick Kids?'

'It's ok,' Gordon replied, his old man's face turning boyish, 'who else would look after you?'

'Certainly not the wife.' Alex cleared his throat. 'Whenever she comes to visit she just says I was a fool to fall into the fire and what a mess the fire brigade made of our bonny fender.'

I left the boys to their old men's tales. It was time to go off duty. Along with the clock, my feet told me the time and when I reached my room, I kicked off my shoes and heard them scream with delight.

Maisie stuck her head round the door. 'Can you still walk?'

I consulted my toes. 'No.'

My pal's curls looked subdued as she staggered in wearily. We swapped notes but she was in a gynaecological ward, so there wasn't much to share apart from throbbing feet and sluice duties.

'Have you seen the others?'

Maisie took off her spectacles and rubbed her eyes. 'A surgeon's asked Isobel to go round the ward with him and the sister was so rattled at a mere first year being seen outwith the sluice, she sent her right back to where he found her.'

'Good Lord! I didn't think the gods sluice-crawled or knew there was a life beyond sore bits and Sisters.'

Maisie's replaced spectacles magnified a twinkle. 'Well, it's not worrying our Isobel – he's asked her out for a dinner date. Oh!' Maisie threw her hand to her mouth. 'I nearly forgot. Rosie phoned. I just happened to answer. She says she nearly died because she had to wash someone's feet and she just hates feet. Jo's ok, last seen climbing into her biker's gear and I don't know about Sheila 'cause she was on late shift.' Curls beginning to revive, Maisie leapt to her feet declaring an urge to tidy drawers and put in rollers. As she left she asked about Douglas.

'I might try and phone him after I've had a quick death,' I said, and did a little practice, falling down a dark corridor of sleep to chase a blue knight trying to save a changeling boy from falling off his air cushions.

When I woke, it was morning.

20

CLOUDS GATHER

It was hard to remember Ward Eight was part of a training hospital. A world away from the classroom, the most important thing here was getting through the work, not killing anybody and being able to stagger off duty without shoes going on fire. Unless I wanted to live dangerously and grind work to a halt, questions that might have helped in the long term remained unasked, and when I remembered Mrs Low's lectures, I couldn't properly follow them through since none of the patients had the enduring patience or painfree zones of the classroom Mrs Brown.

Nor were they lining up to guinea-pig that first injection or stitch removal. There was so little time to persuade them this could be their moment of history, it was amazing I learnt anything at all, but I did. After three weeks I could drive a trolley with skill and precision.

Still, if there wasn't student status in the wards, I wasn't looking for it off duty, so a visit to Beth to find her in her sitting room, but studying, was a disappointment.

'Have you seen Douglas lately?' Sally skittered past on her high heels carrying an armful of books.

'Actually no – I've been trying to phone him yet always seem to miss him.' I aimed for cool and disinterested. 'Of course, I'm pretty busy myself.' Then hedging bets, 'It'd be nice to catch up though.'

'If I see him in the library, I'll tell him I've seen you. Bye!' Sally sounded rushed.

'He's there a lot.' Beth raised her head and gave me a long look. 'It'll soon be exam time, and for us too.' The remark was pointed.

The heavy front door slammed. Beth bent her brain-stuffed head over her work and shuffled her papers.

'Maybe I could catch him there then.'

Beth clicked her teeth in exasperation. 'For one thing, you wouldn't get in, as it's the university library, and Douglas probably needs to get on with his studies, and for another, you've just arrived in Aberdeen and shouldn't be chasing the first bloke you meet.'

I was insulted. 'Honestly, Beth, you take the biscuit. I've seen you snogging that bloke from chemistry – and he comes from Brora! You're such a Holy Willy, you'd think you were my keeper.' Lost for further words, I stomped off to find Mrs Ronce, who was in her sitting-room mulling over *The Scotsman*.

'Ah! Janey – the very one! Come and help me with this crossword. What's two words for relatively annoying?'

'Try pesky sister.' My tone was sour.

Mrs Ronce giggled. 'Beth's just anxious. She's conscientious and wants to pass her exams really well, and she's certainly not sitting one on your feelings.' She threw aside her paper. 'I know, since we're not getting very far with this,' she picked up the Scrabble box and rattled it, 'this looks like a better option.'

I was still smarting from my spat with Beth, so I was glad of the diversion. I had picked up some new words from the ward and thought it unlikely Mrs Ronce knew them.

'You forget. I shoved a W.R.V.S. trolley round the wards and I was also married to a sailor,' she triumphantly got rid of an x and two letters, 'and it was one of the reasons for my divorce. Oh look! I've got a treble score.'

As she totted up the final humiliating score, Beth came in. 'Can I make you two a cup of coffee?' She sounded conciliatory.

'No, let me. I'm needed in the kitchen to boil fish for my poor starving cats. You sit down, Beth, and I'll make it.'

The Roncers must have heard her for they appeared out of nowhere and shepherded her into the kitchen with rapturous purrs. At least they seemed happy.

Beth cleared her throat, 'Um, Jane. I shouldn't have said what I did and I'm sorry.'

'That's ok, but tell me, Beth, is Douglas seeing somebody else?' Unsure if I wanted the answer I looked out at the sodden garden where, huddling in the rain, the shrubs bent together like gossips.

'No, but he'll be up to the eyes in work. Next year's the finals and that's grim stuff. You're at the beginning of your training and he's coming to the end of his. The summer break's coming up and he'll be away home for three months and it's no use you sitting round moping when he's away and probably having a good time,' she paused for a moment, 'if he's any sense.'

I could have mentioned nurses' monopolies on good times but Beth's apologies were rare.

'You're probably right and what'll be will be,' I sighed. I thought about my own pre-exam anxieties, and how Douglas might have his own set of worries and plans, and that three years training was a long time. Then, linking arms with Beth, considered the fire embers. 'Maybe I'll write him a letter. Tell him whilst he's planning being prime minister, I'll be concentrating on becoming the next Florence Nightingale. You could tell me about the Brora bloke. Do you think Mrs Ronce would mind us putting on some more coal?'

21

SISTER GORIGHTLY

Back in the ward, Alex was making such progress he'd been forced to look at brochures of mantelpieces about which his wife would question him during the visiting hour. His face was clear and his eyes a guileless blue, though his chest remained a constant violet. Still, the pink, healing, surrounding skin was a sign he could soon get home. Then, out of the ward's earshot, he and his wife could discuss future living arrangements in a proper manner.

'It's my homework,' he sighed, throwing down the pamphlets. 'I do miss wee Gordie. When he was here the wife didn't like to shout at me in front of him in case she upset him and the Beano made a better read than this lot. Anybody know how he's getting on?'

Gordon had been found a bed in the Sick Children's Hospital and by all accounts he was recovering; he had put on twice the weight taken away with his burst appendix and infected entrails, replacing the old man look with a cheeky young one.

'Different laddie.' Mrs Cockburn advanced on Alex with a steaming bowl and assertive air. 'Popped in, saw him last night. Ok.' She gave the thumbs up.

'Well that's great news, and if you visit him again you can tell him I'm allowed out of bed now, so somebody else can have that wash,' said Alex, morphing into a blue flash.

'What were the air cushions for?' Mrs Ronce had asked, enchanted at the idea of a small boy ruling from on high.

'Bed sores,' I said briefly, aware that Mrs Low considered such things a scandalous dereliction of duty by nurses unwilling or unable to move patients from one position to another so that blood didn't lie, turning into bruising and worse. Our tutor had made an hour unpleasant describing its aetiology.

'It's such a busy ward. There never seems to be enough staff, time, laundry or equipment to meet everybody's needs; our tutors would have a fit if they saw the shortcuts,' I tried to explain.

'Thanks for the warning – it's another incentive to keep healthy, so I'll keep taking this sherry. Cheers!'

I hadn't known then that the teaching department would be sending clinical instructors to make sure we were doing our work properly. In the classroom, improvisation had been frowned upon, but in those first few weeks in the wards we had had time to perfect it. Instructors might have a tough call and word was out they were coming.

'Who's yours?' asked Maisie, as if they were personal property. 'Mine's Maggie Dee.'

As we went on duty she was practically skipping. Sometimes Maisie's early morning, breezy way bordered on the unnatural. 'They say she's ok – better than that Sister Gorightly. Apparently she's a holy terror.'

'I'll find out soon enough but I hope I don't get her. She sounds awful.'

In the ward cloakroom, a limping Mrs Cockburn was the first casualty of the day. She tore off her cap, threw it into a bin, then, taking a large man-sized hanky from the shopping bag in her locker, trumpeted into it. 'That woman,' she said, slamming the locker door shut, 'confiscated my bowl, tore strips off me in front of the patients and said I wasn't to come back until my leg was better. Well, there was nothing wrong with it until her foot got in the way.' She turned the locker key as if she were screwing a lid on tight, grabbed her coat and, before I could say anything, hobbled out the door.

Alarmed by her upset and use of whole sentences, I joined the ward report group, worrying how we could cover her work as well as our own and already missing the clarion call, the chrome clang and the bunion-shaped shoes which bounced her so cheerily round the ward. How would we get our patients mobile now?

As we gathered round Sister Miller for the morning report, I got a flicker of pity whilst the rest of the staff were handed lengthy work slips. Sister Miller's usually blithe expression was grim. 'Nurse Macpherson,' she started to roll up her sleeves, 'the rest of us will have to cover for staff shortages because we've lost a vital team member and you're with Sister Gorightly.'

'Oh God!' I suddenly remembered the girl who'd fled the Nurses' Home, the overheard conversations of nurses scarred by an experience best not shared, and my stomach turned.

Yet out of the sluice, a vision of loveliness appeared whilst Sister and her staff melted away.

But surely this couldn't be the harridan responsible for all those tales of tears and trauma? This was a sweet-faced, silvery-haired angel with a peaches-and-cream complexion and an hourglass figure, over which a turquoise-coloured dress strained in enough places to engage the interest of patients previously considered moribund. Her heeled shoes accentuated the neat ankles now flying in my direction.

In the distance someone dropped a bedpan, breaking the hush that had fallen upon the ward.

'Ah, Nurse Macpherson! I'll be with you today to check out your practical work. I'm sure we will have a very instructive day.' Her tones were dulcet – her smile dazzling, showing very white, if sharp, teeth.

'Now, let's start with something simple. I'm thinking of a bed bath. A basic but essential procedure.' She made for a patient who, in the absence of Mrs Cockburn, had been looking forward to fester unmolested in bed. His smile faded as she explained, 'Nurse Macpherson needs a little practice in the art of bed bathing, so we'll just see how she gets on with you. You'll be happy to help I'm sure.'

'But I'd a bath yesterday and Ah'm getting hame the day,' he protested, a leg making a rapid bid for the floor. 'In fact,' he glanced at the wall clock, 'ony minute noo.'

'Nowsie wowsie, Mr Souter, this won't take but a matter of minutes and you must go home fresh.' Sister Gorightly gave a tinkling laugh whilst transfixing him with a light touch and steely eye.

'Everybody ca's me Dod,' he said in an attempt at cosiness whilst clutching his blankets so that his knuckles gleamed.

A cloud passed over that lovely countenance. 'Oh my goodness, no! We can't have that. Familiarity is not our way. It's Mr Souter, *Mr Souter*, always – we must respect our patient's dignity.'

Unaware he was going to lose it big time, Dod returned his leg.

'Nurse, you go and prepare the trolley and I'll get Mr Souter ready.' Dod's face went as white as the hands pulling the screens round him. The subsequent brisk sounds of tugging and argument suggested Sister Gorightly's lily whites might not be as pure as they looked.

I went to get my trolley ready, managing to swipe enough towels from the shared linen cupboard to start a revolution on the female side. With confidence and the friendly warning squeak of wheels, I trundled my wagon to the bedside.

'Noise, noise!' came a scolding shout. It was discomfiting to find the sister bent double and covering her ears as if in pain, whilst looking straight ahead, our patient held firmly onto his remaining sheet.

Sister Gorightly straightened, took in the trolley and drew breath. 'But this isn't a proper setting. Where are the cover cloths and where last was that basin? Actually, this is a nothing trolley. Dear me! I don't know what the tutors would say to this. It's poor, poor.' She grabbed a metal jug, the only one I could find. 'And this looks as if it came out of the Ark. Look at the rust! It's just as well this isn't an operation this dear man's having, our Mr Souter', – a little coo, a little eyelash flutter, a little playful tweak – 'dear me no! It's just a leetle freshen up. Isn't that what we promised?'

'Ouch!' Dod rubbed a reddening cheek. 'I could easily have hid a dook in the shower on ma ain.'

'What! After all the good work repairing that hernia?' she pointed, and our patient subsided.

'And we certainly won't be needing these.' She clattered away the pile of kidney dishes with waitressing expertise.

I'd been rather proud of them, having had to fight hard to get them off Staff Nurse's wound-dressing trolley. You never knew when they might come in handy, but maybe this wasn't the moment to promote their use as a denture box, even if we had run out of the official ones.

Meanwhile, trying to remember Mrs Low's dictates and keep my instructor at bay, I'd become as nervous as Dod – already the soap was speeding from my grip to land under the next patient's bed.

'Catch!' Right away it was thrown back over the screens. The ward broke into hilarity.

'Pleased to be of service,' Alex's voice floated through talc-laden air.

Sister Gorightly's silence was thunderous.

I replaced the modesty sheet with a towel, which somehow lost its purpose and hit the deck. There was a nursing decree that nothing should fall on the floor barring the odd patient, so I knew things were on a slide, especially as the remaining face cloth Dod was clutching as his last defence was plainly inadequate.

'You don't seem to have grasped this most fundamental of skills. Are you really telling me you passed your P.T.S. exam? Dear me! I'm sure Mrs Low would be shocked to see these breaches of etiquette,' she said, nodding at Dod's trembling form. 'This poor fellow's in danger of hypothermia. Go and get another towel.'

'You can't have any more,' said Staff Nurse who'd overheard, 'they're all done.'

'Really!' said Sister Gorightly as if it were a medical term.

'Ah jist wint ma blankets back,' said Dod, 'an ma PJs. Ah'm freezin!'

I was sharing his cold sweat; but at last, and with enough blankets to flatten him, our patient had a normal temperature return along with his pyjamas.

'So you didn't enjoy that much, Mr Souter?' Sister Gorightly asked and added in a roguish way, 'perhaps Nurse Macpherson will do better the next time. Being such a new recruit, she needs the practice.'

I tidied away my trolley, thinking its squeak had become sad, unlike Dod's wife who was waiting for him with a suitcase at the ward entrance.

'Is he ready?' she asked, all smiles and hope. 'I've got his clothes here.'

I didn't want to be the one who told her he was in danger of a relapse, but already he was at my shoulder.

'Get me ootta here,' he said clutching his pyjamas at the neck and waist-band and looking frantic.

'But, Dod, what about your clothes?'

'Ootahere – this meenute.'

Sister Gorightly's honeyed voice lassoed him. 'My dear man, you can't possibly go home like that. Go and get dressed, there's a good fellow – we can't have you catching pneumonia, now can we?'

'You'd a damn good try,' he muttered, but complying.

Dod's wife was awe struck.

'How on earth did you manage that? He's been enjoying the wee break so much I thought he might not want to come home.'

But Sister Gorightly had no answer. Looking round the ward, a light in her eye, she was on another mission

'I'd like to see you doing the drinks round now, Nurse Macpherson. See if you can do that a little better.' She fluttered a dismissive wave to the Souters. 'You'll excuse us, as I'm sure you're aware, this young proba-tioner is needing all of my time. Come along.' The shove on my back propelled me towards the kitchen.

'I'll give you a few minutes to set up,' she said, brushing a hand across her forehead as though she was feeling fevered, 'then I'll come along and check it before we start. Let's hope you get this right.'

The drinks round was usually a chatty casual trundle with the natural spillage you expect of patients drinking from a difficult angle. I hadn't ever found it difficult and hoped that here at least, my performance might improve.

'Are you setting up for Royalty?' the kitchen maid asked, looking at a trolley loaded with every conceivable drink combination. 'Sorry, but there's no ice. It's been nabbed by the female side. They said it was payback time for the linen raid.'

'Don't worry, with Sister Gorightly around, there's no shortage.' I was too busy looking for a clean cloth to notice she'd arrived and so had Hazel, who was carrying a tray of dirty dishes.

'Ah! How nice to see you, Nurse.' The tutor sounded genuinely pleased. 'You'll see I'm working with your colleague today – though I'm afraid it won't be for the short while spent with you.' She laughed and tapped her fingers together. 'Of course, I know you have a father who's in the business, shall we say, and able I imagine, and keen, to advise you, so I expect that must put this colleague at a disadvantage.'

'But her Dad's a plumber.' I opted for sarcasm.

Hazel giggled, 'Of sorts.'

'A plumber? Oh dear me, no. He's a very important surgeon,' Sister Gorightly, a stranger to irony, puffed out her chest, putting the buttons at risk, 'and I see from your tray that the female side has had their drinks. We must be late. Now, Nurse Macpherson – quickly, quickly.' She looked over the trolley with disfavour. 'Where's the shower cloth?'

A shower cloth?

I'd never heard of such a thing and neither had the kitchen maid, but she took a towel from her precious collection and handed it over as if it were her last.

'I suppose that will have to do.' Sister Gorightly examined it minutely, then, laying it over the trolley with the care of a magician, drove at a spanking rate into a ward full of thirsty patients.

'And high time too,' said Sister Miller. She looked harassed and in need of refreshment herself. 'Hurry up before there's a revolution. Some patients have even been consulting their temperature charts and saying they're feeling dehydrated – though goodness knows where they found that word.' Any medical knowledge beyond its experts was apparently considered dangerous.

'We'll do our best,' Sister Gorightly rocked the trolley as if it were a pram, 'it's just that Nurse Macpherson's rather slow.'

'She's not usually,' retorted that lovely ward sister, and throwing me a smile, hurried away.

The Sister tutor raised her eyebrows and set off. 'We must make this a pleasant occasion. I'll show you.'

I was surprised when she approached nice but nervous Mr Watt. He wasn't long out of theatre after major abdominal surgery, an event he'd approached with some trepidation, and (had) new striped pyjamas supplied by an equally anxious family.

'This can't be necessary,' he cried, now corseted into a tent-sized bib, 'I'm only allowed a few sips of water.' There was a 'Fluids Only' sign above him and enough tubes coming from him and draining into the bags hooked on the bedside to justify his caution. He clutched his head as if suspecting it might be equally trapped.

'Rubbish!' insisted the tutor. 'What you need is a nice cup of tea. Just drink up and you'll be on the mend before you know it.'

She picked up a chart and clicked her teeth. 'Would you look at this! Whoever filled this in hasn't given the proper details. There's nothing written here. See! This is how you do it.' She wrote at length and signed off with a flourish.

Mr Watt swallowed his tea with reluctance and was now beginning to look so upset I wondered if I should do something. Sister Gorightly wouldn't like her authority challenged, so I could only wait until she put it to the trolley before nodding my head and swivelling my eyeballs to Staff Nurse. She looked concerned and went to look for Sister. I just hoped they didn't think I was having a fit. Meanwhile, the circus moved on.

[128]

'I wasn't needing a bed bath,' grumbled Alex, who had escaped all attentions other than a nerve-ridden splash. 'Wee Mac doesn't usually drown us.'

'Such familiarity,' tutted Sister Gorightly.

At last the round was completed and I found the power of prayer when my tormentor wiped her brow and said she'd had enough for the day. She tottered off, presumably to burnish her halo, whilst I retired to the sluice for a bit of sniffing, then returned to the ward to find that Mr Watt was now screened off.

I was anxious about him, but the ward resumed its frantic pace with another twenty-nine patients all needing attention. Eventually, tired, anxious, dispirited, but lacking the courage to look behind Mr Watt's screens, I went off duty.

Feeling a failure and sure dismissal was minutes away, I thought it best to hand in my notice now and was so busy concocting the words, I hardly noticed reaching the Nurses' Home. But it would have been hard to miss Isobel, who was brightening up the entrance hall in a pink dress, mini enough to have Matron reaching for the smelling salts.

'Jane, you've not been crying surely?'

'No, no – it's just a bad cold. I think it calls for an early night. Not like you, you look as if you've a heavy date, you lucky girl.'

Isobel shrugged. 'It's not a big deal. Come on. You're more important. Let me come up with you. You can go to bed and I'll fill a hot water bottle, and what about some aspirins and some tissues?'

'I'll be fine. Look, you hurry on. I don't want to make you late.'

A fancy car had drawn up at the entrance and a good-looking chap I'd seen in the hospital corridor, followed by medical students hanging on his every word, got out. He smoothed his hair in an Adonis-confirming sort of way, looked anxiously at his watch and then at the door where Isobel now was. His face fell as quickly as it had lit up as she smiled, waved, mouthed, 'Ten minutes,' then turned away.

'Don't you worry, you and the bottle filling are of paramount importance to me,' she assured, putting a light hand on my shoulder. 'I'll do it properly and you can give me a score.' She nodded carelessly at her escort now kicking his heels in the car park, 'It'll do him good to wait. Everybody but me seems to think he's God and not a common surgeon for goodness sake. Come on.'

When we got to my floor, Isobel put in a tactful ten minutes in the kitchen whilst I looked from my window to the hospital through a vale of tears. Now that I knew some of the dramas within the grey granite I wondered if, after all, I'd chosen the right career. It all seemed so difficult with Sister Gorightly making impossible the simplest of tasks. At least, I thought, having one last hiccup, Maisie had gone straight home after her shift. She'd been spared the floodworks and I, an off-key rendition of 'Jesus loves me'.

Instead, there was Isobel, complete with survival kit and apologising for having to dash but she was beginning to get hungry and she did have a dinner date.

'Isobel,' I said, recognising grace.

'Yes?'

'Ever thought of taking up nursing?'

'No. I'd rather be a butcher.'

22

SWEET SALVATION

'Are you ok?' Isobel, wearing the concerned look of a nurse on a recruitment drive, was doing a morning check-up.

'Uh-huh, but I wish I'd paid more attention to that lecture on vermin control. How'd the date go?'

She laughed, avoided the question and held the door open. 'Come on then. At least you've got your sense of humour back. It takes a lot to get you down but I just hope I never get her. She sounds awful. Mind, I've got quite enough with my ward sister keeping me stuck in the sluice. She's a right bitch! Says I've got to learn about cleaning first. I'm beginning to wonder what a patient looks like, never mind a clinical instructor.'

That wasn't my problem. On the ward corridor, mine was waiting for me.

'Come along – quickly-do,' the scold-shadowing figure tapped her feet and watch. My heart couldn't make up its mind whether to sink or burst but then Sister Miller came out of her office interrupting with, 'I want to see you both.'

The sister tutor bridled at the abrupt tone. 'We've a busy morning, can't it wait?'

'No. Now!'

The office was a jumble of cheap furniture, strewn papers and filing cabinets haemorrhaging contents onto the lino floor. The cartoons on the wall could have lightened the atmosphere if Sister Miller hadn't sat, like a headmistress, behind her desk.

She picked up the Kardex, a bulletin of patients' progress, and leafed through it until she came to Mr Watt's details with an attached card.

'Do you recognise this?' She took it out and held up the 'Fluids Only' notice last seen behind his bed. 'Do you realise that since your trolley round yesterday, this patient's been seriously ill?' She slapped the card on her desk.

I thought about nice Mr Watt with his troubled gaze and nervous tremor. He'd been very anxious before his operation and the major surgery proved his point. I remembered how weakly he'd tried to argue against taking anything and wished I'd had the courage to challenge Sister Gorightly's bossy ministrations.

'Will he be alright?' I asked, worrying a lot about the patient and even more about the resignation letter in my pocket and when I'd be asked for it.

The tutor stuck out her chin, put her hands on the desk and eyeballed her colleague. 'Surely that's nothing to do with us, we just followed what was on the notice.'

In silence, Sister Miller turned the card, which now read 'Nil Orally'.

'How would we have known that?' The tone was shrill.

'He's had a very bad night. We even thought his sutures might burst with his retching. He should never have had that cup of tea which I believe you insisted he drink.'

'You can hardly make us responsible for your errors.' Sister Gorightly's tone dripped contempt. 'I can't believe you've allowed out two different notices on one piece of cardboard,' she wafted a hand at the paper piles and general office muddle, 'but then, of course, it's not really surprising considering this and the fact that you don't allow me access to information. I've always had a problem getting it in this ward.' Her voice had moved up a scale.

Sounds of the ward cranking into its usual frantic pace had begun but, compared to the office, it sounded like a beacon of calm. Sister Miller snapped her pencil in half. Then she stood up and pointed it at Sister Gorightly who stepped right back. I stepped right forward. Was I to witness a stabbing? Much as I might like to see the back of my tormentor, I drew the line at murder.

'I've got a ward to run and not endless hours to do it in. My first concern is for the patients – that's what I'm here to do. Anyway, any *trained* member of staff should have used their observational skills and seen that this patient was,' Sister Miller itemised with a nicotine stained finger, 'newly post-operative, poor in colour, frail in general condition but cogent, and I also understand he insisted he only wanted a sip of water and it was you who made him drink that cup of tea.'

The tutor gave a deep sigh, then, eyes swimming, turned and put a chummy hand on my shoulder. 'Yes, that's true, but you have to remember I was keeping an eye on our young friend here.'

'Don't you try and blame Nurse Macpherson. I gather that she tried to alert Staff Nurse to her concerns. She's a good team member, so much so that in fact I will admit her training needs may have been overlooked.'

Gosh! This might be the Aberdeen equivalent of praise but it didn't impress Sister Gorightly.

'She's a long way to go yet. But why don't we see what Matron has to say.'

Face aflame, she headed for the door until Sister Miller said, 'That's a good idea, and I'll take this shall I?' She held up the fluid intake chart. 'I see your signature here.'

Sister Gorightly stopped and went white.

'But will Mr Watt be alright?' I persisted, sensing further combat and anxious to escape.

'Yes, and so will you because I shall personally supervise you and now I think Sister Gorightly has other wards she can attend to,' some papers were shuffled by way of dismissal, 'and please close the door. I have a ward to run.'

[133]

Dealing with the next emergency of the day, she went to switch on the kettle whilst I flew out in the tail wind of Sister Gorightly's exit.

'I can see you're feeling better,' Isobel observed as we walked off duty and I recounted my tale. 'It's amazing what a difference a day can make, and guess what, good news for me too.' She squeezed my shoulder. 'I've been allowed out of the sluice. I think James must have had a word with Sister.'

I tossed my letter in a bin, feeling happy and hearing birdsong. 'What it is to have friends in high places, though my swotty, literary-minded sister would say that's a cliché.'

'Even if she spends a lot of time keeping you right,' Isobel bent an amused glance in my direction, 'you're lucky to have one – being an *only* is hard work. Somebody else to annoy the parents would be great.'

She should have been there when I went to visit Beth, thinking she might like to know my career was still on course, but it was clear she wasn't in the mood for drama and suggested I go and tell Mrs Ronce. 'She likes your stories. I reckon it's the blood.'

She was getting as monosyllabic as Mrs Cockburn.

I went and looked hard at my sister's side.

'What's wrong?' she asked.

'I was merely looking for a sympathetic ear.'

'There's one downstairs,' Beth said, and with a righteous sniff picked up one of her innumerable textbooks.

At least she was right there for Mrs Ronce really did seem to like hospital tales and the more gore the better.

'Well! That's some story and you certainly see life,' she said at length, menacing the fire with a poker. 'So how's the patient now?'

'One week on and he's like a new man. He's even helping with the drinks trolley, says he's served his apprenticeship.' It was hard to equate the joking helpful person with that previous shadow connected to livelier looking tubes.

'And Sister Gorightly?'

'Gone to Glory I hope.'

Mrs Ronce giggled. 'And what about the blue knight?'

'Went home last week.'

'My word, Jane, despite your best efforts, they all seem to be getting better,' Mrs Ronce hugged her knees, 'and how are you managing without your bête noir?'

'Actually, I think she did me a favour because I'm now being shown how to do things properly and I even get on the occasional doctors' ward round. Sister Miller may look scatty and smoke like a chimney, but she knows her stuff and is a good teacher.'

I was going to be sorry to leave a place where there was so much action and drama, where people went home feeling better and where, having been released from the sluice, I'd learnt to do more exciting things.

'Well, here's to your next triumph. What's next?'

'In another week, Jo, a classmate, and I are going to Ward Four, Woodend. It's geriatric, a different world from surgical and more like somewhere in Grantown I know, so I suppose I should manage it alright.'

'I think the mannies in Ward Eight'll miss you, but hearing your stories makes me want to keep well. I'm reaching a dangerous age. Let's have another medicinal sherry.'

I went to Sister's office to say this was my last day. She gave a vague smile.

'Your time here's not been without incident.' She rubbed her brow. 'I must remember to fill in your ward report.' With the clink of her teacup, she returned to the more pressing chore of ward surgeon hospitality, emptied her ashtray and closed the door.

She didn't even say goodbye and I had to settle for returning the enthusiastic waves of a ward full of suddenly ambulant patients advanced upon by Mrs Cockburn, now walking well and reunited with her big bowl.

That report would be important. I hoped it wasn't too inclusive.

23

GOLDFISH AND GERIATRICS

Apart from its low-slung, modern-looking Nurses' Home, Woodend Hospital looked like the Ian Charles but with bigger henhouses and a jumble of prefab buildings clustered round it. Nearby were fields full of cattle and the sound of tractors replaced that of cars. There was a long stately drive to the main entrance where oak double doors with polished brass handles led into the main building, but a stone's throw away from the Home was the back entrance, which was handier for Jo and me to get to our ward.

'How d'you like your new bedroom?' She squinted back. 'It's really rustic round here, isn't it? It must be more your scene than Foresterhill.'

I said I supposed so but I was just getting to enjoy work in Ward Eight when I had to shift not only work, but my room as well.

Jo rolled her eyes. 'Don't tell me! Remember, I'd to do it at the end of P.T.S. and even if a van actually shifts our stuff, we've to pack it all away in the first place.' She sighed. 'And I suppose when this ward stint comes to an end, we'll be off somewhere else. Makes you realise that settling anywhere's daft and travelling light makes sense. I'm going to leave most of my stuff at home.'

'Easier for you than me but I suppose change is supposed to be healthy and we need different experiences. Still, going anywhere new makes me nervous.'

'Me too,' Jo had such a capable air she surprised me, 'but Rosie says the ward's fine. She even managed to get over her foot phobia; everybody's so moribund, the only bit of action is their toenail growth, so we've just to close our eyes and let the nailbrush do the rest.'

'I like living dangerously. Anything else?'

'The ward sister's lovely but loopy, more interested in racing results than hospital corners but that's maybe because the patients aren't moving. She's very caring; apparently even the goldfish is on oxygen.'

'And what about the work?' I recalled Rosie screwing her nose.

'We've to remember the colonic lavage lecture.'

We reached the geriatric floor. It was a world away from surgery, wore a close atmosphere of quiet decay and was small enough for staff to cover both wards. No glittering surgical contraptions invaded and there was no purposeful bustle. Sister Gordon would have had a fit if she had seen the dust on the zimmers parked on the corridor down which the frail pipe of a patient's demands and the querulous snap of one tiring of another's company floated ghostlike in the air.

'Bit gloomy isn't it?' Jo whispered. Her knock at the office door seemed very bold.

'Ah! Lovely!' Sister looked up from feeding her goldfish. 'Our new girls, Fishie,' she beamed and patted the bowl. 'I'll be back in a minute after I've shown them around. Weren't we just saying the other day how much our patients love a change of face?' Pausing for a moment to adjust the oxygen supply, she led the way.

She was small and had the look of a kindly, aged dumpling, but so fit we had to move fast to keep up with a whistle stop tour finishing at the male ward where a ward maid was processing the betting slips of a couple of patients unusual in their alertness. The rest seemed lost, hopefully just in slumber.

'Meet Shona, our most important member of staff.'

Shona's quiet smile brought life to the place. 'Sister's aye at me tae interest the wifies in ha'en a flutter but ah canna persuade them.' There was a placid kindness in her tone, a solid measure to her tread.

[137]

Sister gave a fat wheeze. 'Too much excitement maybe.' She consulted her watch. 'Gracious! You'll need to go and place these right now. That race is on soon. Did you get mine?'

'Aye. Just a sec. I'll jist water these afore ah go.' Sticking the slips under one arm, Shona took a glass of water from a patient's locker and poured it over a pot of plastic flowers. Untroubled, the bed occupant dozed on whilst the ward maid padded off, taking all feeling of action with her until two old men came shuffling out from the toilet shepherded by an auxiliary. We were introduced.

'Hello, I'm taking Jock and Willie to the Dayroom,' she explained, steadying their zimmers. 'They like it fine once they get there.'

The old men passed, muttering maledictions.

'Are the patients ever taken out, or,' Jo took in the sombre silent surroundings, 'are they not well enough?'

Sister patted a patient's sleeping form and looked surprised, then thoughtful. 'Now that's a good point. Certainly some of them could go – it's just a question of persuasion. Maybe you could coax those two, but as you can see, most of these patients don't even know they're here,' she whispered as we tiptoed out. 'Mind you, they may well look as if they're far away but they could easily be hearing us, so please treat them with the respect they're due.' She sucked her lip, adding in a pensive way, 'Of course, it's as easy to say as it is to forget, especially when you're busy. Now it must be time for Fishie's coffee break – yours too.'

She sped back to her office and when we passed, we overheard her confide, 'Nice girls, Fishie, but I bet they don't get the boys to go out. Let's open a book on it.'

We'd to go back to the Home for the break, the walk in fresh air marking the contrast to Ward Four's supposed ambience. Rosie joined us in the dining room.

'Well?'

Jo bit into her floured roll and put three large spoonfuls of sugar in her cup.

'We'll certainly need energy to get that lot out of bed.' Over the cup rim her eyes had the sparkle of sun shining on a brown pool.

Rosie rubbed her hands, apparently better pleased with her new ward. 'It's all a bit dead isn't it, especially when you consider that the two girny old mannies are the liveliest there. How're you finding it, Jane?'

'I think it'd be easy to get ground down with all that helplessness, and the basic nursing stuff is hard work, but at the very least we'd like to get more up and about and some of the women into the Dayroom.'

'You'll be lucky. That's the preserve of Jock and Willie.'

'Oh, we'll be taking them outside,' Jo said in a determined way.

'I bet they won't go,' Rosie got up.

'That's funny. That's what Sister said.' Wiping her mouth free of flour, Jo stood up. 'We bet they do.'

We headed back to the ward. 'I suppose we shouldn't go in all guns blazing?'

'No. We'll give them a day or two.' Jo was confident.

But it was a fortnight before we were back on duty together and by that time had learnt that whilst the work could be back-breaking and the patients apparently comatose, they could still put up a healthy resistance when it came to change. By comparison, the Ian Charles pace was dynamic.

'But, Annie, you could be sitting in a comfy chair watching TV in the Dayroom,' I cajoled an arthritic patient, her joints so stiff, they creaked, her swollen hands lying balloon-like on her lap. My own back ached with the labour of helping patients to move, and since she couldn't, I thought her pain and frustration must be unbearable.

'It's Mrs McGillivray to you, and even if I did get up and go through there, those two old miseries make the place smell like a lum.'

'Ah!' Jo put an arm round her. 'But we're going to take them out for a nice bit of fresh air.'

Annie shook her off. 'You'll have to drag them. Anyway, I bet they won't go.'

'Has Shona asked you about putting on a bet by any chance?' I was suspicious.

'Yes!' Annie said, showing the first sign of spirit and interest outside the pill round and bowel chart.

The ward overlooked a scene of green. In front of the hospital there was even a rose garden with some sloping winding walks. They led through a gate to somewhere unknown. If you looked out from any window, the great outdoors beckoned. How could anyone resist it?

As well as making sure bets, we reckoned we should make a nice spectacle of loving care to grateful patients and maybe even acquire a small suntan without the doubtful aid of Fantanstic, yet cynical Annie kept asking us when we were going to admit defeat.

'Not today,' I said. 'Just you watch us.'

She chuckled – a rare and lovely sound.

Acting on an agreed plan, Jo and I marched into the Dayroom.

'It's a bonny day out there, wouldn't you just love to be out in it?' Jo knelt beside Jock and looked up at him in a winsome way.

His contented expression behind a smoke haze changed to one of horror. He put down his pipe in spluttering disbelief.

A copy of a Landseer painting of a stag, kippered after years of hanging in this male bastion where the only female welcome was Shona with a lackadaisical duster, might have suggested there was a great and wild life outside, but Jock wasn't having any of it.

'Naw – jist leave us in peace.'

Meanwhile, Willie was showing a previously unknown aptitude for speed and would have escaped had I not been quicker.

'Honestly, it's wonderful out there. Goodness me, it's stifling in here.' I caught him by the outstretched arms of his overcoat and before they had time to reach the alarm bell, both men were dressed, bundled into prepared wheelchairs, smothered in blankets and out before anybody could hear their pleading shouts and call the police.

'They'll be fine once we get outside,' Jo shouted above the complaining din while opening the outside door.

Now, we were bowling along in good style. Our plan of surprise attack had worked and we were finding it liberating being outside as opposed to being stuck inside. Certainly the men's grizzling took away some of the ambience but this didn't feel like work. The roses were coming into bloom, the sky was blue, the grass was green, somewhere far away we heard the shout of seagulls, the raucous sound softened and carried on a balmy wind. It really was a perfect day.

'Ah'm needin' hame,' Willie piped, his bonnet down about his nose and emanating fury. 'This is a disgrace! Wait till I tell Shona.'

'Aye. Hame – noo!' Jock was no less forthright, slicing the air with a stick he had grabbed as a defence mechanism.

'Nonsense! We've just arrived. Look at the bonny roses – and what a view we get from here. Now, where do you think that road leads?' We had travelled most of the paths and still didn't want to return. The sun continued to shine, the air was clear, why on earth would we go back to that stifling hospital air? I pointed the wheels towards the gate. Jo followed, uttering calming words to patients now bordering on the apoplectic.

Through the gate we went, finding a long winding sloping road edged on either side with bramble-entwined bushes. We paused to savour the view. This was the life!

'Stop!' cried Willie, filling his lungs with nice fresh air; but it was too late, his pleas had momentarily distracted us, lessening our grip as the chairs, lined up at the top of the hill as if at a starting point, took off on their own. The Grand National had nothing on this. The once heavy chairs, gathering speed, seemed now to be flying, and as they headed for the first hurdle, their riders' screams grew fainter by the second.

'Oh my God!' Jo proved she could run as well as shout, but not unfortunately as fast as our charges disappearing round the first bend. We'd been told nurses shouldn't run unless it was an emergency. This qualified.

It was easy racing down that slope. Miss Jones had once told us that the autonomic nervous system took over at times when the brain was disconnected and had asked us to think of an example.

'Your hair stands up to break the wind,' Rosie had volunteered.

She was referring to arms made goose pimpled to entrap warmth and, once we had all finished laughing, was proved smugly right by Miss Jones. Jo and I could now vouch for fear of doing the same to the head. Still, the hairgrips worked, tethering on our caps, leaving us just dishevelled and anxious but not half as much as our patients, whose bleating sounds came from under some bushes. The passing minutes were recorded by the wheels downside up, still turning and making a startled bird scold in alarm.

'How long for manslaughter?' Jo whispered and bent her head like a supplicant.

I followed. Once more, the future looked bleak. I hadn't thought of prison as a career break, and there and then I made a pact with my maker never to be experimental again, if only our patients would be in one bit.

And there, miraculously, were Willie and Jock, uninjured apart from a few battle scratches gained through unfriendly bramble fire.

'Thank you, God,' I whispered, already beginning to regret the deal.

'We'll take you home and will never do this again,' Jo soothed, but our patients had been struck dumb, a prospect more ominous than all their previous complaints. Somehow we managed to wheedle them back into their chairs and soberly returned them to the ward, where they were helped into beds with promises of endless tobacco, no physiotherapy and certainly no fresh air for a very long time.

'I suppose we better go and tell Sister.'

'You go first.' Jo pushed me towards the office door.

I gave a tentative tap.

Sister, looking up from Fishie maintenance, smiled in her benign way. 'Come in.' She knocked on the bowl. 'And here's the girls, Fishie. We've got to congratulate them for getting those two old rascals outside. We never thought they'd do it. What a good thing we backed them, but I'm afraid the rest've lost their bet and what about the boys?'

Jo prodded me and considered the floor.

'It didn't go very smoothly,' I said, then threw myself into a career-saving story where we became heroines snatching patients from the jaws of death.

Sister covered her mouth, then turned, shoulders heaving, to a wall cupboard and took out a biscuit tin and a bottle of brandy. Fishie eyed me with his bulbous stare, then flicked his tail and, untouched by drama, continued his circuit. Well, at least he wasn't searching for a reviver.

'I'll get Doctor to check them out, but it sounds as if they're alright,' she said as she dabbed away tears, astonishingly of laughter. 'You certainly know how to spin a yarn, Nurse Macpherson, so I won't ask too much about the real facts and yes, I did hear a bit of a commotion when you came back, but they're able to complain and that for them's Heaven.'

She caught Fishie's eye as he completed his umpteenth round. 'But maybe you need some training in proper wheelchair use. Then you could take out some of the others. We really do get stuck in a rut here. Now what about giving out some of this nice tablet I've been making and asking Shona to make you a cup of tea. I expect you've had a bit of a fright. I'll go and see if the boys would like a glass of this.' She pulled the bottle cork out with a practised flourish, poured two generous measures into a matching pair of medicine glasses, set them on top of the biscuit box and, using it as a tray, left us figuring out our tablet quota and wondering how to tell Shona she'd lost.

24

MISSION ACCOMPLISHED

Along with the other staff members, we concentrated hard on the wheel-chair lecture in a wheelchair department big enough to test drive a Daimler. Jo's biker status was an advantage and the demonstrating technician, impressed by her questions, all but pirouetted, transforming these bulky unlovely barrows into chariots of fire. I hadn't realised the fascination of spokes, hubs or even punctures, nor the range that a wheelchair could offer in the hands of an expert. Diligently, we took notes and did trial runs practising how to corner, steer, brake and get up kerbs without losing the passenger.

I missed Douglas. He might have liked my geriatric stories but the university was having its summer break. He must have got my 'let's save the world but do it independently' letter. The last time we met, he'd pointed his nose in the opposite direction and jumped on a number twenty-two bus. He'd be back in Alness, where his political inclinations might be making him plan a protest march on behalf of Labour, peaceniks or the workers. My own politics being sketchy, I thought it was good somebody had the time to do it on our behalf.

'It'll be Monte Carlo next,' said Annie. Word of a new tour operation had reached the female ward. She struggled to sit up, the effort making her joints creak and her voice breathless. 'I'd give anything to get a wee hurl,' she said, sounding wistful.

'Me too,' said her neighbour, 'and we've been talking about going along to the Dayroom as well. We could watch racing on telly.'

Jo arrived with a wheelchair. She parked it beside the bed with the expertise of Ben Hur. 'Your chariot awaits, Mrs MacGillivray. You too shall go to the Ball. Nurse Macpherson and I are taking you and your pal. Sister says we're allowed.'

Annie's face lit up as she shoved herself forward, her hands paddling the bed clothes in a big effort to shift them. 'Well! Just look! I think I'm moving better already – all I need is a little help.' A straight leg stuck out from under the blankets, followed, with much grunting, by the other. Then, with a shout of triumph, Annie launched herself into space, making a perfect landing into a wheelchair whose recently pumped tyres held firm.

'There. I did it!' Panting but jubilant, she turned to her friend. 'Hurry up or we'll miss the sun and the two-twenty at Doncaster. I wonder if those two old devils know we might want to change channels.'

'They'll be wanting into our chairs next,' grumbled Jock, sitting hard on the best-placed chair and drawing heavily on his pipe.

'Aye, and making us put these out,' added Willie, stoking up. 'Mebbe it's time we wis hame.'

Changes were afoot for us too.

'Did you see we're going to theatre?' asked Jo. 'We're back in the A.R.I. – it's up on the board. You're going to the Ward Nine's and I'm in Ward Eight's.'

'I hope you don't meet Sister Gorightly then. Have I ever told you about her?'

'Jane! The whole hospital knows about you and Sister Gorightly, but haven't you heard? She's suddenly got a calling and she's off to do good works in a leper colony.'

'What?! She's off to Edinburgh?'

'Don't be daft – Glasgow!'

'Are we talking a missionary position?'

'Ha ha! I've heard that one before.'

We went to tell Sister we had a shift.

'Fishie and I are sorry you're going,' she said, whilst Willie and Jock might have celebrated had they not decided they had had enough of hospital life; it was quieter at home especially since the Dayroom had become full of women pondering the racing columns, recalling the joys of the Tea Dance and eyeing up the men bounced out of bed to join them.

'I never thought I'd be sorry to leave this place,' Jo said, taking off her apron and draping it over her arm.

'Me neither, but I don't know why you're being so careful with that, we're going to be out of uniform for the next few weeks. Still, it'll be nice to be back in the A.R.I. Woodend's fine but lacks the action. Let's go! Don't you just love flitting!'

25

FOR THEATRE READ DRAMA

Back in Foresterhill, I knew what theatre staff wore was a far cry from the swaddling prescribed by Matron; but then, theirs was a world separated from the real one by swing doors and a red line painted on the floor over which you dare not cross. Across it, gowned, masked and otherwise scantily clad aliens would transfer onto their beds post-operative patients, unconscious, labelled and with a list of instructions as if they had been remodelled.

I'd learnt this was the first and scariest part of recovery, and I couldn't cross the Rubicon red until I was allowed. So now, I dithered.

'You must be our new nurse?' A figure approached, her cotton frock closely hugging her slight figure's every move. 'Hello. I'm Kathy.' Introductions apparently didn't need a mask – seeing her smile was as encouraging.

'You'll need to put on overshoes before you come over.' She pointed to a nearby cabinet stuffed with canvas slippers as big as clowns wear. I chose a pair and put them on, thinking Kathy's sandshoes looked light while mine promised trench foot.

'Can I come over now?' I asked, ignoring them.

'Sure. Don't know where your shoes were last so the overshoes keep down infection. Sister asked me to show you around. I'm actually the auxiliary but they allow me to do everything but operations,' she grinned. 'I had to draw the line somewhere. Now, you'll need to get changed first.'

She was young, friendly and helpful, and took me to a room just big enough to allow chest expansion. 'Let's see.' Frowning, she picked a frock from a bundle on a shelf. It was similar to her own: flimsy to the point of muslin and perfect for accentuating bullet-proof underwear.

'Fat on display,' I griped.

'Not at all – it's nice to see a curvy model. And don't worry, it gets so hot here, you'll find even this gets uncomfortable.' My dresser dimpled and, as I struggled with the change, handed over some safety pins. 'Sorry about the buttons or lack of them. The only one who seems to notice is Dr Stewart the anaesthetist. You have to watch him, he's a right lecher.' A sigh hung behind the laugh.

'I'm overheating,' I said, aware of my feet's continued cross messages.

Kathy picked out a pair of large sandshoes, which would have had me jumping for joy had I not been trying to be invisible. Even the barren changing room reeked of disinfectant, sending enough antiseptic signals to wipe out all forms of life.

'You'll be alright this morning. We don't start operating till this afternoon, so I can take you round without anybody bothering us.' She reflected for a moment, then added without enthusiasm, 'That is until Staffie comes along.'

'Staffie?'

'Yea – Staff Nurse – we just call her that. She says she likes it, says it's better than the way we pronounce her name. She's Indian.'

Kathy continued the tour.

The theatre had an overall air of clinical gloom. No cheery chit chat here, apart from my advisor, who also fell silent as we took in the bare walls, grey tiled floor, gleaming chromes and some fearsomely complicated-looking machines. I'd have given anything to do a bedpan round in Ward Four instead of gazing at anaesthetic machines and getting a lecture about an operating table worth the attention of a Marquis de Sade.

'It's important you learn how to work it as sometimes you need a quick response, especially if the patient chokes.' Kathy demonstrated its versatility with a practised foot and accomplished hand. The bed shot up, down, and tilted back and forth at such a rate, just watching gave me vertigo.

'This is the sucker and it takes away excess blood from the wound site so that the surgeon can see what he's cutting.' My instructor waved a relaxed hand in the direction of yards of plastic piping. 'If you don't get genned up on this, some of the surgeons will go off their heads.'

I felt faint.

In a small adjoining room, there were sterilisers and enough dazzling chrome to bring on a migraine.

'All the instruments have to be done like this.' There was a tray-load of instruments waiting beside a machine reminiscent of Ma's Burco boiler. The auxiliary placed them in and with a deft flick of the wrist and scrutiny of monitoring dials, she switched it on. 'If I do this now they'll be cooled down and ready for this afternoon.' She spoke as if they were a batch of scones.

'Operations? Today?'

The auxiliary nodded and I added panic to my illness list.

Quick tripping sounds alerted us to a newcomer.

It was Staffie. I gazed at her with respect, particularly since Kathy alleged she had had her appendix removed under local anaesthetic; maybe she'd lost a few inches of height in the process, for despite the clumpy-heeled white shoes, she was so small I could see right over her head.

'Having a big operation like that without a general anaesthetic's certainly putting faith in the firm,' I had marvelled, but Kathy said this miracle had been done in India and was unlikely here where the surgeons preferred their patients unconscious.

Staffie didn't seem so brave today. She trembled and fluttered like an exotic butterfly, her dress like gauze, her eyes gleaming and anxious. 'The operating list has been put forward, the surgeons are going to be here any minute – we'll need to have the instruments ready. It is just our luck to have a new nurse today and Sister with another day off.' Shaking her head, she headed for the sterilising room, beckoning her second in command. 'Come on, we must be quick.'

'The instruments are already on and should be ready any minute now.' Kathy was calm; her hand described an invisible halo.

'Good! They take ages. We'll leave Nurse to take them out whilst we look for the surgeons' gowns.' Staffie fluttered away, followed by Kathy at a more leisurely pace.

I didn't want to add scalding to my sick list so, knowing the instruments would be too hot to handle, and mindful of haste, I filled a sink with cold water and tumbled them in giving them a nice brisk swirl to ensure even cover. 'What on earth?' began Kathy, alerted by the metallic clatter; her brown eyes went as round as Maltesers. 'You must have forgotten me telling you that tap water isn't sterile. We'll have to do them all over again. Drat!' She seized the tray and started flinging the instruments back in. It sounded like a bad orchestral tune-up. Was deafness another hazard?

Staffie too had come to investigate. 'You stupid girl – they'll never be ready now – Mr Milne will go mad,' she screeched, then lapsed into her own dialect, the drift of which was perfectly plain.

'This place sounds like Bedlam.' Mr Milne the surgeon had arrived. 'Where's Sister?' He was small with eyes as cold as the North Sea and a manner best suited to someone unconscious.

'She's a day off and there's going to be a delay as we're having a bit of trouble with the sterilisers,' Kathy lied fluently. 'We'll be ready very soon – but you know what equipment can be like.' She shrugged expressively and widened her eyes. 'Why don't you have a cup of coffee with Dr Stewart and we'll get things going as soon as we can.'

'And you will not forget that we have with us a new nurse,' Staffie put in, 'so she's not up to what you call speed. All of these things make life for me difficult.'

'Just get on with it then.' Mr Milne, aiming for authority with a magnificent glower, departed.

'Hard to look impressive when you're that little,' Kathy observed. 'Why don't you go and lower the operating table to fit him whilst we get the other stuff ready.'

'Yes, yes, and do it properly – for me too – this is an emergency.' Staffie danced about in a lather of excitement.

The operating table had a pedal that I remembered was like an accelerator capable of performing many tasks. Gently I stepped on it. The table inched up. I tried again. Up it went. Beginning to panic, I gave a quick pump. Another few inches with a column of steel previously invisible emerged whilst the tabletop neared the ceiling.

'How are you getting on?' sang Kathy, and without waiting for a reply, 'As soon as you're finished that, come and give us a hand getting the trolleys ready.'

Mopping sweat from my brow, I gave another sharp foot jab and shut my eyes. Was nursing really worth this anxiety? Maybe I should just leave before the heart attack.

Some irate clanging from the sterilising room said things were heating up, so I left the table to its own devices and hurried to the call.

'These are ready now and this is what you do.' Busier than a chef, Kathy took huge forceps to lift out the instruments onto a sterile-clothed trolley, then pulled over the surplus to complete their cover. 'Take that through to theatre, but mind how you go. If you bang into anybody, the whole thing'll be contaminated,' she frowned in concentration, 'them too.'

'Kathy,' I began, but she was in a hurry.

'Sorry, can't stop now – Staffie's going mad in the scrubbing up.'

Most carefully, I wheeled through the trolley and whilst there, gave the table another pump on the off chance it had decided to cooperate. The table rose another foot. Now I couldn't see its top.

'Nurse Macpherson,' Staffie's voice sounded muffled, 'come and see how you do this.'

Both she and Mr Milne were waiting, scrubbed, gloved, masked, capped and with their sterile gowns on, which had to be tied at the back. Kathy extended her arms and made nice long distance bows. 'If I go too near,' she explained, 'they might have to re-scrub. Now they'll need me to open the operating theatre doors for them. I think the patient's coming through too – we'll all be in theatre so join us once you put on your mask and cap.'

'Um – about the table,' I began, but already the cavalcade had started and there was nothing I could do to stop either them or the patient now being wheeled in by the anaesthetist.

I walked as if on eggs to the changing room, drew my cap down and my mask high, leaving just an eye slit. I could hear raised voices coming from theatre and considered making a run for it.

'Nurse Macpherson. Come in here!'

Slowly, I walked into theatre. The operating table had grown into a rather grand bus shelter. It even had a queue of irate passengers sheltering under it.

The words were out before I could stop them.

'The number twenty-three will be along any minute,' I said, horrified by an escaping giggle.

26

A LITTLE REVENGE

'Are you home?'

'Uh-huh, take a pew.'

Maisie was lying on top of her bed reading a hospital romance and clicking her heels in pleasant idleness. Her room was such a haven of order and calm I should have felt guilty about disturbing it, but then she hadn't had any flittings had she?

So –

'I've had the most awful of days.' Throwing myself into a chair and drumming my feet got her attention. 'Theatre's awful! I'll never last – if it's not a sterile vacuum one minute, it's high drama the next – and seeing people under the knife . . .' I drew breath, squeezed shut my eyes at the memory, and was about to continue when there was a knock at the door and Jo bounced in.

'Ah, Jane! This is where you are. How did you get on? Hi, Maisie.'

'Come in, why don't you?'

'Thanks.' Jo was breathless. 'What a great day I've had. Theatre is brilliant, miles better than geriatric and I've even been helping the surgeon.' She slid onto the floor, her hands folded in beneficence, her face wreathed in smiles.

I was dumbstruck and jealous.

Maisie put down her book and sighed, 'I don't know why I'm reading this stuff when I know the reality is us lot tucked away into cupboards, toilets and sluices as soon as anyone medical appears. You must be in a special category, Jo.' She looked at the book cover with its nurse gazing up at her medical hero. 'You'd wonder who's inspired this rubbish.'

'Yeah, it's a well-known fact we cannae speak – nay even proper.' I was sour, wishing the surgeon's fury had subsided as quickly as the table under Kathy's expert foot. It had been humiliating being thrown out of theatre too.

Jo looked holy. 'We've still got to remember they're human. You know I'd to tell my surgeon to use a different scalpel after the first incision.'

'But the man's near retiring!'

'Fancy nobody pointing it out to him before.' Jo was shocked.

'I'll never reach these heights.' Despair crept into my voice. 'One moment we're told to love and cherish our patients and the next, we're carving them up.'

Saint Jo clicked her teeth and sounded impatient. 'Your trouble is your imagination. You just have to forget that's a person lying there and remember Miss Jones' lectures.' She looked into the middle distance as if admiring a landscape. 'It's just the same only the colour's better.'

But theatre continued to be a nightmare where the best I could do was avoid collision and try not to be intimidated by a surgeon, as short in size as he was in fuse, and a Staff Nurse who resorted to hissing when the language barrier became insurmountable.

Anyway, what was normal about wearing a next-to-nothing theatre muslin and tying those small fierce presences into sterile gowns? These intimate encounters were fraught with peril lest a human hand would touch and the scrubbed person be forced to go through the whole laborious sterile dressing procedure again. Swinging Sixties? I mused, tying Mr Milne in one day and so close I could have had him quivering and defrocking by a careless gesture. Swinging Sixties hinted fat lazy Dr Stewart, who inevitably dropped some piece of equipment he was far too busy and important to pick up himself, but who always made time for a leisurely look down the front of our dresses as we returned it.

And it was useless complaining to Staffie since she had managed to stay his hand and drop his jaw with some Hindi jabbering, but Kathy understood and had had enough of sly nips, gropes and innuendo. She said she'd a cure.

We'd become good friends and theatre was fine at the weekends when there were no operations. We could catch up on hospital gossip whilst mending the linen, and cleaning and oiling the surgical instruments to help them withstand the sterilisation rigours.

'This is what we'll do,' said Kathy, spitting on scissors to shine them, putting them aside and picking up a pair of theatre trousers. 'Now tell me, Jane, have you a boyfriend?'

'No – you?'

Kathy's expression became remote. She said she had been crossed in love – a phrase so quaint, Maisie's book must have been doing the hospital rounds.

'Och, he was a fine lad, Johnny,' she sighed after a good tirade on his infidelity, 'but I'll have nothing more to do with him, not even if he crawled all the way from Inverness. Mind you, it's a long way away. I think I'll try Mintlaw next – they've good dances there.' Her big brown eyes filled with tears and she wiped them away on the back of her hand. 'Staffie's had a bad experience too and she's had her thyroid out.' The comparison seemed to cheer.

'I thought it was her appendix.'

'That as well.' Kathy snipped, scissored the air, then put aside the trousers. 'This should sort out that lech.'

The next operating day, we got near Dr Stewart and his anaesthetic machine. After the usual ogling, he knocked over a couple of rolls of strapping.

'Oh, dash! Pick that up, you two, will you?' He pushed his wheeled chair back, crossing his arms, ready to enjoy the view.

They went some distance but we dashed to get them, handing them over just far enough away for him to have to stand up to get them.

'Oh!' Suddenly, and in embarrassment, he clutched the trousers and stumbled from theatre.

'Oh dear, I think he must have dropped something.' The auxiliary was merry-eyed and innocent.

'Who loosened Dr Stewart's buttons?' asked Sister afterward on one of the rare moments that she left the surgeon's side and came out from behind her mask. She seemed amused.

Jo's theatre work wasn't like mine. Apparently she'd been allowed to hold forceps, and presumably the fort, whilst the surgical team drifted off for a break or the next bus home. At this rate, she would soon be dispensing with the formalities and disappearing with the best of them herself.

I was never going to reach these levels, but now that Dr Stewart was concentrating more on his patients and the saucy columns of his magazine, I was managing some crash-free days and even darting the odd glance at the wielded scalpel.

'At last, Nurse Macpherson! You shine so.' Staffie pattered round in an approving fashion. 'Another six weeks and you will make the hay.'

'Not here, sadly,' I tried to sound regretful, 'I'm going on holiday next week and then it's another shift, but at least your next student can't be worse.'

'But we need the rain too,' said Staffie in her gnomic way.

'Where are you going next?' asked Kathy, pondering the Mintlaw bus timetable.

'After my holidays, it's night duty.'

'Well if you go dancing in Inverness and meet that Johnny, just you tell him Kathy's asking for him but she's got a new boyfriend from the country, a steady boy – and, Jane . . .'

'Uh-huh?'

'I'll miss you.'

'And I'll miss you, Kathy, but not Theatre Nine.'

27

NIGHT DUTY CALLS

It was good to be home. I'd forgotten how quiet it could be, and apart from the usual tractor breakdown, the most dramatic event of the week was Tommy arriving with his van and news.

When he did, I asked about Mrs Spence and Mrs Fotheringham.

'Oh, fine, fine. Always cheery!' he said. 'Sending their love and hoping you're on your way to getting plenty letters after your name. You should go and visit them. They say they miss your breezy voice.'

But Grantown seemed a lifetime away and I didn't go. Instead I was entertaining Maisie who'd come to stay for a spot of country life far away from the seagull city.

We didn't miss its noise and bustle. Over the next few days, we walked the hills around and discussed our lives and futures, whilst at night we enjoyed sitting, having a meal at a table for only four, and by way of contribution, delighted in recounting some of our finest hospital stories.

'I don't think your parents appreciated that story about the patient and the suppositories,' Maisie said as we tramped towards another stunning view. Far away, the Moray Firth marked the horizon with an indigo coloured and glittering shawl whilst a lark opened her throat and sang high up in a cloudless sky. For the moment our own horizons looked no further than the next joke.

'The one where he put them in his ears? Ha ha!'

"Yeah – but I noticed your Dad went off his food a bit. Of course, it could have been that story about the boil and how far a burst one can go.'

What a laugh! We'd look out a few more rib ticklers bound to entertain. How dull meal times would be when we left.

'I think we've heard quite enough about bowels,' my mother eventually snapped, 'surely you must have some clean stories.'

We were stunned. How could anyone possibly not be entertained? These stories and jokes were, in the face of occasionally grim medicine, what kept nurses in touch with humour. Everybody loved them, not least in the Nurses' Home where they would make their rounds, corridor after corridor, bursts of raucous laughter marking their journey.

Maisie thought hard. 'What about the time I went to spray a wound with Acriflavine spray. It's a bright yellow antiseptic and I missed because my nose got in the way. I'd to put up with jokey "Lady of the Light" comments from the whole ward until it wore off.'

This story got the approval ratings and Dad, perked up and showing interest for the first time, asked if Acriflavine would help cure orf, a sort of impetigo affecting sheep.

'I've been putting on gentian violet,' he said, 'but it's awful messy.'

Maisie gurgled, 'But you've the world authority on that. She'll tell you how to do it. She's not called Gentian Jane for nothing.'

Oh good! Another clean story from Maisie. How hilarious.

'So you could help me with the sheep?' Dad asked once Maisie had gone to spread sunshine with her own folk and he was herding me towards his flock. 'It's really a two-man job.'

Maybe I should have chosen to do art, I thought, dabbing on the gentian. Yet there was the same satisfaction helping an animal as a patient and I watched, heartened, as those treated reconvened in a bleating purple-faced group. They seemed surprised but pleased as they started, with an exploratory nibble, to be able to graze again.

'So you're enjoying the nursing? Truth to tell, your Mam and I didn't think you'd stick it,' my father admitted as he straightened his back and shared the view.

Bob lay on the ground bright-eyed, with lolling tongue and alert for the next herding whistle, but Dad was waiting for an answer. It'd been good helping on the farm again. I'd forgotten my home's freedom of space and the loveliness of its surrounds, where even the animals seemed to sense my familiarity and trust it. Life in the city and training in the hospital was a world away. I could hardly imagine that hectic place, let alone that I lived in it.

And then I remembered why I'd left home in the first place. How could I forget the patients, friendships, everyday dramas and parties, and when Douglas had been around, his reminder there was also a life beyond nursing.

'Yes, Dad, it's awful hard work and there's some bits I've hated whilst other bits have been great and yes, it's still what I want to do and I'm going to stick it. I think I'd like to be a district nurse; we'd a talk from a right cheery one. She was the happiest of the folk who came to give us career ideas and she had a car and a dog and a house.' I'd been impressed.

'Good girl. I think that's a grand idea. Right! Bob! Let's round up another patient.'

The holiday had come at the right time and even if I was blue about the nails, it was time to look forward. It would be night duty – a whole new world with long hours, but also good time off to explore those elusive Swinging Sixties.

'So how's the Highlands?' asked Sister Cameron, welcoming me back in her bright way and handing over a new bedroom key. 'The sun would have been shining and the midgies biting.' She slapped her arm as if just bitten. 'You can use the lift to take up your stuff; it's a fair old haul to the night duty top floor.'

'No thanks,' I said, trudging past and fully loaded, 'I don't trust it.'

She laughed. 'Once bitten eh? But suit yourself. What ward are you going to anyway?'

'Female medical.'

'Och now! You'll be needing all your strength for that. Sister there runs a very tight ship.' In a cloud of peppermint, she hurried away as if she had already said too much.

We'd a couple of day hours to get to know our ward's layout, the patients and how the ward sister liked her place run. Mine was partial to a ward tidy as a miser's larder, with patients enclosed in clutter-free zones, their lockers bare and preferably angled out of their reach. Happiness was really an empty ward where no one could kick the bed wheels out of alignment or disturb the regulation sixteen-inch sheet turnover.

Sister's love of order didn't bode well for a naturally untidy person, but at least I was getting to know the patients and earning some brownie points by strategic bed wheel kicking. Whilst sluices tended to announce their own presence, oxygen for the breathless patients was a 'Must See' item, as was the drug cupboard.

Sister held up a bunch of keys padlocked to her. 'These are for the drug cupboard and your senior will carry them except when she has her break. Then you'll have to look after them.' She didn't say it was an honour but I got the message.

I wanted to ask more, but there was something about this steely sister with her cap perched on hair like corrugated iron that discouraged questions and kept patients immaculately pinned to their beds. 'And please remember that when I come on duty in the morning I like to see a tidy ward.' As I left, she added, 'I hope you'll get some sleep as you'll need all your wits about you if you want to keep daytime standards.'

All the woes of a cleaning staff using their clattering brushes to tidy up their working rights were outside my bedroom, but I was polite.

'Excuse me, but this's my first night of night duty and I really need to get some sleep. Do you think you could talk elsewhere?'

'Sorry,' they said, before resuming dialogue.

'Would you lot belt up,' cried Rosie, jerking her door open. She stood in the Highland Fling first position then stamped her feet. 'I can't get a wink's sleep,' she cried, then slammed her door shut with such a bang you might have thought she was somebody important.

The cleaners, looking suitably chastened, crept away and I thanked the stars Rosie was my next-door neighbour and back in harness.

In bed, I tossed and turned and worried about not sleeping now when I might be very good at it later on. The alarm clock was so loud I felt like shutting it off but how would I then count the minutes? The hours drifted past until at last the bell went off and I dressed feeling sluggish and ill prepared, with the companionship of Isobel working on the male side the only cheering prospect.

'Well?' I asked Maisie, as accompanied by Rosie we headed for supper.

'Never slept a wink,' she sounded bitter. 'And you with your shouting match didn't exactly help, Rosie, and I'm also worried about these.' She pushed her spectacles up. 'I'm hoping they won't mist up when I put on a mask.'

Smarting, Rosie replied, 'At least if there's an operation on, there'll be no danger of you falling asleep.' I was amazed that Maisie's anxiety about working in the emergency theatre was just confined to her sight.

In the dining room, we joined our group at their table. But for Isobel and Hazel looking frail and needing a month's vacation, it was as if it was our first day again and we were all together apart from Sheila still in Woodend — and not even on night duty.

'I wish she was here,' said Isobel, 'I haven't seen her for ages. She's really good at keeping us calm and she's so sunny too. I don't know how she does it. I'm beginning to think she's further away than Morag in Tain.'

'Oh for goodness sake, you'll be fine. I don't know what you're worried about.' Rosie maintained her course, fluffing her feathers and ready to take on the world. 'After all, we're going to be the juniors in the ward, so somebody else will be taking the hassle.'

Obviously not cheered by the prospect, Jo ate steadily and silently, then held up a finger as a charge nurse appeared and conversational buzz dropped.

He strode into the middle of the dining hall with all the majesty that a clipboard conveys and got immediate attention. He cleared his throat and started calling out names like a school roll.

'Daddy says that for night duty, we only need to keep our patients alive, comfortable and nightmare free,' whispered Hazel, who was finally admitting her insider knowledge owed much to her doctor dad, 'and I suppose that's why there's fewer staff around but they do need to be sure everybody's here.'

'What do they do then?' I asked, half listening and waiting for my call.

'Panic, paperwork and twice as much work for the suckers who answer the call. Oops! You nearly missed it.' Hazel stopped for a moment to allow me to quaver my presence, then continued, 'Of course, there is one Night Sister for emergency back-up.'

'What constitutes an emergency?'

'If you're about to murder your patients,' Hazel gave her laryngeal laugh, 'and you're feeling brave enough to tell her.'

'Joking apart, the total ward responsibility must be a hellish burden,' I suggested, trying holiness to catch out Hazel.

'Huh! Don't you believe it. She manages stress by snoring away the trying hours between her ward rounds and then she wakes up to look for patients who might come from Banchory, her hometown. Believe you me,' Hazel stretched luxuriously and yawned, 'you'll soon find out what a good address means.'

'Nurse Green! Medical ward,' called the charge nurse. A heavyset girl put up her hand.

'I wouldn't like to meet that one on a dark night.' Rosie cocked her head to one side as if considering a threatening cloud too large even for her.

'Well, Jane's about to and she certainly looks grim,' Maisie observed. 'Maybe it's the prospect of working with her new junior.'

'Or maintaining her standards,' I retorted, cross to be the reason for such unusual harmony.

Personally, I was hoping for a relationship based on equality, but that's not how Nurse Green saw things. When we met in the cloakroom, she made status her first responsibility, whilst putting the final touches to a smile-free zone with her powder compact mirror.

'I've heard about you, Nurse. You sound disaster prone.' She drew down her black monobrow, passing a licked finger over it to maintain the line. She mouthed a sad little mist over the glass. 'Let's hope you can work.' She snapped the compact shut.

We weren't going to be on first name terms, or even second come to that. I was just Nurse and I thought of her as just Green – no wonder she was so sour.

At the respectful distance I would give to Dad's horned cattle, I followed her into the ward where Sister gave us the day's report. Nothing had changed since daytime except now she seemed particularly offhand. Maybe it was on account of Nurse Green's gum chewing, scant attention, and lack of interest on the subject of bed wheels.

'And just watch Mrs Graham,' Sister concluded, at last showing some emotion. 'If she falls out of bed once more I shall have to report night staff for negligence.' She glared at my senior who scuffed her feet to show she'd heard.

Casting a hopeless gaze at her perfect ward like an emigrant unlikely to see these pristine cornered shores again, she sighed and left.

As soon as she had gone all the patients perked up like naughty children freed from parents. Bedclothes were thrown off, pillows chucked into comfortable positions, and a cacophony of bells rung to convey urgent needs.

'How on earth are we expected to keep patients from falling out of their beds if that bloomin' Sister won't let us put up cot sides. That old dear gets so dottled at night, I think she might just take off and land anywhere.' Green looked in exasperation at Mrs Graham, already limbering up for a busy night and rooting about in her handbag, presumably looking for the fare home.

Oblivious to other obviously frail patients teetering on the edge of their beds and threatening to make a bid for freedom, my senior prioritised. 'You've to give out the drinks, wash the supper dishes, arrange the flowers and answer these bells whilst I do a round of the patients and see if there's anything Doctor wants done.' The strict voice went up a note as a ward doctor came into view.

'Start off with the drinks.' She hurried me into the corridor as if I could be a major distraction.

I cantered off, eager to please, and met Isobel in the common kitchen. I told her that my nurse let patients fall out of bed and made eyes at the doctors.

'My nurse's really nice – she smokes,' Isobel said as if that was the ultimate decoration.

'Mine too – but not fags.'

My caring angel flew in. 'Nurse!' she said, presumably to identify me from countless other of her minions. 'Mrs Brown wants a bedpan – and now!' She dashed off, her cap flapping behind her.

I trailed off to the ward and attended to the patient with my wet soapy hands.

'That's a cold bedpan,' she whined, 'The last nurse always heated them to a turn.'

'Hot bedpans are awfully bad for you.'

'The last nurse –' she began.

'Excuse me, I've got to dash. I've left on a pan of milk.'

'You'll have to throw it out if it's singed, of course. The last nurse . . .' perched high on her bedpan, my patient was low in expectation.

'Back in a minute.' I hurried past the house doctor giving him a bright smile, just to remind myself that I could, and to my surprise he followed; the smell of burning milk should have put him off.

Isobel had been doing a rescue job whilst trying not to spoil her nails. He leant against the sink and watched as if there was nothing else in the world he had to do and the ward wasn't full of needing patients.

'The last nurse –' he began, taking in the view, Isobel in particular.

'If you think we're going to follow that saint's footsteps, you're very much mistaken.' I, too, was going to try out a little of what I had learnt. On the medical social ladder, ward residents weren't even on the first rung and I was no longer impressed by any old white coat. Had Maisie not taken one round the ward to see a patient only to discover he was a painter? Resisting this white coat's dazzling teeth and the way his smile made his eyes dance and the cute shock of black hair, I eyed him beadily across the drinks trolley.

'I only wanted a cup of coffee,' he said in an injured fashion.

'Help yourself then,' said Isobel, drying her hands, 'we're busy.'

When I'd finished my list of duties, with the floral art bit an especial challenge without vases and the male ward's urinals declared out of bounds, Green and I worked round the ward to settle the patients and hear how much they would miss the last junior nurse. Pillows were fluffed, under-sheets straightened, sleeping tablets and medicines given out, lights were dimmed, talk was hushed.

'I feel like a nanny,' I said.

Green's laugh, though mirthless, was progress.

It all took time and it was nearly midnight before we sat down at the desk in the middle of the ward lit by a shaded light. Funny to be sitting down at all: if that happened on day duty, we'd have been sent to clean a clean cupboard.

Nurse Green got down to hard facts.

'It'll be a terrible rush in the morning, you'll be doing all the bedpans, giving out wash basins, washing faces of those who can't do it for themselves, getting and testing samples of urine. Doctor says he'll give us note of them just as soon as he can. Oh look! Here he comes,' she patted her hair and checked that eyebrow, 'you stay where you are.'

She came back with a list, which she handed over. She released a smile, proving the power of seniority. 'Doctor says that as I'm so good at delegating, this is for you.'

It looked so long I might have challenged it, but he had gone, a tall figure swinging his stethoscope in a jaunty manner suggesting victory.

Mrs Graham crashed out of bed yet again. 'Go and help her will you, I'm sick of picking her up and I'm due lunch.' My senior unlocked herself from the keys and handed them over with a reluctance suggesting a responsibility too far. 'With a bit of luck you'll get Night Sister. I just hope you remember all the names and diagnoses.' She left me to Mrs Graham, who was already climbing back into bed with lithe ease.

'Now that you're in bed, I'll tell you a story,' I said. 'Do you know the one about the naughty little girl who kept running away? She was a right wee pain.'

'Not like you I suppose. No – you're a good wee girl.' My patient snuggled down. 'I'll mebbe stay the night here after all. It's quite comfy and I think I've missed the last bus home anyway.'

'Quite right.' I tucked her in. She looked so comfortable I nearly joined her, but to keep her in and me out, I searched around for cot sides and was lucky to find a set just like the Ian Charles ones ultimately fitted to kennel Mrs Davidson. They were fiddly to fit and so engrossing to assemble I never heard Night Sister arrive.

She appeared not to notice the equipment scattered round Mrs Graham's bed. 'Come and tell me about your patients, Nurse Macpherson.'

At least she had my name. Maybe it was easier for her to remember one when, no matter how new we were to the ward, we were expected to recite at each bed that patient's name and diagnosis.

We made our way round the ward. I wasn't going to remember everybody and had developed an imaginative strategy.

'There's no patient there.' Sister peered at an empty bed I'd just named and diagnosed.

'She'll be in the toilet.' The lie was frighteningly easy but Sister had wandered off and was now shining her torch on the chart above another bed.

'Ah! From Banchory! The Capital of the North and my ancestral home.' She ran the beam over the patient's face, who woke with a start, surprised to see a stranger peering at her.

'It's alright, dear,' was the soothing remark, 'just you go back to sleep now.'

She turned with a disappointed air and said, 'I thought I might have known her. Now she's awake you'd better make her a hot drink and tell her she's had a nightmare.'

'Too right, Sister!'

Green must have been lurking in the corridor, for as soon as Sister left, she returned.

'I've looked out cot sides. We can take them down before Day Sister comes on duty,' I suggested, 'they're dead easy to fit.'

'Well ok – but you can do them.' Green settled at the desk and took out her knitting.

'I'm off for my break now and there's bolts and nuts just under Mrs Graham's bed. If she gets out of bed she could hurt herself,' my tone was firm, 'and I suppose that would be your responsibility, wouldn't it?'

Isobel was waiting to chum me to the dining room.

'How's that awful senior of yours?'

'She's going to have a right job putting up cot sides without these.' I showed her the nuts and bolts secreted into my pocket.

Isobel's peal of laughter was like a ray of sunshine and an encouragement to get through the night without a war, and so, on my return, I ignored my senior's complaints about nipped fingers, instead admiring the way she had used crepe bandages as a securing alternative.

'I'm surprised you didn't find the nuts and bolts. Look! There they are.' I pointed to the essential bits quietly relocated and far enough under the bed for Green to crawl to get them just to prove her athleticism.

'That's very strange.' For the first time, doubt crept into that strident voice.

Dawn broke with its shortening of time but lengthening of footsteps. Our relationship was never going to be based on trust but my senior wasn't going to mind any short cuts getting through the morning chores.

'What's that smell of burning?' she asked, tanking past with an armload of syringes.

'That's my poultice.' I left my patient and rushed to the kitchen, putting out the flames before the alarm went off.

'I hope you don't intend putting that on me,' the patient exclaimed when I approached her with the charred remains, 'and you've got the wrong arm as well.'

'That woman can be right difficult.' My grumbles came between basins and bedpans.

'You've put soap in my eyes,' yelled a patient as I wearily slopped a face cloth in her general direction.

'Just rise above it,' Green recommended, surveying her charges with a jaundiced eye.

'Nurse, I must have a bedpan now!'

'Yes, yes, coming.' Could life return to leaden feet, air into collapsed lungs?

Night Sister arrived to do a last-minute check, looking sweet, slept and like everybody's favourite auntie. Harassed and tired, we stopped arguing with the women until she left the ward in a waft of Banchory Lavender.

'Didn't you want a pan when it was offered to you a minute ago?' The tacked-on smile ached.

'I'm afraid we're too late, Nursie. Sorry.'

'Don't worry, it's no trouble,' I soothed, trying for sainthood and hating the tears coursing down an old face.

And then at last, it was morning proper and staff were arriving. They sounded bright and cheerful but my concern was Sister, whose gaze was fixed on the beds. With a courage I thought remarkable, Green popped some chewing gum into her mouth before slouching towards her whilst Mrs Graham asked to get her gates back – they'd been handy for leaning on.

Somehow I had managed to get all wheels straight and, this essential duty accomplished, got a barely perceptible nod of approval that allowed me to creep off duty, exhausted but feeling triumphant that not only had I stayed awake all night but that I now had all day to sleep.

Actually, and at last, this was something I could do! So could Rosie and Maisie, but the others had problems and as our nights on duty progressed, so did their air of exhaustion and look of pallor. Isobel's fragility seemed on the verge of serious and she began to sound depressed.

'I'm beginning to think Morag had the right idea,' she sighed, yawning as we began another shift. 'I'm starting to feel so like a zombie, I'm frightened I make mistakes with the insulin injections in the morning, then I lie awake all day worrying in case I have.'

I tried to cheer her up. 'At least your senior allows you to do them. She must think you're safe enough.'

'Mine takes sleeping pills from the drug cupboard and that seems to help her. She asked me if I'd like some. There doesn't seem to be any check on the numbers,' Jo said wearily.

'I think they should. Some of them are bloomin' dangerous and you don't know what they might be doing to you. I certainly wouldn't take any of that stuff.' Rosie nodded at some nearby nurses with shadowed eyes and sluggish walks. 'You could be taking anything. I heard of someone who took yon appetite suppressant, Dexidrin, by mistake and she never stopped running all night. None of the patients could sleep for the sound of racing footsteps up and down the corridor.'

'Thanks for the advice, Rosie – you've just missed your name.' Hazel stood up to let a flustered Rosie dash off. 'And if I was really desperate, I think I'd be popping a few myself, though at least I don't have a problem staying awake.'

'Why?'

'Andy Cargill.'

'Ah!' We all laughed, knowing the male nurse's reputation.

Then one morning, despite the fact that we couldn't all share the perilous joys of the linen cupboard with Andy, my feet skipped and I began to sing. The lungs felt good too as I flew round the ward with ease and efficiency. My brain answered the morning challenge in such a way that the poultices, toast and boiled eggs were a joy to deliver, as were the on-time bedpans, done to a turn. Even the urine specimen jars had all been collected and stood in as neat a row awaiting the resident's attention as did the bed wheels.

'You're very happy this morning,' a patient observed.

'Well, I am,' I admitted, handing over a cooked-to-perfection hot water bottle. 'I've got nights off and am going to see if I can get my pal from the male side to hit the town and see if we can have some fun.'

I could have said I needed to be off before the resident tested that extra specimen jar filled with Lucozade and labelled Mrs Sweetpea, but thought she might not see the joke.

28

HOME FROM HOME

Mrs Ronce was putting nails into her sitting room wall. The frying pan made an unusual hammer. 'Great tool this. You get a bull's eye every time.' She laid it on the sofa and stepped over a couple of framed photographs lying on the floor. 'Now where's my graduate lodgers? Ah!' She picked them up, then slung them on as if hanging coats on a peg.

'What do you think, Janey?'

'They look happy,' I said looking sideways to see them properly.

As well as hanging on Mrs Ronce's wall, Sally was in Glasgow and Beth in London. With exams behind them now, they were free to explore the world of actual work.

'And that's when education starts,' Mrs Ronce observed, her toothy smile giving her the look of a benign rodent.

'Would you take on Maisie and me?' I asked, loving this house with its fascinating clutter, cats, heaps of newspaper and landlady. It was a world away from the Nurses' Home whose charms on night duty were beginning to wear thin with sleep deprivation.

Suddenly, my acquired skill was becoming as elusive as dreams. Despite sentinel Rosie's best efforts, small sounds escaped, amplified in the long darkened corridors and waking me with curiosity about them. Somewhere we could forget work, get to sleep and escape from the impersonality of a huge, terribly clean and highly polished establishment was appealing, despite Sister Cameron doing her best with cheerful briskness and a care she tried hard to conceal.

Mrs Ronce weighed the hammer thoughtfully. 'I don't really need lodgers you know. I just like young company and I could get that in the pub.'

I was crushed. I thought she'd have jumped at the privilege. It was a job scouting about for selling points but then one of the cats came in and wound himself round my leg. I picked him up. 'My friend Maisie comes from Peterhead,' I stroked his head, 'and she could bring you fish from the market.'

Mrs Ronce laughed. 'Ok Janey, let's give it a go. I hope she's good at crosswords.'

'She should be, she knows her Bible.'

Delighted, I went back to the home to tell Maisie.

We'd been having fun. Beatlemania had hit town with the *Hard Day's Night* record giving a more exciting meaning to the darkness hours. We went to a dance where Isobel met a new boyfriend who made her laugh. Maisie meanwhile set about loosening more than the corsetry of Aberdeen's social scene. Maybe that accounted for her red eyes.

'It's these contact lenses – I'm sure they'll be fine in a year.' Maisie blinked hard into her bedroom mirror. 'I'm going to dye my eyelashes next. How did you get on with Mrs Ronce?'

'We can move in anytime but have you a fish-proof suitcase?'

'How soon can we move?' Maisie was already rifling through her wardrobe. 'Let's go and ask Sister Cameron.'

She was in her office.

'Your compulsory year's up at the end of next week,' she said after a diary was consulted. 'You can leave when you like after that.' She put our names down against a date with an exclamation mark making it official. 'Next year when I retire, I'll have my own but and ben.' She looked out of the window with a dreamy expression, as if already glimpsing hills and glens.

Even though we had the time to sort our possessions, the flit was a series of full suitcases and bags trudged down the stairs and crammed into a taxi.

'You could have used the lift,' said that mischievous home sister in her Highland way, putting her hands behind her back to oversee better, 'but you've managed fine, by Jove yes!' Strains of a Gaelic farewell came from behind the door she had closed on us.

Another milestone.

'My lassie wants to be a nurse but I've told her it's hard, hard work,' said the driver, squeezing in. His tone inferred that he'd rather she took to the tidiness of the Aberdeen streets.

We did not look back, probably because we couldn't.

Mrs Ronce had been looking for us. As soon as the taxi drew up, she was out and, with an imperious gesture, stopped an oncoming bus. 'Come in, come in.' Her welcome was warm. 'My, but you've plenty stuff! Look, Pussies, there must be something here for you too.'

The cats pulled up their chairs to watch as, in front of an irate bus driver, we disembarked. Under pressure from his steady horn blast, the taxi driver became so agitated he started helping.

'Speak about making an entrance.' Maisie grabbed an armload of stuff and aimed for the door. 'I'll die of affront if anybody in that bus recognises us. Mind out, cats.' She staggered into the house, dropping something small and frilly as she went.

'If it was all that size,' the taxi driver grumped, 'I wouldn't be holding up the traffic.'

But at last we were unloaded. Mrs Ronce waved on the bus whilst the driver made a gesture making her slam shut the door.

'Common!' she snorted.

'Starters.' Maisie handed over a brown packet from her handbag before negotiating stairs so narrow, and with a load so cumbersome, she went as if blind.

'Fish!' Pleased, our landlady clasped her hands round it, then, heavily escorted, disappeared into the kitchen.

She'd lit a big fire in the sitting room a floor above hers. In many ways it was a miracle. I'd envied Beth and Sally this snug little room with its faded, creaking, saggy yet comfortable furniture. And now it was ours, along with bedrooms each overlooking the garden, a tangled green world of long grass, overgrown shrubs and trees hung with ivy. Beside an abandoned garden rake was a brush, which Mrs Ronce said was handy for sweeping back small boys who, during the apple season, would climb over the walls to get them.

'Silly little blighters. These apples are so sour, I've a good mind to make them eat at least one and then they'd really know about belly ache.' The thought seemed to please her and suggest care best confined to a hospital far from here.

With basics bought and our unpacking done, we celebrated with cocoa and toasted Mrs Ronce who, surprised by the concept, excused herself on account of a pressing drinks and Scrabble date.

'This is the life,' sighed Maisie, happily kicking off her shoes and sprawling on the couch.

We stared into the flames, soothed by their flickering movement. Outside, the rain pattered friendly noises on the small windowpanes. We pulled the dusty red velvet curtains to shut in a world where the fire cast moving pictures on the walls.

With the occasional bus rattling past and its own individual creaks and groans, there were more noises in that little room than were ever heard in the top floor of the Nurses' Home, but we both dozed off and when we woke, had the virtuous feeling of sleep perfected.

It was odd coming on duty from a different direction. Even the dining hall seemed a cheerier place.

'Crikey! You're looking fresh,' observed Jo, sinking her chin onto her hands as we waited for the roll call. 'The sooner I move out, the better.

I'm going to have a word with Sister Cameron as well. I got hungry the other day and went to make myself some toast and she leapt out of a cupboard accusing me of boiling eggs in the kettle. I'm really sick of being treated like a kid.' She rubbed her eyes. 'I hate to admit this, and even though I wasn't going to, I've had to resort to sleeping tablets.'

'And much good it's done you,' chirruped Rosie. 'You look like death warmed up, but listen girls! I've got good news.' She patted the table with her hands, then, beaming with the air of an angel bestowing favours, said, 'We're all coming back on day duty and into Block. Fancy! We'll have every weekend off for the next four weeks and not have to run after anybody, whilst sitting down in the lecture theatre during the week. It looks like we're all going to be back on days and just like a big happy family.'

Isobel waited until we were on duty sorting the drinks trolley in the kitchen. Softening the clatter by laying the thick white cups out as if they were bone china, she sighed. 'I didn't want to hurt Rosie's feelings. She's got such a kind heart and given me so many tips from her Granny's precious sleep remedies it's a wonder I'm not comatose, but now, just as I'm beginning to feel alive again and getting the hang of night duty with its lovely time off, it's all change.'

She loaded her trolley with enough sugar to turn the ward hyperglycaemic and put her diabetic patient over the edge, then, trundling out, groaned, 'Is that not sod's law?'

Nurse Green was of the same mind. 'Just when I got you trained,' she complained. 'I was even beginning to think you could see there were more important things to do than having straight bed wheels.'

I took that as a compliment and in a bid to continue the goodwill, wished her luck for her finals.

She got a sheet of paper and holding a pencil over it said, 'Right! You do the injections whilst I make up a new list of duties for the next junior. I've just thought of a few more things to add to it.'

29

TYPHOID TAKES ME
TO A SPECIAL CLINIC

Typhoid had come to town. It came in a box of corned beef tins from Argentina and brought screaming, doom-laden headlines about Aberdeen to papers as far away as America. They were as dramatic as they were inaccurate. Still, it was a nasty outbreak and even if the Aberdonians weren't lying heaped high and dead in Union Street and were instead treating the situation with their customary phlegm, the disease was going to need some clever medicine and a lot of nursing staff to contain.

Matron and Dr MacQueen, the medical officer of health, took centre stage in the lecture theatre where, as predicted by Rosie, we were very comfortably sitting.

Dr MacQueen came straight to the point. 'Well, Nurses, today we are in a very grave situation. Typhoid is a killer unless it's dealt with immediately and by professionals. It's seldom in recent years that we have had to deal with anything so infectious.' He cleared his throat and looked about, which was unnecessary; he had all our attention. 'As a direct result of typhoid, patients have swinging temperatures and will rapidly lose fluids, I'm sure you know what I mean.' He had the dismal look of a plumber with a small washer confronting major leaks. 'We will be dealing with many acute cases who will have to be monitored very carefully. Fluids need to be replaced very quickly and of course the patients will need barrier nursing,' he looked around, 'which of course you will know all about.'

Matron interpreting to cover some blanks looks, said smoothly, 'Of course. All our students have had a grounding in its importance, and know how easily contamination is spread unless protective clothing, masks and gloves are worn at all times, not to mention hand washing. Very like theatre work in fact.'

Dr MacQueen returned to his theme. 'We are going to need all members of staff to help contain the infection, which is why I have come to explain that we will be cancelling your Block until such time as we have stamped out this contagious disease.'

Matron, with a sheet of paper in her hand and a business-like air far removed from her usual twitter, took over. 'Dr MacQueen has kindly arranged for you to be included in the staff immunisation programme afterwards and whilst I realise we are asking you all to put your studies on hold, I know you are capable of great sacrifices and will be only too happy to help wherever you can. I don't imagine anybody has any further questions?'

Unless they want their heads examined, I thought, not liking the idea of being at the wrong end of a needle but flattered that we suddenly had become a vital part of a professional team. Matron, meanwhile, began to read from her paper, ensuring complete attention. Ward changes were important and this one especially so. This called for professionals. Didn't Dr MacQueen say so himself? I hoped I'd rise to the occasion.

'Nurse Macpherson, please report to the Special Clinic.' She gave me a keen glance as if conferring an honour.

'Special Clinic?' Goodness! That sounded important. I felt especially privileged until, waiting in the queue for my jab, I asked Maisie what it actually was.

'Venereal Disease.' She said it so loudly, nearby people started listening. 'I worked with a nurse who was there. She said it's definitely different and she'd some stories I know your folk wouldn't appreciate. Personally, I'm glad it's not me that's going,' she twitched her nose, 'try telling folk at the Palace dances that's where you work. Barrier nursing it ain't.'

I nearly asked for my arm back but already the injection was in my system, shortly after to give me such a temperature I had to be thankful that the clinic didn't need me immediately.

Woolmanhill was a centrally located antiquated building in town. It used to be the Infirmary but was now the Casualty Department with Outpatient Clinics nearby.

The Special Clinic was sited discreetly over the road and handily placed for the street punters who could have found themselves in the Leg Ulcer Clinic had they not been acquainted with this less exciting place.

It had the avuncular ease of an old gun dogs' retreat, occupied by two bloodhound technicians, their sagging eye bags reflecting a world-weary tolerance. In charge was an elderly springer spaniel doctor in leather patches, who waved a welcome whilst putting put down his paper to have a better look.

'We thought you were business.' The technicians looked disappointed. 'We don't actually need a nurse, you know. There's not an awful lot of work. Patients are just examined, tests carried out, there's the occasional injection to give and of course, you'll be needed to chaperone the female patients when they are being examined.'

I thought it was a bit late for that but didn't get the impression they needed a witty newcomer.

'Make yourself at home.' They waved their newspapers towards the waiting room.

'What should I do?'

'You could give the trolleys and instruments a dust.' They relocated to the columns of the sports section where an occasional outbreak of animation indicated serious discussion of the city football team's fortunes.

There was a grubby instruction card of duties under the bread bin in the kitchen and I carried it with me as I explored. The small print was the most interesting bit.

'There is no special time during the day for patients to come. They will be seen as they appear. They must be treated like other patients.

Remember! Sexually transmitted diseases can happen to anyone.' The card was so grimy it carried its own health risk.

Disappointed at the lack of custom, I performed my cleaning duties desultorily.

A bell rang. Ah! Somebody!

Before I could unroll the welcome mat, the team swooped upon an anxious-looking man and bore him off to an examination room.

I dithered outside, anxious not to seem curious and dying to know what was happening. The card had instructed discretion – hard, when there wasn't even a keyhole.

'Thanks very much,' the patient said as he came out, scuttled past my discreet presence and then disappeared.

'See, we didn't need you, did we?' the technicians jeered.

'True – what did you do to him?'

'We took some samples and gave him a jag.'

'A jag?'

'Penicillin of course.'

'I could've done that.'

'He said he didn't want to drop his trousers in front of you, but we've taken a special sample for the microscope, thought you might like to see it. Come on.'

I peered down on a glass slide and could see little other than a wriggly comma.

'What's that?'

'A sperm!' They sounded like a pantomime act.

I peered again but it had disappeared.

'It's gone.'

'Well it must be somewhere,' the doctor replied looking round the room.

Between worrying about the lost sperm and getting a dawning awareness of the importance of football, the days drifted past. Even if typhoid raged, with any patient found collapsed taken to Casualty, immediately presumed to have the disease, then carted off to the City Hospital – the designated hospital for treatment – I saw none of it and heard even less whilst Aberdonians, trusting their medical services, just went calmly about their business.

The class's feeling of importance dwindled too when we realised we were only covering wards to allow more experienced staff members to work in the typhoid wards. My work seemed especially limited but at last the great day came when I was allowed to take off venous blood.

Mrs Low had given the impression this was akin to brain surgery. She said that we could mistakenly inject air into the patients' systems and floor them – surely a contradiction in terms. I'd been anxious about doing it, even though neither patient nor technician considered it important enough to take their attention from the seemingly eternal fascinations of the Dons and their fortunes. I located a vein, closed my eyes then pressed on the needle of my hypodermic.

As the blood welled satisfactorily into the syringe, it was acknowledged that this was my first time.

'Same with me,' said the patient, grabbing back his arm, 'and yes, I'll tell the wife she'll need to come in as well.'

I watched the spivvy, swaggering, macho figure leave, adjusting his story-line and righting his brilliantined coif in some window glass, discreetly darkened but surely not designed for that purpose.

'What do you think he'll tell her?' I asked.

'Oh, the usual yarn about toilet seats, though the more imaginative can blame bicycles. We have been known to put in bicyclitis as a diagnosis if people can't accept the official line. Still, we should be glad he's told her. She wouldn't know otherwise – not until it's too late and nothing can be done. Venereal disease is not a pretty sight.'

There followed much sighing and rustling of newspapers. A knuckle was thoughtfully chewed.

A small young woman appeared next day, as bedraggled and dowdy as a wet sparrow. She crept into a far corner, neat, cross-ankled and anxiously clutching a red plastic purse like a talisman, bright against the darkness of her worry. She looked an unlikely partner to yesterday's bold boyo but her concern for him was real.

'My James's right unlucky. He catches everything that's going,' she said, meekly surrendering her arm, 'and I suppose I'll have to have the examination as well?'

If only she had had some of the self-confidence of Bella Bliss, our most dedicated regular. If a howling gale had met her up an Aberdeen close, it would have been the first to change direction. She had the lines of a majestic ocean liner complete with multi-national flags, handy for helping with ambassadorial hospitality in this seaport city. Even her magnificently sculpted hairstyle had been nailed into submission, remaining constant despite the many 'wee clinic checks in case I catch typhoid' she insisted on having. She appeared at least once weekly, more if it was raining, and was never in any hurry to leave. I was reluctant to challenge such frequency, as was the staff, since Bella's black, flashing eyes and mighty hands ruled out discussion.

'Why do you think Bella comes here so often?' I asked as a bang, crash and curse announced yet another appearance.

'It's a break from her street work, she likes the warmth, the attention, and of course she takes home the magazines. You know we always send you out for replacements after she's been. We'd have thought you'd have noticed that – you read plenty of them.' The doctor was condescending, then he folded his own intellectual paper and scratched his head in a perplexed way. 'But truth to tell, she's coming in just a bit too often – she's killing off our other trade. They're terrified of her. We're going to have to tone her down a bit.'

Stung by his observation and my lack of it, I should have realised why in all weathers she wore a red coat so massive it must have been bought in a tent shop. It could probably hold a bookshop. The sparkly butterfly fastener could have come from a less mundane outlet, but the toning down of Bella Bliss defied imagination.

'I'm just thinking of my clients and with this typhoid thingie you can't be too careful,' she explained as she made her usual entrance accompanied by jangling bracelets and high heels so staccato she could have been a flamenco dancer.

I fully realised then the role of chaperone as I caught Bella giving both technicians a measuring eye. She headed straight for an examination room and seemed surprised I was following.

'I think you're only due a blood test, Bella,' I said, hiding behind her medical notes.

'Miss Bliss to you,' she returned, stepping out of her fishnets and continuing to undress. Big knickers crashed to the floor. 'Now just you run along like a good little nursie and tell the boys I'm ready.'

I didn't fancy arguing with an Amazon and neither apparently did the boys, for they were showing all the signs of a pack on a planning mission and far too busy to attend their sole patient.

After some discussion, the doctor was transformed from a friendly dog into a wise but impersonal clinician whilst the kindly technicians became Rottweilers.

Dr Dog stood outside the examination room and spoke in a voice loud enough to be heard in Casualty: 'Nurse Macpherson, on no account are you to leave this patient's side. We'll also get a staff nurse from another clinic, and we'll attend to you in just a moment, Miss Bliss.'

Silence fell as he shut himself away to make a private phone call. The guard dogs planted themselves outside his office, ears cocked and grim of countenance.

'What's keeping the boys?' said Bella at last, her sighs and gusts of irritation beginning to reach gale force. 'See – if I've to wait any longer, I'll start looking for them myself.' Her hands curled into steel balls.

Incarcerated with her I began to panic. I was trapped with an impatient woman who took up so much room it was getting sweaty. The outside silence grew louder. I mopped my brow.

'There better be somebody here in the next five seconds,' Bella growled, 'or –'

I was planning an exit strategy when the staff nurse appeared at the door, so large, she blocked it.

'Miss Bliss?' She approached, running a practised eye over our patient, who was already regarding the big feet, bigger hands and suggestion of a moustache with a suspicion that made her reach for a blanket to cover her shoulders, her sledgehammer hand protecting the seafaring tattoos.

'Right, Miss Bliss, we'll have you out of here in no time at all. The doctor here has been giving me training for examinations and it'll just take a second. I don't think we'll need anybody else here other than the student nurse. She'll need to learn too.'

Had she done an air kick and cracked her knuckles she couldn't have been more threatening as, donning the biggest size of rubber gloves and picking up the clinic's most treasured female investigative gynaecological/gardening kit, Nurse Powerful advanced.

'Well maybe I'll just not have anything. You can just go and find another guinea pig.' Bella flew off the couch, flattening me against the wall whilst tussling to put her clothes back on. A fish scale, bright as a sequin, fell at her feet. 'Ah'm off!' Her coat flew behind her like a parachute but didn't slow her. Perhaps being magazine-free helped to speed the process but certainly Bella could shift.

'You're killing trade but I'll be back, see if I won't!' she yelled, shaking her fist at the kennel door. 'And I'll be taking my sailors with me.'

'Good. That's what you must do,' growled the doctor, all but marking his territory.

30

THE JOYS AND JINGLES
OF CASUALTY

Maisie and I were supposedly studying. In the face of ferociously good hygiene and practice, typhoid had packed up and left a city with a clean bill of health, immaculate public toilets and us back in Block. If we passed its exam we would graduate to purple belt, second-year status.

'We can't fail this. I couldn't stand repeating another month of sitting in a lecture theatre hearing doctors droning on. Speak about being bored to death!' Maisie slapped down her textbook, her hand searching in the digestive biscuit packet beside her. 'At least the nursing tutors kept us awake. Who'd have thought there were others as good as Jonesie and Mrs Low and that learning to set a trolley for a lumber puncture would be such an inspiration?'

Flames danced in the fireplace. I was lost in a reverie wondering where the year had gone.

'You're thinking about eating that last biscuit.'

'No, I'm not. I was just thinking how depressingly relevant the lecture on varicose veins was.'

'Well, I suppose sitting down for a month will have given them a rest.' Maisie made the ultimate sacrifice. 'Come on, Jane, take the biscuit and just think of the ignominy of failure and Rosie in a purple belt.'

With incentives like that, we couldn't, mustn't, and didn't, fail.

In triumph I rang home with the good news.

Mum sounded pleased. 'We've been more worried about the typhoid business. The papers made it sound like the plague, but there's you getting through it as well as passing another milestone. Good girl!' Then unable to resist it, 'We never had such good news when you were at school.'

To celebrate I bought an apple-green velvet dress with a price tag so large I could have worn it instead, and some might have preferred it if I had. With the city banning public gatherings and the Palace Ballroom dances cancelled, medical parties were the only social outlets.

Unfortunately, I'd been asked at the clinic to take the occasional walk well away from it. 'We're frightened you might recognise the person coming in,' the technicians had explained. Swapping curiosity about clients for distrust and remembering Matron's morality lecture, I wasn't keen on anybody in the medical profession getting close.

In a bid to cover suspicion with sophistication, I practised smoking in front of a long mirror.

'You just look silly,' said Maisie. 'Have you seen yourself?'

Still, I persevered whilst the purple belt comforted. It meant I must know something and surely entitled me to lord it over any grey ones. However, my next move was to Casualty where lack of accommodation in Woolmanhill meant there weren't any.

I began to worry about running the department. I was, after all, a very new purple belt, but as soon as I passed through that busy main door Mr Morgan, the charge nurse, put me straight.

He was bald with compensatory bushy outcrops covering his ears, a luxuriant moustache and an easy air of command over the exciting world that, in earlier days, I'd believed was everyday hospital life. With a nice line in music, he would sing in a pleasant tenor to divert the afflicted from the copious blood, vomit, broken bones, buckets and basins that were the everyday ingredients of this busy place. Ambulances, their blue lights flashing and horns blaring, were forever screeching to the main entrance, and always there was Mr Morgan or his staff who would restore calm from chaos, and knew when to despatch the most dire emergencies back into the ambulances and onward to Foresterhill.

Sometimes I'd get to be the accompanying nurse and felt guilty that flashing through red traffic lights at break-neck speed made my pulse race with excitement on a par with that of a patient in a serious condition.

Meanwhile, Mr Morgan would be in full voice. 'A wandering minstrel I,' he would warble, then, just as his patients were leaving, restored and smart in neat herring boned bandages, he'd despatch them with another refrain, 'A thing of shreds and patches –'

'Can I get a shot?' I asked one day, as he was set to treat a patient's sprained ankle.

'I'd rather he did it.' Uneasy in these surroundings and suspicious of my interest, the old man nodded at Mr Morgan, whilst his hand beat its own trembling rhythm.

'I cleaned the windows and I swept the floor,' sang the resident vocalist, 'the lassie has to learn, otherwise, she'll never learn.' He handed over the bandage, still crooning, 'and I polished up the handle.'

The patient looked doubtful. 'I think it's getting better.' He struggled up, his face bright red with the exertion, then fell back in his chair, the air whistling in his lungs and making him gasp. 'Well, ok then, but only if you don't start that confounded racket again.' Mr Morgan looked hurt and stroked his moustache as if to comfort it.

I advanced, crepe bandage in hand and wound, like carding wool, a yard of it round the purpling foot.

'You're trying to mummify me,' grumbled the patient, 'and how'm I going to get my sock on?'

'I'll flipe it for you. See?' I turned the rancid article half inside out.

A gold tooth gleamed as the old man relaxed. 'I hivna heard that word since ah wis a loon.' He leant forward in a matey way. 'Ye must be gey auld fashioned.'

'Jist a country quine,' I said, feeding the sock over his toes and stretching it so that it covered the bandaging. 'Look! It'll act as a compress too.'

'Take a pair of sparkling eyes,' burst out Mr Morgan, helping him to his feet and out the door.

I improved so much at bandaging that the arrival of the tubular bandage with its neat, bombproof way of application was a great blow. Maybe I could shine at reception skills.

'That's me off for my lunch break,' Miss Lettuce and Yoghurt announced, coming from behind her glass screen where, in her secretarial capacity, she recorded everybody's particulars. 'Somebody will have to take my place.'

'Let me,' I said and put my cap aside. I had neither her figure nor face, but once ensconced I found it easy to find out the necessary details.

'Married?'

'Yes.'

'Age and occupation please.'

'Why do you need to know that?'

'Just curious.'

A young man, immaculate in a better-living sort of way, approached. Even the hanky wrapped round one hand was spotless. Carefully, he wiped the ledge before laying down his injury.

I took his particulars.

'I'm a missionary,' he said by way of occupation. 'Praise the Lord!' His look was fanatical as he raised his good hand in jubilation, its descent, however, hampered by the counter. There was a painful sounding crack.

'And your employer would be,' I bent over the admission form, 'God, I suppose – one *d* or two?'

My customer was shocked. Reviewing his status, he checked the hanky, waving it like a health warning, and seeming surprised his hand was still attached. Then he checked the palm of the other and noticed it now had a red mark. As if in revelation, his brow cleared, his face lit up and he exclaimed, 'Stigmata! Excuse me, Sister, I'm in the wrong place for I have much work to do. This is a calling and I must share it with true believers.'

He left in such a rapid burst of Hallelujahs even Mr Morgan couldn't join in.

'Fancy him thinking I'm a Sister.' Charmed, and adjusting my friendly mode to efficient mode, I got ready for the next patient.

'Name please,' a pen was poised. This beat bandaging, no matter how simple that had become.

A small man, dungareed to the hilt, gave a coy smile, then transferred his gaze to everywhere but my helpful self.

'Name please.' I didn't want to shout but maybe he was deaf. A queue of ailments was beginning to form behind him. Somebody nudged him.

'Ah'm cried Cherlie,' at length he conceded.

'I have to know your full name,' I pointed out irritably.

'Ma freens a' ca' me Cherlie – an' if it's gud eneuch fur them, it's surely guid eneuch fur you.' He wasn't giving an inch.

The receptionist returned and resumed normal service.

'Name please.'

'Charlie Broon – spelt wi' a *w*,' the little rat said, then, leaning over, whispered, 'Yon maidie wis affa personal.'

'Whit maidie?' she asked, dropping her plums.

'Yon ane afore ye – it's surely nane o' her business asking sic stuff. She's jist a wee maidie.'

Mr Morgan now extended his repertoire to include 'Charlie is my darling' to much accompanying thigh slapping and common hilarity. I hoped, since Matron was famous for everything but humour, that this wasn't going to be warbled into my ward report. With a bit of luck it'd be forgotten and, tiring of its regular jingle and with some relief, I was eventually able to say, 'You'll have to change that tune 'cause I've been put on night duty.'

'So fare ye well,' came a staff chorus in dubious harmony.

Night staff cover was a doctor, staff nurse, student nurse and porter. As the door to the main entrance was locked at night, he was armed with a big stick – a useful diagnostic tool if anybody rang the bell.

Although accident pile-ups, mugging victims and the odd little headache made the place hectic at times, there were quiet spells which were supposed to be spent cleaning out sterilisers in the clinics, and tidying up after day staff.

Whilst the doctor grabbed sleep when he could, Staff Nurse did jigsaws kept for the entertainment of children in the warmest waiting room, the porter dozed peacefully at the admission entrance and I loitered through the other rooms carelessly dusting and letting sterilisers overflow.

The old building creaked in a friendly way and must have had some healing ghosts because the long dark corridors felt welcoming and safe. Even if the night sounds of motor and human traffic were muffled through the thick walls here, it felt right at the heart of a happening city.

Policemen, often responding to traffic accidents with casualties, brought an unruffled manner to any crisis, whilst we were handy for making them tea.

'Does that whistle work?' I asked a constable who, attacked by a sudden bout of thirst, had dropped by.

'Certainly.' He handed it over.

'Help ma Bob! What did you do that for?' he wept after I gave it a disbelieving blow.

Several of his colleagues came rushing in, leaving a bewildered porter gazing at the entrance door now hanging on one hinge.

'Now then, now then, what's going on here?' they demanded conventionally, opening their notebooks and searching for their pencils.

My policeman blushed as if caught in a compromising situation whilst Staff Nurse was sufficiently taken up with her puzzle to wonder if anybody had seen any missing pieces – and she didn't mean the door.

Then one of the hospital residents, celebrating his stag party and spying it was open, decided the casualty department was the hottest spot in town.

'Come on, chaps! This'll be fun,' he encouraged his entourage.

'I'm off,' said Staff Nurse, under-whelmed at an invasion of happy revellers and no blood.'Just see if you can get rid of them, there's someone there I can't stand.'

'You've always been far too aloof,' shouted Staff Nurse's least favourite person, and pounced on her as she was trying to fit into the brush cupboard. As it was full of cleaning equipment, I was surprised she even knew it was there.

'Get lost,' she said and shoved. Unfortunately, her strength matched her reluctance and he staggered back. His foot landed on a brush, making the handle swing forward to whack him on the back of the head. In a daze, he stumbled forward and hit his forehead on the side of the door. Blood began to flow.

'Tsk tsk!' said Staff Nurse.'I suppose I'll have to get Doc up now. Blast!'

'Amazing how when it's their own blood it's a different matter. Still, I think a couple of stitches should fix it,' she advised him remorsefully, then with a bigger regret,'and I can't find the local anaesthetic, you'll just have to do it without.'

The doctor, none too pleased at having been roused from his sleep, did just that whilst most of the party, sensing trouble, disappeared.

'Two stitches? I can only get in one – so, let's see . . .' with care, he snipped.

'Hey! You just cut me!' roared the patient, recovering sobriety.

'Yes, Staff said you'd need at least two.' The resident was anxious to clear himself.

'You certainly know how to make chaps welcome,' said the patient,'but maybe I should go before I really get hurt.' He nodded at the bridegroom, now his only companion,'And you can point him in the direction of home when he wakes up. I'm blowed if I'm carrying him. Not with the injury I didn't have before I came here.' As he left, the place fell silent with our remaining guest dozing in the waiting area and clutching a fire extinguisher as if it were his bride.

'I think we should take that off him,' said the porter.'Oh my Lord!'

The bridegroom had slid off his chair – the emergency knob struck the ground – there was foam everywhere and our only patient had just disappeared.

'There's nothing like a white wedding,' said that unflappable Staff Nurse, 'but I suppose we'll have to get him out of there, then we'll have to hose him down.' The idea seemed to please her. 'That should wake him up – better than a gastric lavage anyway.'

'Yeah, that should work. I don't particularly want to see the contents of a washed out stomach and see, after he's gone, let's barricade the door and put off the outside light, it seems to be attracting trouble,' said that caring doctor.

31

A GRIM NIGHT

'Did you know our names are up on the notice boards again?' Maisie was persevering with her new contact lenses, so maybe the red eyes didn't mean bad news. 'You're an extra and I'm off to the Eye Ward – suitable, eh?' She blinked hard.

Recently Mrs Ronce had been praising the past glories of Beth and Sally's cleaning skills and now it was getting harder to ignore the scrubbing noises coming from the bathroom and coinciding with our homecoming.

'Maybe she's ill.' Maisie's hearing was obviously affected by her sight.

I sighed. Being an extra didn't mean sitting in a tidy corner knitting. Instead, it was the huge anxiety of being sent anywhere an extra hand was needed to deal with big trouble in an unknown ward, with strange patients in uncertain circumstances.

Suddenly, cleaning seemed a simple and rewarding task.

'I think I'll do a wee hygiene turn.'

'That'll be a relief,' Maisie laughed coarsely as she dabbed her eyes and I went to help Mrs Ronce before going on duty.

Those halcyon and exciting days in Casualty were lost and I was now back in Foresterhill. The uncertainty of where I was to be working made me anxious and irritable. Sitting waiting in the dining room for roll call, I fretted, envying Jo's serenity as she glided off to the Intensive Care Unit.

'Have you noticed that even the back of Jo's shoes sparkle?' Maisie was full of admiration.

'Not as shiny as our bath now is and I think your contact lenses must be rose tinted.' I was sour.

Maisie snapped, 'What's wrong with you, Jane? You're like a bear with a sore head; you'd think you'd to carry all the cares of the universe.'

'I hate being on extra – you haven't a clue where you're going to be sent and if it's a strange ward, you never know where anything's kept either.'

'Bet you'll have to "special" Mrs Joy tonight.'

'My oh my, Maisie! You really do cheer a girl.'

'Nurse Macpherson, to special Mrs Joy in the kidney unit.' The charge nurse sang out as if it was a conspiracy.

To 'special' was to care for a seriously ill patient all the time. For some, this was the most rewarding aspect of nursing, but I didn't relish the prospect of having to be fully functioning with a brain at low ebb and little likelihood of back-up support for any emergency.

'Good luck.' Maisie was so cheerfully set for a night of knitting in a ward noted for the encouragement of lying very still and eye rest, I wouldn't have been surprised if she'd time for putting back in her rollers.

In no hurry, I made my way to the kidney unit. I could see that an emergency was in full swing with sisters dashing about after doctors pushing impressively complicated-looking machines. Staff nurses flashed past with handfuls of syringes. I was beginning to think my humble presence was a pleasant mistake when a doctor yelled at me, 'Get Tacky!'

'Who's Tacky?' I asked a nurse.

'One of the doctors,' she rushed past.

'Dr Tacky,' I called and yet another white coat appeared.

He gave a funny look whilst I pointed to the room where there was so much activity. I presumed this was Tacky for he disappeared into the chaos within.

'That's an odd name for a doctor,' I said to a ward maid, who was leaning on a brush watching the action with leisurely interest.

'Hey! That's not his name,' she laughed, 'that's only what his nearest and dearest call him.'

Great way to start, I thought, making a timid appearance in the unit.

There was just enough time to register the minuteness of the room and the patient when a sister grabbed me in a thankful way.

'Ah! Night staff!'

You might have thought I was manna from heaven.

She reeled off a list so full of technicality it was like a foreign language. I just concentrated on looking intelligent.

'Yes. I think I've got that,' I lied in plain English.

Thanks to hospital talk about Mrs Joy, I already knew she was a new, very ill mother, whose kidneys weren't functioning, making her blood toxic. Student nurses all had an especial concern for young patients, probably because we could relate to them. Tonight, it felt as if the onus for Mrs Joy's care rested on my shoulders.

'Her heart is considerably weakened,' Sister added as an afterthought.

Oh God! More bad news for Mrs Joy.

Cardiac massage was in progress, bringing with it a tension-packed concentration directed on a pitiful thread of life. Surgeons tersely spat orders to subordinates who obeyed with the manufactured efficiency of the desperate calm. As the only available nurse, I was shoved into the middle of the team, whilst Sister, worn and worried, collected her day staff.

I wanted to cry, 'Don't go,' but recognised I couldn't. Day staff didn't so much leave, as evaporate. I felt sick with the inadequacy of my knowledge. My purple belt felt like a burden.

'Cardiac needle,' one of the team of doctors demanded.

A second froze as everybody stopped. They all looked at me and, as one, roared, 'Nurse!'

I shot off through the nearest door and found myself in a sluice. Blindly,

I hared out again with the roars of, 'Hurry, hurry,' in my ears, and raced to the nearest theatre.

It was clear by the sounds of chat that the staff were taking it easy and equally clear that they were in no hurry to answer my frantic bell ringing.

I varied my call to Heaven: 'Oh please, Lord, hurry them,' I prayed.

'Well, what is it?' a staff nurse appeared, chewing.

'Cardiac needle for kidney unit.'

'The last time we gave anything there, it was never returned.' She prepared to defend her patch.

'Cardiac needle!' I screamed, changing her 'I've just done the inventory' expression to a degree of cooperation.

'Thanks.' I grabbed it and ran.

Now, nearing collapse myself, I padded towards the doctors. 'We don't need that now.' A doctor pushed the needle aside like an unwanted toy.

Breathing heavily, I tried out my pulse whilst summoning some energy to transmit to my legs. Revival became complete on discovering that Mrs Joy had rallied and even regained consciousness.

Gradually the crowd dwindled and soon the only people left were Tacky, whose proper name I just wasn't going to discover, and me. Mrs Joy wanted to know where she was and what was going on and I, mindful of her frail heart, tried to reassure her that all the frightening equipment surrounding us was irrelevant and nothing really to do with anybody.

I must have been boring, for Tacky fell asleep, making it hard for me to fight off the waves of engulfing tiredness as his rhythmic snoring and the patient's light breathing harmonised to a lullaby.

'Now, now! What's going on then?'

Night Sister's voice cut into the heavy atmosphere, making us start.

'I never saw you coming.'

'You mean you never heard me.' She was triumphant that she'd caught someone napping. Tacky's snores continued unimpeded, but she seemed reluctant to tackle him.

'Should anything untoward happen, will I let you know?' I asked after an update.

'I don't know where you get your terminology – untoward surely isn't a medical word,' she made a line of her mouth, 'and no, don't call me – I wouldn't know where to start in this place. You're supposed to be capable and with some common sense. After all, you're a second-year student and should be learning to cope without too much hand-holding, and you've got him.' She pointed to Rip Van Winkle.

She left me in a frenzy of anxiety, which at least cured the notion of sleep. I longed for my grey belt.

'How old's your baby?' I asked Mrs Joy, now disposed to chat having been thoroughly roused by Sister.

'She's just six weeks old. The doctors said I shouldn't have family, but what do they know?' She looked into the distance, the ghost of a victory smile lighting her face. 'My man's looking after her – she's lovely and I can't wait to get home to see the pair of them.' She gestured towards the equipment. 'I'm only here for a few hours more, surely?' Her sunken eyes were alive with longing.

I saw the flushed cheeks and held her temperature chart against me as if warding off evil.

Tacky, now awake, went to get coffee. We didn't joke about his snoring but I watched him go, a fellow traveller on a dark night. Anxiously, I kept up small talk with Mrs Joy with the foolish idea that if we kept everything to the normal, nothing would divert. One easy passage to the next. Morning with its fresh hope would come, certainly? Curious thoughts, simple to ridicule in daytime, were easy to imagine during the watches of the night, when the wait for dawn could be tortured and too long. I hadn't the expertise of the medics but like Mrs Joy, I clung on.

A little time off delivered by a blue belt, equally reluctant to shoulder responsibility, allowed me some respite in the dining room. I gave Maisie a blow-by-blow account of the night's work.

'Mrs Joy's young, pretty and uncomplaining but she's so anxious to see her baby, she'd do anything to get home. Everybody's heard about her. I couldn't stand something happening to her on my watch, I'd feel so guilty.'

'Och, I'm sure she'll be fine,' said Maisie. 'She's managed to hold on so far and that must be a good sign. Now, do you know how to turn the heel of a sock? I'm getting stuck with my knitting.'

Jo was sitting beside us saying very little. She had plenty on her mind but I was too preoccupied to care. Nurses always thought their own dramas unbeatable, and I couldn't think that Jo, with her matter-of-fact approach, was having a worse time.

When I got back, the familiar signs of emergency were only too obvious and with a hollow feeling, I hurried towards it. The blue belt, pleased to see me, left. Once more the fighting team was back with all the accompanying rush, but this time the thread of life was going.

For several hours we fought a losing battle. I tried to stifle images of a six-week-old baby crying in the night as I searched shelves, poured out lotions and scoured the cupboards for what the medical staff demanded.

'Give mouth-to-mouth resuscitation,' Tacky ordered.

I gazed at him aghast. Yet I did not find it difficult to place my lips on the airway over ones vomit-spattered, foam-specked and blue, and do what we all had laughed and joked about in the safe and healthy quarters of the classroom.

But to no avail. Just as dawn crept in, the pitifully slight figure convulsed and Mrs Joy died.

32

CHARLES BRINGS SUNSHINE
TO NIGHT DUTY

'Well, at least you're not on as an extra.' I too was getting ready for duty but with a light heart.

Maisie, however, wasn't consoled. 'I don't suppose I'll get to read this tonight. Apparently Orthopaedic's hectic.' She threw a textbook into her carrier bag. 'Changes! And we're still stuck on night duty with everybody else on days exploring the far-flung outposts of the A.R.I.'s training empire. We'll miss Jo, though I don't suppose she's complaining. She hated Intensive Care. Said theatre stress levels were nothing compared to somewhere crisis bells went off every five minutes. She'll find Sick Kids a breeze. As for Sheila, I've forgotten what she looks like.'

'I'm just delighted to be back in an actual ward. I'm replacing Rosie in male medical.'

'Well, she'll have knocked them into shape! Now she's gone to the T.B. Ward in the City with Hazel, I believe she's about to wean the world off spitting, not to mention fags.'

I said, 'She didn't get very far with Charles the auxiliary. On her watch and during his break I saw him reading tea leaves in the smoking room. He got through a packet at a sitting – speaking of which,' I felt in my pocket and took out my own cigarettes and lit one with a small coal from the fire, 'you?'

Maisie shook her head; the curls danced. 'And you shouldn't. I don't know why anybody would want to go into that awful staff room – even if you don't smoke, you come out smelling like an ashtray.'

A lecture loomed. A change of subject was needed and having lately noticed a sprightliness in my flat mate, the furry mules and even the hair net banished, I was curious. 'For all your complaints about night duty, you're looking pretty perky yourself.'

'Am I?' Maisie refused to bite, then looked so shifty it made me suspicious.

'You're definitely up to something, Maisie. I don't care what you say and I think at the very least you could tell your old pal what it is.'

She sighed and threw up her hands. 'Well, ok, I'll tell you. Since you're so snooty about my voice, I've taken up Talkin' Blues. Listen, here's one, I've just heard it. She patted her head as if adjusting a Stetson, coughed twice, then managed, 'Smoke, smoke, smoke that cigarette,' before I grabbed her and dragged her out the door.

'I'm sorry I asked. Come on, Tex Williams, duty calls. We'll be late if we don't hurry and I don't want Charles hanging about getting a chance to tell me about the joys of the last nurse.'

Once Day Sister had given us the patients' reports, I readied for responsibility with a list of duties for him to which Charles responded not at all. Maybe his thick specs blinded him to efficiency.

'I'll just have a wee faggie,' he lolled across the office desk, 'and what about a cuppa? Everybody needs one before starting the night.' He waved languid nicotine-stained fingers towards the kitchen and blew a perfect smoke ring to the left of my right ear. He appeared oblivious to a ward full of shouting patients and ringing bells, and deaf to the call of a kettle switch I expected him to throw.

Much as I was dying to light up, I felt I couldn't yet, so I returned his pale blue gaze, vaguely discernible behind the bottle ends, and aimed for a cool, 'I've got the Kardex to read.'

I'd tried to sound dismissive, but Charles just tapped his cigarette in the direction of an ashtray and continued to inhale with the enthusiasm of a dedicated fan. I gave up and went round the ward, hoping that at least the patients would recognise me as a person of some authority.

'Where's Charles?' everyone asked whilst someone handed over a slip of paper.

'What's this?'

'It's our list for who wants tea and when.' A patient, so breathless and cyanosed I thought he'd been gentian-attacked, seemed surprised by the question.

'But it says two o' clock!'

'Aye.'

'So – who makes it?'

'You! Och! Canny! Mind my back,' he grumbled, unappreciative of a brisk pillow pummel. 'Now you've gone and moved me, just as I was getting comfy.'

'You need to sit up to help your breathing.' Bossiness was tempered by the knowledge that he would soon wriggle back down to navy blue.

When Charles eventually deigned to appear I asked about catering, which seemed to reach peak level at 4am.

'You've got it,' Charles beamed. 'Gives the boys something to look forward to. It can be a long night.'

He added that all previous good and caring senior nurses were happy for him to have a well-earned nap, and yes – they had made the tea.

I was shaken, 'Even Rosie?'

Charles smiled as if in fond memory. 'What a girl! One of the best. I'd only to tell her once that I don't take sugar. I hated being such a nuisance but I just had to keep her right.' He yawned largely.

There was no time to dwell on the miracle that was Rosie, for the first night turned hectic with emergency admissions and tea-making was relegated to a place called later. Charles turned into a surprising hero. His long legs covered the ward in half my time as he willingly answered the call of tired men made anxious by the approach of night. Jokes had never figured in our lectures but Charles could have majored on their medicinal value, evidenced by ribald laughter and the feeling of fun he brought to bedsides.

But at last, everywhere and everybody became quiet, allowing us to draw breath sitting in the middle of the ward at a small desk, its light shaded like an air raid precaution. Charles took up a lot of room but left enough space for me to write the morning report.

Just before recording a perfect sleep all round, including my partner, I looked up to be surprised when someone waved. I waved back but the waving persisted.

I nudged Charles, but his snoring grew louder, so I got up to investigate. 'Yes?'

'Do you see the time? I've slept in.'

'No you haven't. It's not morning yet. Go back to sleep.'

'But it's time for tea.'

I'd forgotten all about it, but Mr Time and Motion looked so upset, I went to the kitchen, where I hoped the loud crockery sounds would wake Charles. They didn't; but did everybody else.

'Just in time,' they chorused, sitting up looking bright as children at a midnight feast.

I should just have thrown in the towel and done a full trolley round. It would have saved an endless tray trek, but then, stealing over the ward, came the sound of so much spitting you might have thought we were in a chest ward.

I allowed myself a smile as weak as the tea, meantime slumping into my chair, feet throbbing and with lead-weighted eyes.

Charles woke.

'Tea?' he beamed.

'You can blooming well make it for yourself.'

Charles muttered something about the past pure reign of perfect seniors and stomped off to do his share of crashing around the kitchen.

I was dreading morning. Rosie had been coy about working with Charles, so I didn't know about his two-speed approach to work and how the 'Go' one would make light of the usual slog. The half hour before handover time, in an immaculate ward with every patient and every strand of hair in place, was such a bonus, I began to feel petty about the tea making.

'Crikey, Charles, you're amazing. I've never been in a better organised place.'

Charles smoothed a lock of hair to the side and gave a careless shrug. 'I like a tidy ward. Makes the men feel things are right.'

'Hey, Nurse! You forgot to do my wallies,' a patient shouted, pointing at teeth as brown as the inside of a well-used teacup.

'I'll sort that,' said Charles. 'You go and tidy yourself up, Jane – you look a right mess.'

Amused but reluctant to be on the end of Charles's universal hairbrush, I went to repair the ravages of a night of responsibility and on return was met by Charles with a smile as big as the false teeth ones grinning up from the bottom of the pink basin he was holding.

'I thought I might as well do everybody's and save time.' He jiggled the container so that a sound like chatter reached up from its depths. 'Now, where's the Eusol? It's just the ticket for a batch clean.'

Somehow, we got off duty before a nervous breakdown and before war broke out between those patients delighted with new and better-fitting teeth and those who might never eat an apple again. Such, however, was their loyalty to Charles that the muttering was confined.

Somewhere in a nearby sluice, things would be settled later. However, the men were more vocal about the responsibilities of a senior nurse, the necessity for her to anticipate disasters, concentrate on making a decent cup of tea and most importantly, her vital role in not upsetting Charles.

33

HAZEL NEEDS A HAND

'How's Charles?' Maisie asked.

I told her I'd left a ward of folk with mouths like horses' teeth and letterboxes, was worried this might figure in my ward report and worst of all, I'd upset Charles.

'Golly! How did you manage that? It's one of the unwritten hospital rules. Nobody likes to do it. Not even Rosie.' As if reassuring herself she still had hers, Maisie sucked her teeth. 'When I think of all the cups of tea I made when I was a junior, I'd have thought I'd done my share, but my junior's a right weedy Alice. Last night it seemed easier just to make her one on the off chance she'd perk up a bit.'

Even if Maisie resented being on night duty, she was definitely up to something and it wasn't singing lessons. She should have been moaning more about her new ward and weedy Alice. I was getting really curious but forgot when Mrs Ronce, anxiously waiting for us in the hall, handed over the phone.

'Glad I caught you. I've just had your friend Rosie on the phone. She says to tell you that Hazel's been rushed into hospital with a burst appendix. She's in Intensive Care and you're to visit her this evening before you go on duty.'

Oblivious to the smell of burning milk, she tapped her head as a memory prompt. 'Oh yes – she said you might not get in to visit because Hazel will be poorly but to try anyway.'

A bus rattled past, shaking the house, making the grandfather clock chime a discordant reproach and scaring the cats upstairs.

'Did she say any more than that?'

'Well she said she'd see you tonight and not to bother the ward in the meantime.'

''Typical!' snorted Maisie. 'She's so bossy she wants to be in charge all the time. It's a good thing I've got the hospital number. Now, let's see . . .' already she was dialling.

Mrs Ronce went off to rescue the kitchen, whilst dithering in a state of anxiety, I thought about Hazel with her easy humorous way. Hard to imagine her lying ill and in pain.

It could only have been a few minutes but it felt like an eternity before Maisie put down the phone.

'Well?'

Maisie grimaced. 'She's in Intensive Care because she's got peritonitis. She's on a drip and in an oxygen tent. Apparently she didn't complain about the pain until she collapsed on duty in her ward, and by that time the damage was done.'

'She must be bad if she's in I.C. and why the oxygen tent?'

'She's got a chest infection,' Maisie was short, 'good thing she's not a smoker.'

'Maybe we should get to bed now and be ready early.' I headed upstairs, not wanting a lecture, but Maisie was making another phone call so I left her to it, considered lighting up, but instead fell into bed and a dreamless black pit.

Hours later, the sound of a drill and a heavy weight on my chest woke me. For a moment I thought I too was in hospital but it was just a purring cat making himself at home.

'Come on, Puss. I need to get going,' I moved him to one side, 'or Maisie will be chasing me.'

'I heard that.' My flat mate stood in the doorway. 'But you're right – let's get on the road,' as she turned, she called over her shoulder, 'and leave those fags behind.' I stuck my tongue out at her retreating back and put them in my bag.

Jo's bleak description of the Intensive Care Unit was accurate.

'We might have a job recognising Hazel here, you can hardly see the patients for equipment.' I was looking into a glass-fronted place where its occupants were lost to another world, but then Rosie came out from a side ward and signalled to us.

'She's here,' she whispered. She looked flushed and anxious. 'At least she's conscious, but she's not able for too many visitors – best you two go in together but make it quick.'

Hazel was propped up with pillows. Despite her breathing difficulties, her smile was valiant.

'You're like a princess in your palace.' Maisie gestured at the clear polythene tenting her.

'Home from home and they say I'll be out of it soon and I'm even going to live,' Hazel gasped, 'but I don't know if I'll survive the treatment.'

Maisie grinned and pointed to the cylinder pumping oxygen into the tent. 'Well you certainly don't want anyone lighting up here anyway.'

Hazel beckoned to me, then, pointing to Maisie, croaked, 'Has she told you her news?'

'No.'

'Not that she's the best practical nurse of the year? Dad told me when he came in this afternoon – thought it would cheer me up. He's on the board of management that decides that kind of thing. Seemingly they base it on ward reports.' She drew a laboured breath, 'They say she's a very mature approach.'

'Isn't she a dark horse!' I was delighted. I looked at Maisie, who had the grace to blush. 'I've been wondering why she's been looking so pleased with herself lately,' then, substituting guilt for a lie, 'I thought it was because she gets up so early she always gets the cream off the top of the bottle.'

Hazel clutched her side as she laughed, then turned grey as she coughed a hard, unyielding bark.

Maisie looked at her in concern. 'Remember and put your hand over your wound when you cough, it'll save your stitches.' She patted the air like a pastry maker with a light touch. 'We'll go now but d'you want a nurse?'

Hazel shook her head and since talking seemed insensitive, we waved instead. Looking back, I saw she'd closed her eyes and was so grey I worried that if she retreated to another world it might be hard to get her back.

Rosie was waiting. 'I've told the others to come tomorrow but as you two are working here, it'll be easier for you to pop in and give us news of any change.' She wrung her hands. 'She's not very well is she?'

Maisie spoke in the firm voice she kept for Rosie. 'No – but she's got plenty smeddum, and before you ask, it means guts.

'But maybe a bit less than before,' I tried for a light touch.

'Huh!' United in disapproval, the girls marched off down the corridor in a flurry of tut-tutts, allowing me the chance to regret levity and look for a bin.

There was one beside the exit. Taking out the cigarettes, I crunched the packet into the shape of a big chewed caramel, then, stuffing it through the bin's big mouth, hurried to make my peace with the others before going on duty.

34

LOSING A PATIENT

'Mr Dick was admitted this morning. He's in for blood sugar tests tomorrow so he'll need to fast.' Sister looked up from her day report and nodded at a patient skipping past. With his pink cheeks, white curls and chubby form, he looked like an elderly cherub on a placement. Sister, momentarily uncertain, cleared her throat. 'Since ever we mentioned fast, he's been flying round the ward like a rocket. Maybe we should have explained we meant he's not to eat or drink.'

'So that'll be one tea less, Nurse Macpherson,' said Charles, watching the patient complete another lap. 'We should call him Speedy. I'll go and tell him that if he's been on the go all day, he'll need a rest.' He raised his hand like a torchbearer and loped off.

'I think his deafness doesn't help and this place has been going like a fair all day. Maybe he'll settle now,' said Sister, closing the Kardex with the satisfaction of one finishing a good read, 'and I know he's in safe hands. Charles is very caring.'

I toyed with the idea of bringing up the subject of teeth with Sister's paragon but there never seemed a right moment and when at last everybody was settled, it was break time.

'It all seems pretty quiet now,' I squinted round the ward, 'even Speedy's sleeping. Will you be alright?'

'Of course.' Charles made for a chair, stretched out his long form and folded his arms. 'Honestly, Jane, you'd think you were in charge.' He yawned deeply, crossed his ankles and closed his eyes.

Maisie was toying with her food when I joined her in the dining room. 'I'm thinking about Hazel,' she said. 'She really didn't look well, did she?'

'It's early days and she'll be getting the best of attention.' I tried to sound reassuring. Jo's Intensive Care replacement joined us.

'I think we've one of your crowd with us,' she said, pulling her plate near her and grabbing a fork. 'She's on the mend and should be better once she's had some blood.'

'Blood!'

The girl speared a potato before replying, 'Yes, but she's going to be alright. She was making heavy weather of recovery so they decided the blood might help.'

We watched, slightly nauseated, as she stuck in.

'Are you sure she'll be alright?' Maisie pushed her plate away and rested her elbows on the table; a finger twiddled with a curl.

'Of course, but she's worried about losing training time. This'll set her back a bit, that's for sure.'

I was snapped out of thinking about this unsatisfactory remark by Charles, who was pacing the corridor and looking anxious.

'We've lost Speedy Dick,' he said.

'You mean *you've* lost him.' I was stuck for a more positive remark.

'Well it's your responsibility – you're in charge.' Charles used his full height to make the point.

'He can't be very far away.' I looked down the quiet corridor, at the end of which was the female ward. Usually there would be a faint chatter coming from there but tonight it was like a morgue. 'Have you tried the toilets?'

'Twice and before you ask, I've looked everywhere else too.' Charles sounded faintly aggrieved.

'Has Night Sister been?' Panic was making me squeak.

Charles looked at his watch. 'No. But she should be any minute.'

I cast around desperately. Where on earth could Speedy be? And not to put too fine a point on it, if we didn't find him, where might I soon be? I was sure that losing a patient was dismissal territory.

In the distance came the click of Night Sister's cubed heels coming our way, their owner about to have a pleasant night ruined. I felt sick. The corridor held not so much as a shadow. Charles took off his spectacles, breathed on them, tie-cleaned, replaced them, then looked around. But still no Speedy.

'How on earth did he get past you?' I asked, rather knowing the answer, but Charles was saved the lie as a blood-curdling scream broke the silence. It came from the female side.

'The old devil!' Charles shot down the corridor. Sister was now coming through the swing doors common to both sides and I could see her torch swinging in a gentle arc. I went to meet her, unsure what I would say.

'Good evening, Nurse, but what are you doing out of your ward?'

Resembling Fishie in his bowl, I opened my mouth, then my jaw dropped.

'Excuse us, I've just been taking Mr Dick for a stretch of the legs – a bit of a sleepless night,' by some miracle Charles, carrying Speedy like an airlift, had appeared, 'but now he's ready for bed.' Sending a smile round the world, he passed at breakneck speed.

Speedy's air of dishevelled confusion might be hard to explain, but Sister was already looking at her watch and frowning. 'Drat! I'm running short of time and should be at the I.C.U. They've a bit of an emergency there so I haven't time to do a round here, but you've no problems have you?'

'No, Sister,' I chirped. 'I'll run and help Charles.'

'Don't run unless it's an emergency,' she said predictably.

Hoping the urgent visit was nothing to do with Hazel, I went into the ward where Charles was reintroducing Speedy to his bed.

'I lost my way,' Speedy clutched his pyjamas at the neck, 'and couldn't see there was a wifie in the bed already. I got an awful fright.'

'Uh-huh,' Charles agreed, tucking him in so tightly his breathing could have been compromised, but already Speedy was settling onto his cloud. 'Nighty nighty – sweet dreams,' he piped and was so quickly asleep he must have been exhausted.

We went to the office to allow peace in the ward and, curbing a need to shout, at least speak aloud.

'Crikey! That was close – I never associated medical wards with such dangerous living,' I said, relief mixed with irritation. 'I don't want too many experiences like that.'

Charles obviously worked on attack as the best form of defence.

'And you shouldn't have, but do you know that pair of nurses at the female end were asleep at the time and didn't notice a man coming in to their ward? I think that's shocking.' Charles shuddered. 'Am I needing a fag!'

Wanting one myself made me teachery. 'You're in more need of a meal. Best to go now and whilst you're at it see if you can find out anything about my pal Hazel.'

I explained about her whilst Charles, half listening, checked his pocket.

His face cleared. 'Ah! There they are.' He flourished his cigarettes. 'Tell you what, rather than asking anybody – you never know what stories people think up – I'll just do a teacup reading. I see you've left yours unwashed in the kitchen. I'll take it with me, seeing as you're connected to Hazel by anxiety.'

He was on a mission, making it impossible for me to stop him carrying the cup off and just providing another proof of lunacy.

Whilst he was away, I pondered over the Kardex, lost in creativity until he came back flourishing the cup. 'I see blood.'

'That's my lipstick.'

'Well in that case, and if that's how you're going to be,' Charles threw himself into a chair, stuck out his bottom lip and looked moody, 'you can jolly well wash it yourself, but I think you'll find your friend's on the mend. That *blood* must be doing her good.'

We were in the changing room. Other workers were readying for home and chat centred round the joy of sleep: but Maisie had other plans.

'Before we go, let's see how Hazel is. We're more likely to get news if we're in uniform.'

'That's a good idea, even if Charles and the runes say she's getting better,' I was tired but crammed my cap back on again, 'and I think on account of your mature approach, you should be the one to ask about her.' Lack of nicotine was making me scratchy.

Maisie looked hurt, which made me feel worse, but I continued, 'Why on earth didn't you tell me about that prize? Didn't you think I'd be pleased?'

She straightened herself, as if expecting confrontation. 'To tell you the truth, Jane, you're always going on about your ward reports and how they're likely to sink you, I didn't think that hearing I had good ones would do much for your confidence. In fact, I'd to make a call to the management folk yesterday about accepting the prize and even then I didn't want to say anything.' Her finger wagged, 'Anyway – we never know what's written about us, so I think you worry for nothing. If they were all that bad, you can bet Matron would have been the first to let you know.'

She took off her apron, stuffing it into a laundry bag like she had a grudge against it. 'Goodness knows why I've won it, maybe I got maturity in my last job persuading Peterhead wifies to climb into one size smaller. But enough about me, let's find out about Hazel.'

A staff nurse met us at the ward entrance. 'You're not relatives, so I can't tell you much and you can't go in and see her either.' Seeing our concern, she relented a bit. 'She's actually had a good night and she's out of the oxygen tent. She's a great patient, but she's not off the worry list yet and her folks are with her.'

We exchanged looks. 'Still sounds a bit serious,' Maisie murmured. 'Thanks, Staff, we'll not hold you up. Maybe we can visit later.'

'Phone first,' the nurse advised.

At home, a robin was being stalked in the garden by a Roncer.

I got cross thinking about something so dedicated to taking life. 'Scoot, cat!' I shouted, knocking on the window, unaware that Mrs Ronce was hiding in the bushes with a water pistol. She must've been on a training mission and didn't look too pleased at the interference, but then the phone went and I ran to answer it.

It was Rosie.

I told her about Hazel and that it was unlikely she'd be allowed visitors.

Rosie was in full administration mode. Her voice chirped down the line, 'Nonsense! We're her friends after all. She needs us. Look, I'm going to contact the others and we'll all go tonight. At the very least she needs cheering up. A visit's exactly what's required.'

'Let's hope we get in then. And what about Sheila? Any chance of getting in touch with her? Maybe you could take your magic wand and see if you can track her down. I'm beginning to think she's been swallowed up by Inverurie.'

Rosie sounded surprised. 'That's easy. She's at Sick Kids. Didn't you know? I always know where everybody is. I've got a list.'

'You're just a wee wonder,' I said, impressed by such loyalty to the group, but replacing the phone before she could answer.

In the evening, we all met outside the I.C. unit.

'Well it's great to see everybody. I was beginning to think you'd left the planet, Sheila, but it's a pity we've to meet here,' said Isobel. With her black hair in a frizzy halo and her scarlet mini, she looked exotic enough to change the surroundings into a place more colourful, but Jo just shivered.

Rosie, a whirr of organisation, rounded us up. 'Now mind, we've not to let Hazel see we're worried about her and I'm not sure we'll all get in, but if we do, nobody's to hog the conversation.' She cocked an eye at Maisie. 'Now, Jo, you've worked here and know the staff – they're bound to like you – so you go in first.'

'Speak about damned with faint praise,' Jo muttered as she was pushed through the swing doors with Rosie at the rear, urging us forward.

A ward sister met us and looked stern until, recognising Jo, she smiled. 'Come back for more punishment?'

Jo explained about Hazel and that we only wanted a few minutes with her and that her health was our every consideration.

'Ours too but alright,' Sister was dubious. 'Of course, you know she's had a rotten time but I'm trusting you not to upset her and know you won't let me down.' She looked at the rest of us as if this might not apply, then added, 'but you'll have to be quick, mind.'

'Thanks, Sister.' Rosie resumed leadership whilst we trooped behind.

On the locker in Hazel's room was one red rose, identical in colour to the blood dripping into her arm in the otherwise clinically white, window-less space. It bore out Jo's description of an alien planet with Hazel its sole occupant, pale, but bravely waggling her fingers.

'Goodness! I must be ill!'

'No. We just reckoned you were researching life on the other side and might have some info of paramount importance to pass on, but this is a bit extreme isn't it? I never thought you were that dedicated.' Isobel draped herself on an oxygen cylinder whilst Sheila pulled up a chair and, with the care and bright attention of a clocking hen, laid a hand on the cover pane. 'Hey, Hazel, is't nay aboot time ye were oot o' that bed? My bairns are fleein' aboot the ward five minutes after getting oot their appendix.'

Unable to do much else, Hazel rolled her eyes. 'Bully for them!'

'Look, I got everybody here,' boasted Rosie. 'I thought it'd cheer you up and Sheila's right, it's high time you were back and working in the chest ward. You'll be able to tell the patients how much worse you'd have been if you'd smoked.'

Hazel's cough commanded a minute of respectful silence whilst Maisie, settling for non-verbal communication, made wound-protecting gestures with the bright smile of someone playing charades.

'That must be really painful,' offered Jo, 'but I expect you're on antibiotics, so you'll be better in no time.' She spoke with such authority I nearly stood to attention. 'But this is the gloomiest ward in the block.' She gestured at the surroundings and wrinkled her nose. 'I'd have thought you could've chosen a better place to spend your time.'

'But at least you can ask for the Suggestion Book. That usually guarantees great attention,' I said, knowing it was used more to register complaints.

Hazel lay there, exhausted, but with a faint smile playing about her bleached lips. 'No, but I'm thinking of it. I'm going to suggest they've a rotten system for filtering out unwanted visitors.'

35

CORPSE ON THE LOOSE

'So, how's your friend now?' I was back on duty with Charles and we'd settled the patients. Speedy had been discharged so I almost felt relaxed. 'Think she's on the mend. We got a bit of cheek – always a good sign.' Charles gave a complacent smile. 'It's all in the stars. I knew she would be alright, but you wouldn't believe me.' He pointed to a patient whose bed was at the ward entrance, never a healthy sign if you were the occupant. 'She's not like Mr Tully. He's been in and out of this ward so many times, he's just like an old friend. But with his bad heart, he's really got something to complain about.'

I looked at my patient, who was searching for air in quiet gasps, and deliberated. 'Do I dare leave him in your hands whilst I get a bite to eat? He is poorly but no worse than before. Tell you what, I'll grab a quick meal break and be back before Sister's ward round.'

Charles opened one eye by way of reassurance and I rushed off for a quick glimpse of the dining room, bolted a meal and hurried back, wondering if I was really up to being a senior and whether I should have left Charles in command.

I was right to wonder and wrong in the other decision, for when I returned, the screens were round Mr Tully's bed, with Charles in a dead faint under it and a dead Mr Tully on top. 'I've just arrived and this is what I found,' a flustered Night Sister explained, her torch making shaky arcs over their faces. 'I can't imagine what's happened but I'll have to phone the resident to ask him to confirm there's a death, whilst you see if you can revive Charles.' Giving instructions seemed to perk her up. 'And then of course you'll need to assemble the final offices trolley.'

Diagnosis of death apparently beyond the remit of nursing staff, she went to make her call whilst I whispered a message to Charles: 'I'll have to give you the kiss of life.' It was enough to galvanise him back to reality.

He came to and stood up, swaying enough for a whiff of Mr Tully's oxygen – I was sure he wouldn't grudge it. Then, casting an anxious look over the corpse and crossing his arms as if warding off evil, Charles said in a relieved way, 'Oh, thank God, he's still dead.'

'What!?' Sister was back. She searchlit the auxiliary with a still-quivering torch.

For a ward normally full of patients lining up for a tea round, it was remarkable how well they were pretending to sleep. The whole place was silent apart from Charles, who hurried to explain, 'Yeah, soon after Nurse Macpherson left, I thought there was something missing and it was Mr Tully's breathing, so I took a look and saw he was dead.'

'Nurse!' barked Sister. 'You mean you couldn't feel his pulse?'

Charles shrugged. 'Um – well – I noticed he was very still. As I was looking, I knocked his paper off the locker and went to pick it up, but Mr Tully's hand flopped over and hit me on the head. I thought he'd come back to take me with him. It gave me an awful start – I nearly died as well.' Charles put his hand to his brow and staggered a bit. 'This oxygen isn't much good. Don't you treat shock with brandy, Sister?'

There were some more theatrical effects before Sister relented and gave him a small tot. 'I think you can manage now, but you'll have to wait for the resident.' She was in tutting mode. 'My My! But this is a busy night. I wonder where the name Tully comes from. Not Banchory anyway.' She looked at the ward. 'You'd better put him in the side ward and not disturb the others; it's good it's so quiet.'

In the poor light she looked like a tired auntie but I chanced my luck.

'Before you go, Sister, and I know we're not supposed to ask, but can I ask how my friend in the I.C. is?' I couldn't have been more humble.

'No, you can't ask. It would be highly unprofessional of me to tell you she's on the mend,' she replied and tiptoed away as if her presence might attract more work.

We moved Mr Tully in time for the ward resident to come, place a stethoscope on his chest, pronounce him dead, then leave and allow us to do one last service for our patient.

'I could do this myself, you're due a break,' I said, wheeling through the final offices trolley.

Paying no attention, Charles spoke to Mr Tully. 'You did tell me you were sick to death of struggling for breath all the time and no matter whether you were in bed or up, you were never comfortable and you'd reached the stage that after years of never feeling well, you wanted out of it. And now you are, so the only thing left for me to do is to make sure Nurse Macpherson does the job properly.' He took a face flannel from Mr Tully's sponge bag and handed it to me.

Touched by his words, I set about the task whilst Charles chatted as if he and Mr Tully were mates in a quiet pub. I'd dressed dead bodies before but never in such a personal atmosphere.

When the job was almost finished, Charles decided to help. 'I think she's having a wee problem with your shroud. You'd think she was tying a parcel. Here, let me.' He took the long straggly ties and made them into perfect bows. 'There! That's the best we can do.' He stood back to admire his handiwork.

Less impressed by what was now presented as an impersonal bundle, and preferring to remember Mr Tully as a stoical hero, I said, 'Come on, Charles, you need some food. I don't want you fainting again and if you don't go now, the dining room will be closed. I'll go and phone the porters to come and take the body.'

'I'm sure I'll get something, but I see the mortuary trolley's been left on our floor.' Charles upturned his huge hands. 'Just call me Atlas! Why don't I take him down with me when I'm going? You tell them I'll meet them on the ground floor – it'll save them a bit of hassle.'

I remembered the vagaries of a single-handed trolley from our P.T.S. days. 'Will you manage just yourself?'

'Of course!' Charles was already and assuredly steering this one to the side of the bed. Once the body was transferred, we shut the lid, which gave such a clang it could have wakened the hospital. I was glad to see Charles set off with it, even if it was at a rate unbefitting a hearse.

The phone call made, I was back into the ward and about to do a head count when Charles was back – and in a hurry. 'You forgot to label him. Quick! I've left him in the lift.' He grabbed the slips I scribbled on and was gone leaving me to wonder how long it would be before somebody clever asked whether the running footsteps meant haemorrhage or cardiac arrest.

Again Charles was back and in a froth of anxiety. 'He's gone!'

'I know that – but what are you doing here?'

Charles beckoned me out to the corridor so that he could shout, 'No! What I meant is that somebody's pressed the lift button and released the lift from our floor.'

For a moment I thought I had drifted off and was having a nightmare, and part of it was the sound of a lift door opening with the approaching sound of screeching wheels accompanied by trotting footsteps. I clutched my heart. Had Mr Tully miraculously returned?

'Nurse Macpherson!'

This was worse than a bad dream. I had never seen Night Sister so stressed and out of breath, nor a trolley so expertly driven. At that turn of speed, Banchory should know it had a rally driving expert.

'What's the meaning of this?'

I took the plunge – after all, what had I to lose apart from my dreams? And was nursing worth all this anyway?

'It's all my fault. I should have left the porters to do their job but I thought I'd save them a trip.' It was hard avoiding hysterics. 'And I forgot to label Mr Tully and I forgot to put the lift on hold and . . .' Appalled by how things must look, I threw caution to the winds blurting, 'I'll work my shift until you get a replacement.'

Charles swallowed hard, then cleared his throat. 'Actually Sister, I don't think you should blame Nurse Macpherson. The truth is, it's all my fault. I shouldn't have left him in the lift, but I didn't think there was any risk of anybody else using it since staff's not supposed to use it unless it's an emergency.'

Both careers at stake, we hung our heads whilst, in the distance, the early sounds of morning stole upon us, with the cries of oystercatchers trawling far away conveyed by a wind surely from Siberia. Amazing how you could hear them when Aberdeen's beach was so far away. Soon, I thought, I might be hearing similar dawn sounds, but more permanently at home. What a long way to come to develop hearing skills but lose patients!

'It's not a competition,' said Sister irritably, 'and stop that silly talk about replacement. It's just lucky for you it was me who found him. I thought for a moment he must be on tour. Still, and I want you to understand this even if you know nothing else,' her voice went up a pitch, 'patients are not to be left lying about like lost luggage – dead or alive – so go and phone the porters now and let them do a job that they at least know how to do properly and don't you dare let that trolley out of your sight until they come for it. Understand?'

'Yes, Sister.'

'Right.' She stomped off.

'That was close,' said Charles dropping his shoulders and stretching his neck. He drilled his eyes at the trolley and after a full second said, 'Heck! This is more boring than watching paint dry. Tell me about your time in the Ian Charles and when you found yon awful wifie under the bed. Now that sounds really exciting.'

36

A PROPER PERFORMANCE

Sister Catto headed the gynaecology ward. She was also a cat. It didn't need to stretch the imagination of a newly-qualified, blue-belted, final-year student – yes, folks, another miracle – to figure out that one. Of course, the nickname Kitty helped, but the slanting green eyes, round face and pointy ears sticking through short jet-black hair clinched it.

I was discussing my new ward with Maisie, celebrating a day off, ironing in the kitchen.

'You'll like her. Remember, that was my first ward. She treats everybody the same and it's a happy place.' She looked down at an orange feline, fresh from chewing a sad little pelt and now insinuating his body round her legs. 'But she's from the caring side of your family-cat – quite a different branch.' She pointed the iron at the clock. 'But if you're not out of here in the next five minutes, Janey Mac, you might find Kitty has claws too.'

I took the lift to the hospital top floor.

Well out of earshot of the rest of the hospital, it overlooked the whole of the city. Far below, gulls wheeled and turned. For a moment I thought I heard their cries but then realised they were the sounds of laughter coming from the ward.

'Ah! And here's our new nurse.' Kitty's face split into a welcoming smile as she came along the corridor heading an assorted team of medics and nurses, 'and she's just in time for the round.' She turned as another burst of laughter split the air. 'Come on! If we're quick, they'll share that one with us.'

I wasn't used to being so included. Usually all but the most senior staff members would be hidden away and work held in a state of suspended animation until a round was over. Going on this one felt like a goodwill tour.

We gathered round the first bed.

The gynaecologist twinkled at the patient over his half specs. 'Good Morning, care to share the joke?'

'You're too young,' replied the patient, giving a wriggle of pleasure and pulling her nylon bed jacket about her as if to contain her mirth.

'Pity,' said the gynaecologist. After a few small pleasantries, then a big discussion about her operation, he said, 'I think we should have a look at your stitches.'

'If that's ok with you and you don't mind an audience?' Kitty interrupted, leaning casually on an over-bed table at the end of the bed and resting her foot on its bar.

'Aye. I'll take the tickets, Sister, you take the money.'

'In that case, we'll need these.' Kitty dimpled and stood back to let the other medics pull the curtains.

'Could I sit up now?' asked the patient after her scar line had been admired.

'Certainly,' said Kitty, 'these nice strong doctors will be only too happy to help you.' She waved her hand at the assembled white coats. 'And be sure and tell this lot what your worries are because they're the ones paid to have the answers, unless of course you want a private word, in which case just tip me the wink and we'll organise that for later.' She moved to the next bed.

Once every patient had been given the proper attention and every question the appropriate respect, the round was over, allowing the patients to settle in a ward that ran like clockwork. There were some squalls but only amongst the most competitive of patients reliving the biggest and bloodiest of operation tales. No wonder Kitty was respected and people loved working here.

'Well, how did it go?' Maisie, ironing piled virtuously high, enquired. 'Or need I ask?'

'It's great and not only that, she's wondering if our group would like to take part in her pantomime. Apparently our P.T.S. dramatics have gone down in the annals and she thinks the patients need something to think about other than their battle scars.' I scratched my head and wondered, 'Why does everyone associate us with drama?'

'Why indeed,' agreed Maisie. 'Would there be a singing part? I've given up on talking blues – couldn't get the rhythm somehow.'

By good luck we were all now back on day duty in Foresterhill, so it was easy to catch up with everybody. Persuading them to sign up, however, was another matter, so I approached Hazel since she had the kudos of a recovery bordering on the miraculous.

'Don't you think I've had enough excitement lately?' It must be all that new blood coursing through her veins, but between that and her blue belt, she had the manner of a general, gracious in victory. 'Anyway, I only associate with winners so who'd you like me to ask?'

'Maybe you could have a word with Jo and Isobel. I think they'd trust you more than me anyway. Rosie's already spoken to Sheila and she's going to help with the scenery.'

'Fantastic! And what about our practical nurse of the year?'

'She wants a singing part.'

'No!' Hazel's hand flew to her mouth, probably to hold back the scream. Still, she wore the thoughtful look of one already mustering her troops. 'It'll be great to do something altogether – should be a larf.'

I wondered how she'd persuade Isobel.

'No problem! She's at a loose end since breaking up with the latest bloke.'

'Is she ok?'

Hazel narrowed her eyes. 'Well, you know Iso – if she'd a broken heart you'd only know about it if you were at her funeral.'

But Isobel sounded fine when we gathered outside Kitty's office. 'I hope we're doing the right thing here. I've suddenly got a dose of the jitters. Still, it stops life from being dull and it's worth it if it means we can have something that takes our minds off blue-belt responsibility.'

Rosie was in a chirpy mood. 'Isn't it good that I managed to get Sheila on board? Now we've only to have Jo and we'll all be together again and having fun. Hey look! There she is. Come on, Jo,' Rosie's hands beckoned, 'Quickly, now!'

Sheila laughed in that lovely comforting way that reminded me of hot chocolate. 'Some things dinnae change. Come on or we'll get a row.'

'And here's the rest of the team.' Kitty came to the door and waved us in. Weaving around some other budding thespians, she levered herself onto a desk, stretching her cat suit enough to inspire awe. After introductions, she went on, 'And thanks for coming, good of you to give your time. I've got the scripts here,' she waved a sheaf of papers, 'so please have a quick read and then we can discuss the parts. And just before anyone starts slagging off the author,' she considered the floor for a moment, 'I think it's only fair to tell you, it's me what writ it.' Only the swinging legs betrayed a playwright's anxiety.

'Great,' breathed Isobel. 'Just the place for professional suicide.'

We exchanged glances. I thought about my ward report and prayed for a good read.

Eventually, Isobel put down her script. 'It's great and I like the idea of a pantomime with germ-laden bugs against the universe,' she spoke as if she too had felt the winds of adversity, 'and it should be great fun, but I'm not sure where I'd fit in.'

Kitty sized her up. 'I need three tall people to do "Sisters," you know, the one the Beverley Sisters made famous. You and Hazel are a perfect height.'

'I knew it'd come in handy sometime, and you're obviously not fussed about our voices.' Hazel observed.

Kitty laughed. 'Charles's going to be the third sister. Need I say more? But we'll need other singers for the bug parts.'

Maisie drew breath whilst Rosie's hand shot up, probably to gag her. 'Ah! A volunteer. Splendid.'

'Er – well, no – actually,' Rosie stuttered, bouncing up and down as if about to take off.

'You don't have to do it well. Bugs ain't toonful. Just as long as you're bold with it and can hit the occasional note.'

'That's you,' jeered Maisie. 'The bold bit anyway.'

'You seem to know each other pretty well,' Kitty observed. 'I think you'll make a good team with one other person. What about you, Jane?'

Already overwhelmed by the informality, I said, 'Is this for the other bug? It's quite a big role.'

'Yes. I need a threesome of nasty little bugs with carrying voices.'

'Sounds the very part for you.' Since signing up with Isobel, Hazel couldn't have been more helpful.

'Ah'll be happy prop building and painting,' Sheila offered. 'Ah've got a few ideas already.'

Kitty gave her a long look. 'Could you paint a celestial scene?'

Sheila's smile was angelic. 'Ah'm better at little devils but Ah'll try. Ah'll need folk wi' muscles though.' A spokesman from a group of burlies Kitty must have found in weight-lifting classes flexed his pectorals. 'We'll help – we're keen to see a real artist at work.'

Sheila, looking pleased, gathered a group and started a conversation so technical that paint was never mentioned.

'I'm not wonderful on machines but I can just about work a tape recorder, would that be enough for sounds?' Jo stepped forward.

'Yeah. Great.' Kitty, wildly confident, handed her a small box. Rather doubtfully, Jo went off to twiddle knobs in a corner.

Kitty continued, 'I've arranged with Home Sister for us to rehearse in the Home sitting room, so I reckon we need to meet there in a week and by that time, you'll all have had a chance to get an idea of how you want to play it. Now, any questions?'

'Have you got a part?' a sly voice asked.

Kitty twitched her nose and all but checked her whiskers.

'My part's not yet in the script but, like you, I'll be working on it. I'll have enough to do backstage. It'll probably be at the end and only be a cameo part.'

'What's that?' whispered Rosie as we drifted out.

'I think it means she'll steal the show.' Isobel was cynical.

'You alright these days, Iso?' I asked.

'Apart from getting involved with you lot, yeah – why shouldn't I be?'

'Just wondered, that's all. I haven't seen you for ages. What about coming down to visit us. Tell us about any new romances.'

Isobel sounded bored. 'I've had enough of blokes. They get all serious about themselves. They don't seem to think a nursing career's worth considering. Why can't they just be friends?' Sighing, she wandered off as if the world had become very complicated.

The following day, patients intrigued by pantomime news asked about Kitty's part in it. I wasn't able to help and when they asked her, she just looked inscrutable and swung her stethoscope with such a majorette-like twirl they had to duck.

Rehearsals got underway and Rosie surprised us with a sweet soprano, attracting the admiration of some male nurses Kitty had coerced into helping.

'There's no point in them falling at her feet. She's got a boyfriend at home. He must be mad.' Maisie sounded surprised and with renewed diligence, went off to undermine those golden notes with her tuneless undertow.

'There's a grave danger those two will kill each other,' I said to Kitty during one particularly fraught rehearsal when Maisie finally knocked Rosie off her singing perch.

Kitty was taken aback and protested, 'But conflict like that's necessary in good drama – they're merely suffering for the sake of art. They're horrid little bugs. You'd expect them to act like that.'

I thought of my own role as the slimy fawning one and felt uncomfortable that it was so easy.

Harmony was more evident in the 'Sisters' routine, a clever parody with Isobel, Charles and Hazel a slick trio. The wardrobe mistress, pinched from the hospital linen store, simply swapped a lifetime of skills battling with nurses to lower hem lines, to providing mini-style sister uniforms that showed Charles's knees to best advantage.

'What about a bosom, Mabel?' he asked.

Silently, she handed him two balloons.

'So what kind of costume will you be wearing?' a patient asked one day when I was recounting some panto tales.

'Green tights and a tunic.'

'Gosh! That's brave,' she said and held onto her stitch line before sharing the joke with her neighbour. 'Wait till our visitors come – they'll have a right laugh. We'll all be coming to it. Not long now.' The words fluted down the corridor and reminded us of how little time we had left. Even Kitty was beginning to get a twitch, and a visit from Matron, reminding her that she held responsibility for student nurses who should be spending every off-duty minute in study, didn't help.

'I'm going to cancel this – it's never going to work,' she said in an uncharacteristic fit of ill temper, after a rehearsal of muffed lines, shaky props and nervous hysteria. 'It's just not worth the anxiety.'

Jo scurried past clutching the tape recorder.

'I think I've broken it,' she said.

'Then you'll have to do the sound effects yourself,' snapped Kitty, definitely wobbling.

'How will I do the sound of a lavatory chain pulling?' Jo worried over a key feature in one of our scenes.

Maisie gave an accurate raspberry.

'That will do!' Kitty shouted. 'Right! That's it. I've had enough.' She swished her tail and put her head in her hands. 'I can't do this.'

'For goodness sake, Kitty, let's cut out the drama – please.' Charles exuded calm. 'Everybody's doing their best, so why don't we all have a break and a ciggie?'

Surrounded by our concern and his words, Kitty brightened. 'You're right. I don't usually smoke but these are exceptional times, and if you lot fail your finals, remember it's not my fault.'

Had she been in a more positive frame of mind, she would have seen there was progress with Sheila and her team transforming the barn-like Nurses' Home hall into a credible theatre. The new Home Sister lost some of her formidability by helping rig up curtains before returning to her stance guarding the stairs leading to the bedrooms. 'Anybody could get up there,' she said with her arms folded, large feet planted at quarter to three.

'What does Kitty think about these?' Isobel nodded at the backdrop of rural scenes, which had well-upholstered cherubs, with the faces of some hospital familiars, frolicking amongst silver clouds.

'She said she thocht they were a bittie pink for the North-east,' said Sheila, looking out some blue and carefully adding those rude little flourishes in which she excelled.

The big night came. There had been a state of High Alert in the ward with a queue of candlewick-clad patients readying for the evening from early in the morning: and there they now were, complete with family and friends, cramming into an already-full hall and easily distinguished by their banter and, 'Already we're in stitches,' a catchy little number they'd been perfecting all day.

'I can see Matron. She's right in the front row. Look!' Rosie was peering unprofessionally through the curtains.

Sure enough, there she was, so unrecognisable in mufti and smiles that Sheila's pinkest cherub, frolicking behind its medals, looked more like the original.

'For the love of Mike, Rosie, come on, we're needed back-stage.' Maisie collared her.

'You're so bossy,' said Rosie and bounced off, allowing Kitty to signal the curtains to be raised.

'Right, everybody, let's go.'

The pantomime got underway. Matron was reported to have laughed at the right moments; the audience was sympathetic. The scenery was standing the test and Jo's sound effects were on cue. Charles brought the house down by bursting one bosom and running agitatedly after the other when it escaped. Meanwhile, Isobel, with Hazel, proving a full post-operative recovery, high-kicked him back to the limelight, completing the number to rapturous applause. Rosie and Maisie brought an unsurprisingly authentic but well-received hatred to the plot whilst the patients from my ward, perhaps remembering who was likely to be taking out their stitches, loudly applauded the sly fly bug.

'I saw your ladies giving you a really big cheer,' Jo observed, holding the sound box as if it were treasure.

'One tries one's best,' I tried for nonchalance, 'but now our part's over and still I don't know how the show's going to finish. I can't remember it being discussed.'

There was a heightened buzz as we moved on to the pantomime's last scene. Not even the last waltz at the nurses' dances had this level of anticipation.

Our own parts completed, we stepped back. The lights dimmed, allowing silence to take the stage.

Then, and to an audience more accustomed to fishnets draped round Aberdeen harbour, the appearance of one wrapped round a shapely leg insinuating its way through the curtains was well received. At the same time, a saxophone held one note. A spotlight shone on the snaking appearance. Assured of everyone's attention, the other leg made a glittering appearance. Who would have thought prune-faced Mabel was such a dab hand at sequins?

Matron cleared her throat as a dancer in a sly smile came through the curtains, completing a routine that would have put the slinkiest feline to shame. The sequins moved and glittered, the figure leapt and twirled, the saxophone whispered and moaned. The audience held its breath.

Then, finally and in a gravity-defying leap, the performance was completed. Helped by flying heels and shooting stars, the dancer disappeared back through the curtains.

The applause was thunderous. It had been some pantomime. A line of candlewick stood up, the better to shout approval and an encore.

So, Kitty – well it had to be – took her curtain call, executing a curtsey which put the fishnets further to the test. Then she beckoned to the saxophonist.

Elegant in a black evening suit, a distinguished-looking musician stepped forward to take his bow.

'Good God!' exclaimed Maisie.

'No,' twinkled Rosie, that stickler for accuracy, 'it's Charles.'

37

FUTURE PROSPECTS

Miss Jones was in the P.T.S. classroom and making the introduction.

'Today, Nurse Macpherson has kindly given up some of her studying time to talk to you about the training here. As she's going to be sitting her finals soon, she's in an excellent position to tell you about it.'

Who'd have thought it!

'Your hair's fine but why do you think you were asked?' Sprawling in an enviably relaxed way on our sofa, Maisie had been puzzled. She waved away the cloud of hair spray created in my stressed pre-talk preparations.

'I dunno. She spoke to me after the pantomime. Maybe it was my stage presence.' I felt my stomach clench. 'No that was a joke, but at least I'd a script then. This is a different kettle of fish, especially as I'm not even sure what she wants me to say.'

'Remember, we'd a blue belt who came and spoke to us when we were in P.T.S.,' Maisie idly filed her nails, 'and I don't remember what she said, so it obviously wasn't particularly memorable, but maybe you could tell them what you're going to be able to do because of the training. Aim for your future as well as theirs.'

I said Miss Jones might not like to hear that I wanted to get as far away from hospital starch as possible. The nurse's cottage in the gloaming, dispensing healing homilies, seemed as good an idea now as had the life-saving, parties and city life of which I had dreamt at the beginning of my career; but maybe the classroom wasn't the place to say so.

'If you want to do district you'll need to do your midwifery as well.'

She eased off the sofa and picked up a form from the mantelpiece. 'Look, I've got an application for Edinburgh. After our finals and all being well,' she waved crossed fingers, 'I might go there. They say Edinburgh's fun and if I'm going to the missionary fields I'd need that qualification.'

'Missionary! Maisie – you must be joking.'

She went pink. 'Well if all else fails, though maybe I'll stay on. I've been asked to be a staff nurse in the medical ward I'm in just now. I could do with the money and it'd give me some experience.'

I wondered why it was that my most interesting conversations with my flatmate were just as I was leaving the house, but in the meantime, I had to speak in a classroom before a critical audience.

'It's hard to believe that three years ago, I was sitting listening to someone like me, and I just wish I'd paid more attention.' The class laughed dutifully whilst I looked round the room feeling an unexpected affection for it and the tutors who had striven to teach us so much. 'But I came here not knowing anything other than that I wanted to be a nurse and now that dream's about to be put to the test. You're about to embark on that same adventure. Treat it like that and expect a rollercoaster. You'll be getting a first-hand knowledge of crisis, the wonder of life, the fortunes of people and of course, don't forget death.'

Miss Jones didn't look too happy at that but I was on such an evangelical roll, I wished I'd brought a baton and the words of 'Jerusalem'. 'Sad – but that's reality – so there'll be times when you wonder if you should just chuck it all. Then again, if you stay the course, you'll learn how to deal with the scariest of scenarios, help people at their weakest times and even be able, at the end of it all, to pass the ultimate test as I've just done,' I caught someone smothering a yawn and with a sudden admiration for Miss Jones' ability to hold her audience, wrapped it up, 'by giving a talk about nurse training in front of a new P.T.S.'

Then Miss Jones asked if anybody had any questions and a hand shot up.

'What will you do if you fail?'

There was a mischievous glint in the eyes of the questioner. I hoped the battle-hardening training wouldn't make her lose that sparkle.

'I'd have to re-sit,' I said, appalled at the concept, and went home to do some studying and tell Maisie that whilst my future might not lie in public speaking, staff-nurse pink might suit her better than being a missionary.

38

CHRISTMAS IN
THE WORK HOUSE

Christmas preparations were getting underway in my new orthopaedic ward. Sister dispensed with the formalities of introduction. 'Ah! A blue belt. Go and fix up a bed for traction will you?'

Somewhere was a recollection that traction was a form of torture dreamt up by someone who had no intention of ever personally trying it out. The theory was that, by clever use of weights and pulleys secured to the body on a Principle of Moments basis, you could realign bone structure into a properly healing position.

I'd seen patients attached to these devices and doubted the strategy as I fixed an iron beam to the bed beside Mrs Jones, who'd been stuck in hospital for ages with a fractured femur. Confined to bed, she'd become the complete authority on all ward, not to mention world, matters, but unlike Mrs Spence and Mrs Fotheringham, my Ian Charles pals, it hadn't made her any sweeter.

'You're new aren't you?' she asked, checking the faded stoat plait hanging over her shoulder. She was old with a creaky voice and a face corrugated in disapproval.

'Uh-huh.'

A weight fell to the floor with a Big Ben clang.

'I thought so.' She pulled at a bed jacket as battle worn as Miss Kerr's dressing gown and settled back, pleased to have live entertainment.

Even though a guardian angel, disguised as a friendly auxiliary, quietly and competently managed the operation, it still looked like an incomplete Meccano set.

'Very good.' Mrs Jones sounded disappointed.

Mrs Jack, for whom the apparatus was being constructed, lay on a trolley nearby. Grey-faced, anxious and prepared for theatre, she eyed the construction doubtfully. 'It's like the scaffolding that fell on me,' she said.

'It's for you when you come back,' Mrs Jones crowed.

Tidying away, the auxiliary muttered, 'What a pain she is. If we got to choose our patients she wouldn't be here, but she's a widow with no family and doesn't get many visitors. It's a shame really, and with Christmas so near she's going to get even worse. She sees the black side of everything. It's already making her even more crotchety.'

It might be hard to divert Mrs Jones, and a pity her thigh bone was taking ages to heal, but I was cross when Mrs Jack burst into tears. She too was old and in particular pain.

I gave the beam a good thump, making the weights swing. 'Look, safe as houses. It'll be fine – we've done loads, honestly.' Mrs Jack watched as if hypnotised.

Sister came along and dumped an armload of tinsel on a table in the middle of the ward.

'That looks great. Now I'd like you to get on with the decorations.'

The ward was full of old women whose brittle bones had broken in a second but were now taking months to heal. They were delighted to have their dreary routines changed and, supposing there was communal deafness, shouted their advice.

Very shortly there was bedlam as Mrs Jones fought her corner. 'Put the tree beside me,' she shouted, 'I could do with the company.'

'I think it should be at the top of the ward,' said Sister, 'then everybody will see it.'

'Oh well, if you can't take advice, see if I care. I'll have a bedpan instead.'

The staff and those patients who were able to get up enjoyed the gaiety and cheer of the decorating. Outside, the sky was leaden with the first few flakes of snow idling past the ward windows. I wondered if Staffie in Theatre had noticed and still been excited by them. I was there when she saw snow for the first time. It'd made her clap her hands and scream, an unexpected and unwelcome action in the middle of an operation and I remembered an uncharitable delight that she'd been shouted at for a change.

Here, the ward was turning into Aladdin's cave. Now, the tree, impressively huge, stood at the ward entrance, laden with parcels and bright with fairy lights. Streamers lowered the ceiling in a cheerful way whilst brightly-coloured baubles reflected the soft lights of the Chinese lanterns hanging over each patient's bed.

'That's Mrs Jack back from theatre and coming round. Mind you, she may think she's in a different ward,' Sister sighed with pleasure as she folded plump arms over her ample self and surveyed her charges, 'and I suppose it's good she's beside Mrs Jones, she'll be the first to report any problems.'

Christmas Day came with excitement running fever-high and an orthopaedic consultant dressed as Santa. After a sherry sojourn in Sister's office, he made a cheery ward round, kissing startled but delighted patients with an enthusiasm surprising in such a normally gruff man.

'See what I've been given.' Mrs Jones stroked a new bed jacket, her fingers lingering on the satin ribbon. 'Betty Jack's daughter brought it in and' – she stuck an emaciated leg out from under the cover – 'look! The plaster's off. The best Christmas present in the world.' Happiness smoothed the corrugated iron of a face, framed with hair washed and stoat free, into soft waves.

Already she was moving around her bed without moaning. She even sounded like a different woman. 'Would you just look at that!'

Seizing a lull in activities, Sister was dancing a light-footed sword dance to everybody's astonishment, especially hers.

'I'll do that soon,' vowed Mrs Jones, 'won't I, Betty?' But Mrs Jack couldn't answer since she was weeping blissfully through the carol singing. The weights swung as if in harmony.

'Merry Christmas, darling!' The consultant dried her tears with a large hanky, harrumphed, then headed back into the office from which sounds of merriment ensued for the rest of my shift.

Going home, I thought it had been my best Christmas in hospital and was especially pleased that Mrs Jack seemed to be surviving all that surrounding hardware with Mrs Jones helping her in any way she could.

I let myself into the house where Mrs Ronce was carrying a shovel with its one lump of coal.

'Maisie not home yet?'

'You've just missed her,' she said, barging past into the sitting room from which there came such a large crash she must have distance-flung the coal.

Then the atmosphere grew past its normal chill with a worry-making silence. Mrs Ronce was never this quiet. Maybe the Christmas period was having the same effect on her as it was on Mrs Jones and she too was feeling lonely.

'Another bally pagan festival,' she'd said, but I felt guilty for thinking she was invincible and in no need of company. The silence was now becoming so unnatural I peeked round the door.

Mrs Ronce, with one arm flung out in an odd position, lay spread-eagled on the tatty rucked-up rug.

'Mrs Ronce!' I rushed through. 'Damn cats!' I had to step over them to get to her side.

'Dratted carpet, I'll have to get it mended and don't speak to the pussy cats like that – they're not used to bad language.' She sat up, grimacing with the effort.

'Don't move!' I shouted, but Mrs Ronce paid no heed and crawled onto the sofa.

'I'm fine. Look!'

'Wonderful if you like a laugh with your arm at a funny angle – and keep still!'

'I can't do very much else and why in God's name do they call it humorous,' Mrs Ronce said, biting her lip and looking diminished. 'Where are you going?'

'To get a taxi to take you to Casualty. Funny bone or not, that arm needs attention.' I was already in the hall and dialling.

It felt odd being on the receiving end of Casualty, but alright to be there whilst she was recovering from her anaesthetic – if not Mr Morgan's Christmas carols. At length and with her arm now in plaster, the staff handed her over as carefully as if she were an old lady.

'If that man sings any more,' gritted Mrs Ronce, 'and if it wasn't so painful, I'd hit him with this arm. It feels like a ton weight and would make a good weapon. God preserve me from ill health and nurses. When we get home, you're going to have to open the sherry bottle. Come on, let's get the Hell outta here.'

But Mr Morgan had the last word. 'We wish you a Merry Christmas,' he warbled and with an operatic flourish, slammed shut our taxi door.

39

AND FINALLY . . .

Was it really three years ago that our crowd had met in the hospital dining room as raw, shy recruits, and I got my wish to walk the green corridor as a team member? Could we really now be people entrusted with the lives of so many ill patients? Could we even become staff nurses in that awful pink? It was as awesome a prospect as it seemed unlikely. At the time, we'd thought we'd never reach this stage, but now here we were and about to put all our experiences to the test.

I had moved to a female surgical ward and it was the morning of my practical exam. Maisie, pleased to have had hers the previous day, helped me get ready with cups of tea and a brief history of disasters experienced by others.

'But it's ok once you get started,' she eventually reassured me and put her arms round my shoulders. 'You've had the practice, and the patient, unless she's really mean, will say you're a wonderful nurse and keep her moans until the examiner's gone and, Jane,' she turned away and mumbled, 'you can do it and thanks for being such a pal over the years – we've had some right laughs.'

'Think nothing of it, Maisie, but just tell me, are my seams straight?'

Once on the ward, it helped that it was so busy, there was hardly time to think whilst a patient I was trying to get out of bed held the monopoly on worry.

'I'm frightened I burst my stitches so don't rush me,' she squeaked, halfway between bed and chair, 'I need plenty time.'

A passing staff nurse whispered, 'You've got Miss Wilson's wound to dress. Sorry, but Sister said she was also an excellent patient to exercise tact and diplomacy on.'

'Mind out!' cried the patient, who might have gone into free-fall, had Staff Nurse's catching reflexes not been better honed than her timing of bad news.

'Just don't drop your next wifie, even if you feel like it.'

Miss Wilson had to be the most difficult woman in the ward. Nobody ever fixed her bandages properly and it was a sad fact that her loud nasal complaints drowned out the kind murmurs appreciative patients often gave. We'd already had words about staff's inability to respond to her every need and whim so, after checking my patient was still in stitches so to speak, I went, with sinking heart, to let my next one know her big part in my future.

'Don't you worry, Nurse,' she gave a gummy smile, 'I'll help as much as I can. Look, I'll even put these in for you.' She fished some plaque-encrusted teeth from her denture dish and slammed them in.

I made a grab for them, 'Let me clean them first.'

'No,' she champed, 'I don't trust anybody with my teeth. I once heard about somebody doing a whole ward's worth in a pail. No, just you do my dressing properly for a change.'

'Nurse Macpherson, can you come now?' Sister's voice fluted down the ward and slowly I went to meet the examiner, a large woman so stern faced I thought my patient might have slipped away that minute and I might be the first final exam nurse ever to have to dress a corpse.

But there was plenty proof of life as Miss Wilson informed the ward, the world and the examiner about the importance of her role in medical history and mine. Introduction then superfluous and a patient the complete expert, who needed explanation? Hoping Mrs Low, my old tutor, would have forgiven the lack of it, I patted the counterpane and managed, despite the artillery of words, 'I'll just go and get the dressing trolley now then.'

'Yes, you do that and I'll tell this good woman about my other operations.' My patient ticked four fingers whilst I pulled the privacy screens. The examiner looked trapped.

An expectant hush suddenly fell upon the ward as, gowned and masked, I took the dressing trolley to the bedside. Miss Wilson now became Miss Chatty But Helpful.

The teeth seemed to have given her a new lease on life, making her so vocal I just managed not to put a plaster over her mouth. The examiner sighed and took notes whilst our patient held forth.

'You must appreciate gallstones are very painful things. I was glad to get rid of them.' She screwed her face in recall. 'There were five of them. The surgeon put them in a wee jar beside the bed.'

'I believe some people keep them. What have you done with yours?' asked the examiner, not really interested.

'Swallowed them. I thought they were pain killers.' Miss Wilson circled her hand over her wound. 'D'you know, sometimes at night I can hear them rumbling round. It minds me of a cement mixer. I'm surprised the others can sleep for the racket.'

'Just goes to show how careful you have to be,' said the examiner, beginning to sound quite human.

At last, I was finished.

'Nurse Macpherson's done a wonderful job of my dressing,' enthused my patient, and then drew breath, 'she's fair improved!'

She was surprised into silence by a swift tucking and tidying up technique that might have impressed the Time and Motion people who had, at one point in our training, given us all sorts of efficiency tips we never had the time to try. The rest of the ward resumed its comfortable buzz of talk and activity.

'Now we'll go over a few points.' The examiner led the way to an empty waiting room, like an executioner with a prisoner. I didn't envy her the job but mine was worse, especially as I tried to highlight Miss Wilson's many troubles in a sympathetic way. I could hardly say she was more of a pain than her wretched gallstones.

'How did it go?' Staff Nurse asked later, at which I burst into tears.

'Go and give that patient a bedpan will you?' Sister bustled past, uncaring.

A week after the practical, we sat our final written exam. The last time I'd been was in this hall it was for the pantomime. Now it was a different place, with the sound of busy pens used by people wearing such an air of concentration, a bomb drop would have gone unnoticed.

It was easy enough writing down the nursing care of a patient suffering from lobar pneumonia and describing the anatomy of the liver meant that we could use lots of coloured pencils. Those of us who had sampled my mother's tonic wine at a New Year's party had felt so liverish the morning after, we had researched the subject.

Then there was a collective sigh as the completion bell went. Tools were downed and we slowly picked up our possessions and began to drift away. Nobody wanted to talk about the exam whilst everybody seemed tied up in private thoughts.

'Will you be coming straight back?' I asked Maisie as we stepped outside.

'No, I'm off home.' She brushed away a red hair tendril. 'Am I glad that's over! As long as I live, I never want to sit another exam.'

'Have a safe journey then,' I said, turning for home and already feeling that Maisie and I were taking different paths.

And so I sauntered along, enjoying the walk, pleased to feel the sun's warmth and freed from the shackles of an exam that would decide everybody's future.

I looked over the Kittybrewster bridge, seeing the railway below and remembering how alien Aberdeen looked on my first journey and so unlike home, I never thought it would feel familiar. Now I knew that under the city's granite exterior were a funny, brave, hardworking people who made light of their illness and faced the future with stoic calm. My pace quickened.

A bus rattled past, bouncing on the cobbles, as I neared Old Aberdeen. I thought how lucky we'd been to stay in this lovely part of town, a planet away from a hospital industry of care and concern, giving us the carefree world of a wacky landlady in her rackety house.

She opened the door as I was fumbling for my key.

'I heard you!' she cried in a pleased way. 'You'll be glad that's over. Why don't you go out into the garden for a little sit down? It's so nice in the sun, and I'll bet it's even nicer in the summerhouse. Now I've got to dash! Do you know, I've been so busy today I haven't even had time to play the piano, and it's such good physiotherapy for this cursed arm.' She skipped back into the kitchen and rattled enough pans to alert the cats, who rushed inside and straight to their dishes. They were beginning to get rather fat and in need of more exercise. They were plainly spending far too much time lounging about in the summerhouse.

I ambled out to where it stood, tucked away in the corner as if it had been there forever and bringing a little piece of heaven to a busy world.

Now, well into the sixties, Aberdeen was getting the hang of them with its mini-skirts and music no longer making ministers lean from the pulpit. Hopefully Belfast swung too. Apparently it had a good midwifery training school, a new nurses' home, and was centrally located somewhere called the Falls Road. If I passed the finals, I planned on going there.

Sitting on the dusty jumble of the summerhouse cushions, I thought it might make a nice wee change.